CLEVER AS A FOX

CLEVER AS A FOX

Animal Intelligence and What It Can Teach Us About Ourselves

SONJA I. YOERG, PH.D

BLOOMSBURY

Published by Bloomsbury, New York and London.
Distributed to the trade by St Martin's Press.

Library of Congress Cataloging-in-Publication Dta

Yoerg, Sonja, 1959–
Clever as a fox: what animal intelligence can teach us about ourselves /
Sonja Yoerg. – 1st ed.
p. cm.
Includes bibliographical references (p.).
ISBN 1 -58234-115-X
1. Animal intelligence. 2. Psychology, Comparative. I. Title.

QL785.Y556 2001
591.5'13–dc21
00-046801

First U.S. Edition
10 9 8 7 6 5 4 3 2 1

Typeset by Palimpsest Book Production Limited,
Polmont, Stirlingshire
Printed in the United States of America,
by R. R. Donnelley & Sons Company,
Harrisonburg, Virginia

To Richard

CONTENTS

ACKNOWLEDGMENTS

I owe thanks to numerous friends and colleagues for help in writing this book. Although I had chatted about my idea for a popular book on animal intelligence to many people over many years, Bob Levenson was the first to suggest that I actually write the thing. He also showed me how to begin – a big hurdle. John Gottman very generously put my proposal in the hands of his publisher, Alan Wherry of Bloomsbury, whose kindness and enthusiasm astonished me. Alan handed me over to Karen Rinaldi who signed me on. Karen, together with Panio Gianopoulos, provided pain-free editorial advice and buckets of encouragement throughout the project. Thanks, too, to all the other folks at Bloomsbury.

I'm grateful to everyone who helped me shape the book or who commented on selected chapters: Steve Glickman, Ellen Frankel, Arnie Leiman, Gail Machlis, and Rich Ivry. Special thanks to Jaz Zaitlin for reading the whole manuscript and digging out stylistic and logical errors. Al Kamil also took the time to read it all, which I truly appreciate. Al was there the first time I thought about animal intelligence and has been the ideal sounding board for both my best and my stupidest ideas. More than that, he has been a friend through all my incarnations. Thanks, Al.

Richard, my husband, gets his own paragraph. He read every chapter several times, critically and with great insight. He displayed an uncanny ability to find the chapter ending where I had buried it somewhere in the middle and also provided many of the funnier lines (but not the *very* funniest, his claims notwithstanding). With Richard nearby, I never lacked for the kind words and loving support that kept me going: for a Brit without pom-poms, he makes a superb cheerleader. Richard, you are simply the best.

Chapter 1

A Dim and Clouded Eye

Perched at the tip of a stunted pine, a Clark's nutcracker gathers a bit of warmth from the morning sun. Most of the tree on which she sits is buried under layer upon layer of snow, and although the green rush of spring has already come to the foothills below, here, near the summit of the tallest peaks, the freeze is still on. Nothing stirs. The nutcracker breaks the silence with a jay-like 'Caw!', listens for the echo, then preens first one wing and then the other. The palette from which her feathers are colored was borrowed from this desolate winter landscape: gray from the boulders, black from the bark of the trees, white from the snow.

Cocking her head to one side, she glances at a protruding rock to her left, glides down to the snow, and begins to dig. In a few minutes she has tossed aside enough snow to expose a patch of ground. She digs in the frozen earth and retrieves a cache of a dozen pine seeds, which she slips from her beak into the expandable pouch that lies along the inside of her throat, designed by nature just for this use. Back up to the surface of the snow, she takes a quick bearing from the rock and the tree, hops a few steps closer to the rock, and digs again. When two more caches have been emptied, her pouch is full; in silhouette she looks as though she has swallowed a golf ball. She leaves the snow and alights on the tree. After a brief rest, she abandons her perch, flying up the slope and over the barren crest of the mountain toward a thick stand of pines miles away, where her nest lies. There she will feed her nestlings the pine seeds – the only meal on the mountain until spring ascends from below to overcome winter.

The nutcracker buried the seeds during the previous summer and fall, making thousands of caches over miles of terrain. Her custom-designed bill allowed her to break open pinecones before they were even ripe, giving her a jump on the other birds and rodents that are partial to pine seeds. In selecting seeds for caching, she weighed each one in her bill and clicked it with her mandibles, listening for the telltale hollow sound of a rotten kernel, judging the seed's density and quality like a fussy shopper lifting and squeezing a grapefruit at the market. After the quality control check, she pouched the seeds and flew as far as fourteen miles from the harvest site to terrain better suited for long-term seed storage. When burying the seeds, she avoided areas prone to drifting and chose instead southward-facing slopes where the sun would shrink the snow. After she put a cache of four or so seeds in the ground, she covered them with some dirt and perhaps a leaf for camouflage.

For several months this was how she spent her days: harvesting, selecting, transporting, and caching the fall seed crop. In an average year, she would make about 12,000 caches, storing as many as 80,000 seeds. She made each cache, noted its location, and flew away. She did not return until winter had wiped everything else off the menu.[1]

A bird with a brain the size of a cashew remembering thousands of locations for months at a time? Most of us have trouble remembering where in the parking garage we left our car a few hours ago. Now imagine drifts of snow covering the signs indicating floor numbers and lettered zones. And yet, experiments have shown conclusively that Clark's nutcrackers (and other bird species) use their memory, and not some lazy trick, to recover buried seeds.[2] Their lives depend on it. The diet of the nutcracker nestlings is

[1] Vander Wall and Balda, 1981.
[2] Kamil and Balda, 1985; Vander Wall, 1982.

2

entirely pine seeds, and only Mom and Dad know where the seeds are hidden. If nutcrackers couldn't remember where they stored their food, there soon would be no more nutcrackers.

Are you skeptical that the nutcracker could have such impressive intellectual abilities? We want to examine that skepticism and use it to begin to understand some of the questions of comparative animal intelligence. Why is it surprising that a bird might have a better memory than an elephant, or even you? What can the story of the nutcracker and our reaction to it tell us about the nature of intellectual ability in people and in animals, about the nutcracker's adaptation to the harsh realities of its niche, and about the biases we apply and the partial truths and naked lies we accept when we look inside the minds of other creatures?

The Intellectual Line-up

Suppose I told you the cache-and-carry story again, but with a different cast: A chimpanzee sits on a tree limb deep in an emerald green forest. After a quick look around, he climbs down and begins digging in the ground at a nondescript spot. He eventually uncovers a small pile of nuts of a kind that ripened during the previous rainy season. Taking two nuts from the cache, he covers the rest with leaf litter. Later in the day, he has similar snacks from other cache sites made weeks before.

Most of us find it easier to believe that a chimpanzee could remember where he left his lunch than to believe the same of a bird. (In fact, primates – humans excluded – don't make food caches.[3]) There are many reasons for this bias toward the chimpanzee, some valid, some not. As an example of an invalid reason, consider the ancient notion of a Great Chain of Being. The central idea, still very active in the popular mind, is that all beings can be ranked along a single dimension indicating their proximity to God. The Great Chain looked something like this in its original form: God,

[3] Vander Wall, 1990.

angels, man, woman, apes, horses, cats, birds, turtles, frogs, fish, bugs. Because the beings nearer the top of the Chain are closer to perfection, they have more of the goods in all domains, including intellectual ability.

While some sections of the Great Chain of Being are being dismantled (that man-over-woman business is on the way out), the idea has persisted that a linear ranking of animals is possible. The use of 'higher' and 'lower' to describe species is an example, where 'higher' might refer to mammals (like us) and 'lower' to squishies and crunchies (such as crayfish and cockroaches – not much like us). The metaphor of an evolutionary chain or ladder carries with it the assumption that evolutionary change brings improvement, that comparing a fish to a person is like comparing a Model T to a Porsche. But that's not how evolution appears to work; there is no support for such unidimensional scaling in modern evolutionary theory. If you buy into the modern view of how species arise, then an automatic judgment (based on perceived distance from the primordial soup) that a chimpanzee is necessarily brighter than any bird is pure prejudice. Don't feel too badly about it: the prejudice is widely shared.

Despite scientific evidence, simple classification schemes like the Great Chain of Being have strong appeal even in modern times, rooted as they are deep in our cultural and religious soil. They continue to influence what we believe in our hearts long after our minds have been won over by an elegant theory or the sheer weight of data. In this book, we will return to this idea repeatedly; our perceptions of the intellectual status of other species will always be a joint product of real scientific knowledge and the fuzzier forces that mold all human endeavors: values, personal and cultural histories, emotions.

The ancient scholar Plutarch, in an essay titled 'The Cleverness of Animals', staged a debate about which group of animals was intellectually superior, those living on land or those living in the sea. During the warmup to the central argument, one team defended the idea that animals had intellectual abilities of any kind. This was a touchy subject in ancient Greece because the power to reason was inextricably linked to moral purpose. Plutarch's position was, however, clear:

> There are . . . many animals which surpass all men, not only in bulk and swiftness, but also in keen sight and sharp hearing; but for all that man is not blind or crippled or earless. We can run, if less swiftly than deer; and see, if less keenly than hawks . . . In the same way, then, let us not say of beasts that they are completely lacking in intellect and understanding . . . what we should say is that their intellect is feeble and turbid, like a dim and clouded eye.[4]

This argument seems logically sound. It begins with the premise that humans are at the intellectual pinnacle of creation. Even without the philosophical link to the Great Chain of Being, most people would readily agree that humans can think circles around any other species. Sure, dolphins and chimps and even nutcrackers might be smart, but none ever earned a Rhodes scholarship or designed a suspension bridge. When it comes to intellect, humans have the sharp, unclouded eye. Plutarch then asserts that, like humans, other species can think, but that their thinking is like seeing with cataracts. Perhaps if we could develop the cognitive equivalent of a standard vision test, we could line up all the creatures from the ark below us according to their abilities. That lineup might even replicate the Great Chain of Being and we wouldn't then have to apologize for our species biases.

But is vision a good metaphor for intelligence? There are different types of eyes engineered to capture different portions of the spectrum for different purposes. A standard vision test, fair to all, would be much harder to develop because a single factor, such as acuity, might not capture all that is relevant to performance, and might not itself constitute a single dimension. Plutarch's dialogue implies that intelligence is a monolithic capacity, that differences among species are always quantitative: variations in

---

[4] Plutarch, Moralia XII, p.343.

amount rather than kind. However, many scientists have argued, especially recently, that intelligence is not a single entity: it's apples and oranges (and perhaps apricots and bananas as well). To grasp the mental abilities of the owl, the pussycat, the tortoise, and the hare and to weigh them side by side will require a commitment to unraveling the nature of intelligence. As will become obvious in the next chapter, few topics in the history of psychology have generated more controversy.

It's All Relative

Ironically, but not accidentally, there is an aspect of the Great Chain of Being that does, at least in part, support the assumption that a chimpanzee will be brainier than a bird: evolutionary continuity. Crudely, the argument runs like this: we know we are smart. Chimps are a lot like us in many ways, birds are not. Therefore, chimps are more likely to be smart than are birds. The logic is not infallible, but there are scientifically sound reasons for believing that closely related species will tend to be more similar (in their bodies, their behavior, and their minds) than more distantly related species. When a new species emerges, it resembles, in most respects, the species from which it was derived. Even people with little formal understanding of genetics can make fairly accurate judgments of relatedness among common species. A mountain lion is clearly just a big kitty. A zebra is a horse with a fancy paint job. A squirrel is an upholstered rat. We are good at detecting family resemblance and using that resemblance to draw conclusions about behavior and mental ability. We know apples don't fall far from trees. We can use this knowledge of relatedness to help understand how intelligence, or the lack of it, is distributed across the animal kingdom.

On the other hand, we only have to think about our own families to realize that even closely related individuals (or species) sometimes differ remarkably. Chimpanzees may be our closest cousins and be more similar to us than any bird, but no one would ever mistake one for a human. Species differ, and the differences can usually be seen, measured, and quantified. If what distinguishes this species from that species is, say, a longer limb or a bushier tail, then we can reliably measure that trait in related animals and try to correlate the differences with things we know might favor or discourage that trait during natural selection. Perhaps longer limbs improve running speed and that bushy tail is effective as a desert sunshade. By comparing species, we can infer how the forces of genetic heritage on one hand and unique environment on the other have altered animal bodies, pushing and pulling species up, out, and along the arbors of the evolutionary tree.

But studying the evolution of ear shape in bats or skull width in rats is one thing, and understanding the evolution of cleverness quite another. If we want to use the concepts of relatedness and adaptation in our hypotheses about which animals are smarter than others, then we have to devise methods that can detect similarities and tease apart differences in intelligence. How do we do that? The first step is to clearly define intelligence (see chapter 2). Then we have to design tests that measure intelligence as it is defined and put the selected species through their paces (see chapters 2 and 5). Finally we have to figure out how performance on the tests relates to ecological pressures and evolutionary history (see chapters 7 and 8). Imagine making a career out of studying events that happened, ever so slowly, millions of years ago (the evolution of the creatures alive today) and the relationship between those events and attributes you cannot ever hope to see directly (mental abilities), which are produced by a structure that doesn't fossilize very well (the brain). How the methods of evolutionary science may be applied to the study of comparative intelligence is one of the most vexing issues of modern behavioral biology.

Of course many types of science rely on long chains of inferences in their constructions of local reality; after all, who has seen a black hole? My message is not that a science of the evolution of intelligence is impossible but rather that we must be ever mindful of the delicacy of the enterprise. If we are building a house of cards, let's be sure we recognize it as such. The assumptions lurking behind conclusions we draw about animal intelligence must be examined again and again. When we see a chimpanzee thoughtfully studying his own face in a mirror, what questions should we be asking in order to learn what his behavior says about his mind? About the differences, and similarities, between his mind and our own? And when we see the nutcracker retrieving long-buried seeds, how do we ask questions of her that are open-minded, that don't rely entirely on how far away her branch of the evolutionary tree is from ours?

A Case of Mistaken Identity

One consequence of our extravagant intelligence is that we run the risk of exaggerating its significance in the game of Life. The vast majority of people in developed nations spend nearly all their time steeped in a complex, varied, and ever-mutating material and intellectual culture. We are so in love with the fruits of our intellect that few of us ever pause long enough from the enjoyment of novels, board games, speed dialing, Web surfing, radio talk shows, and Monday night football to ask what all this brain power is really for. Yet if we are to engage in an impartial analysis of animal intelligence, we must then consider what good it does any animal to be smart. Given our own mental abilities it is hard for us to imagine that there are advantages to being a bit slow on the draw. Nevertheless, many wildly successful species have gotten by perfectly well on fewer neurons than legs. For natural selection to favor a high I.Q., the additional energy-consuming brain matter has to pay its way; being smart must translate into a concrete competitive advantage realized in the only currency that evolution recognizes: survival of more kids.

Throughout this book, the question of the function of intelligence arises. For the moment, I want to take an end run at the question, to try out the idea that one of best ways to learn about something is to see it fail. I want to tell a story of animal stupidity.

Several years ago I lived in a village in central Wales comprised of 300 sheep farmers. I was there studying the Eurasian dipper, a perching bird (like a robin, wren, or sparrow) that makes its living in an unusual way: by diving into rushing streams to hunt for bugs. My research question was simple and fundamental: how do young dippers, who have just fledged, learn to master both air and water, and capture prey that are both agile and cryptic?[5] The first thing I had to do was find nests and figure out when the young dippers were scheduled to fledge. Dipper nests are large, mossy igloos built directly over running water, pitched on a cliff face or under a bridge. They are either impossible to see, impossible to reach, or both. When the nest gets too crowded and it's time for the young to leave, they take a baptismal plunge into the current, and end up bobbing like bath toys under the faucet as the tub fills.

It was mid-May and breeding season was in full swing. I had awoken at four A.M., filled my Thermos with tea, grabbed my gear, and headed for the river. An hour later, I was sitting inside a hide, waiting for dawn to break so the show could begin. The target of my attention was a dipper nest cleverly camouflaged on a moss-covered cliff on the opposite bank. Because this was only a feeder stream for the main river, I could cross the water in one giant step. I had a very good seat for the show. My goal was to keep track of how the parents were divvying up the responsibilities of a nestful of kids. I knew the male was playing house with two other females (dippers are supposed to be monogamous!), and I wanted to see if his philandering was shortchanging any of the females or their nestlings.

The first two hours passed uneventfully. Both the male and female dippers were shuttling back and forth from the main river to the nest, delivering mouthfuls of larvae to the chicks. At the same time, I also had the pleasure of watching a pair of gray wagtails feeding their nestlings, stashed away on the same cliff face only an arm's length from the dipper nest. Wagtails are sleeker and have longer tails than the portly dipper, but their diets overlap so the two species are often found in close proximity.

[5] Yoerg, 1994, 1998.

Soon something strange began occurring. On his way to his own nest with a beakful of goodies, the male wagtail began using the top of the dipper nest as a landing pad before making a lateral move to his own nest. As he passed in front of the mouth of the dipper nest, the dipper nestlings burst into a chorus of begging. For them, seeing movement at the nest opening is like hearing the doorbell when pizza has been ordered. It means food has arrived.

Initially, the wagtail continued to feed his brood, in exactly the way evolution had so carefully designed him to do. Then, I began to notice a slight hesitation in his flight as he passed in front of the begging dippers. Finally the unbelievable occurred: the wagtail approached the dipper nest with his beak crammed full of insects and landed, not on the dome of the nest, but at the opening. The dipper chicks greeted him with raucous begging and he obligingly stuffed the nearest gaping mouth.

Over the next twenty minutes, the male wagtail fed the dipper brood nine times. I was astounded. The first rule in winning the game of natural selection is to help only yourself and those related to you. The second rule is that if you can't do that, for God's sake don't help anyone else! But there was that wagtail, deftly catching bugs and flies and stuffing them into mouths belonging to another species. Between eleven A.M. and noon, the wagtail made three-quarters of all the deliveries to the dipper nest. I watched as often as I could over the next few days. During every hour of every observation period the wagtail fed the dipper chicks more often than the combined effort of the dipper parents. Not surprisingly, visits by the male wagtail to his own nest fell off, and were only partially compensated for by the female wagtail.[6]

While inside the hide, I hardly had a moment to reflect on the significance of the drama; keeping track of the movements of four birds at two nests used all of my processing capacity. At night when the birds were asleep I wondered where all this would lead. Would the wagtail continue feeding the dippers once they had

[6] Yoerg and O'Halloran, 1991.

fledged? (Both wagtail and dipper parents do this.) What would become of those dipper nestlings, the product of a fortuitous cross-fostering experiment? Would they hanker for the winged diet of their wagtail benefactor? Would they find themselves unaccountably attracted to lady wagtails when breeding season came around again? Unfortunately, I never found out. Four days after I first saw the wagtail's misguided behavior, both nests were destroyed, presumably by a mink, a common nest predator in that area. After my disappointment and sadness abated, I couldn't help but wonder if all the commotion I had witnessed might not have attracted unwelcome attention.

What does this story tell us about animal intelligence? To me, the most unintelligent aspect of the wagtail's behavior was his failure to recognize that the dipper chicks were not his, even when his own nest was only a yard away and visited regularly. (An analogous situation in humans would be this: Dad is on his way home with take-out food when he hears some kids in the house next door. He walks into the neighbors' house and says, 'Chinese food all right tonight, guys?' Meanwhile his wife is rummaging through the freezer wondering what to feed their kids now that Dad hasn't shown up. Dad does this five nights a week.) The wagtail's behavior seems unintelligent because it is inflexible, because it reflects the operation of a nestling-feeding mechanism that is highly determinate. I don't know for certain, but the wagtail's behavior is probably governed by some rule such as, 'Once you have a full beak, fly to your nest, and stuff the food in whatever open mouths you find, especially ones that are begging loudly.' My wayward wagtail just didn't get all the way to the right nest before executing the rest of the instructions. But so what? Over millions of years of evolution, the simple feeding rule, or some version of it, worked pretty well or, rather, it worked as well as other fancier, more flexible mechanisms that came with a bigger price tag. If we want to understand why some species are smarter than others, we have to become comfortable with the idea that smarter is not always better. We have to realize that while massive amounts of cognitive wherewithal was just what we needed in our niche, nobody else's niche is quite like ours.

Before leaving the wagtail story, I want to add a footnote that might spare a portion of the wagtail's reputation. When the female dipper (curiously, not the male) saw the wagtail approach her nest, she would usually give an alarm call and chase him off. This happened often enough that the wagtail learned to adjust his Good Samaritan deliveries in response. If he arrived with food but encountered the dipper parents, he would hop around on the bank until they had gone or, if the adult dippers lingered, he would relent and feed his own nestlings. I find this aspect of the story the most endearing and intriguing: the wagtail, while clueless as to how his behavior was jeopardizing his own biological fitness, was exquisitely sensitive to the social consequences of that same behavior.

The encounters between the female dipper and the male wagtail became less frequent because of the irony of negative feedback: the wagtail was doing such a marvelous job feeding the dipper chicks that the dipper parents downshifted their delivery rates in response. As the wagtail enjoyed less harassment from the dippers, he could indulge his bizarre calling more freely. The more the wagtail contributed, the less actively the chicks begged to their own parents, thus providing more feeding opportunities for the wagtail. And I speculate that at least the male dipper, with his other romantic commitments, probably welcomed the relief.

Clearing Our Vision

During the eighteen months I lived in Wales, I spent thousands of hours watching dippers. I didn't watch casually. I used binoculars to read the color-coded ankle bracelets that identified individual birds, and a spotting scope to see exactly what they were eating. I developed a coding system for their behavior and followed strict rules for how long to follow particular birds and what to do if they flew out of sight. During observations I spoke continuously into a tape recorder, then transcribed it all later, getting an accurate record of what behaviors occurred, when they occurred, and in what sequence. Of course, I also read everything about dippers I could get my hands on, and listened carefully to the observations of other scientists who were familiar with them. But if you ask me how intelligent dippers are, I wouldn't have a ready answer. On the other hand, if you ask almost anyone who has more than one pet which one is smartest, I can almost guarantee you will receive an immediate, confident reply, and a few illustrative anecdotes to help make the point. So why do scientists like me, trained to watch and think about animals, hesitate to draw conclusions made so easily by everyone else?

The answer is not that nonscientists lack opportunities to observe animals. In fact, most people interact with animals every day. Nearly every household has a pet and many keep several species. People without pets encounter pigeons in the park, squirrels and raccoons in the backyard, and more exotic species in zoos. Scuba divers meet up with fish, farmers cope with gophers, campers slap at mosquitoes, and drivers swerve around creatures scurrying across the road. Even in the most urban settings, animal life, in the form of cockroaches, ants, and rats, is omnipresent.

We believe that familiarity brings knowledge. Generally, the longer we have known someone, the better we believe we know their abilities, their preferences, their tendencies. We observe behavior, listen to words, read emotions off faces, and learn the patterns that inevitably emerge. When we can readily predict what someone will do or say or feel, we feel we know who that person is. The same principle applies to our relationships with animals. Pets are usually considered family members, and we use our daily interactions with them to draw conclusions about who they are, including the nature of their mental lives. If you own three dogs, you probably would be able to rank them on a number of psychological dimensions, including emotional sensitivity, sociability, and intelligence.

Nicolas Humphrey has argued that people act as 'natural psy-chologists', inferring what goes on in the minds of other people by observing others' behavior and relating it their own conscious experience.[7] In a highly social species like ours, he argues, knowing what is on the other guy's mind confers a practical advantage. We don't stop there, however. We use the same mechanisms to infer mental events in other species. That quizzical expression on your dog's face means he didn't quite understand when you asked if he wanted to go out, so you patiently repeat it. This time he barks in response, which you take for a 'yes'. Does his behavior mean he understood the question? How could you know for certain? Even if you could look inside his head, you would only see his brain, not his mind. In assessing intelligence and other mental abilities, behavior is all we have to go by. Because intelligence is invisible, all of us, whether scientists or not, are 'natural psychologists' in that we only have behavioral clues to solve the riddle of animal intelligence. As you read this book, you will learn what scientists have discovered about how intelligence is manifested in the behavior of various species. You will also learn that scientists themselves are not immune to the limitations that the structure of their own minds places on their ability to be objective about minds that are so different.

What we know about our pets and about other animals is not purely a result of direct interactions with them. Our intuitions about which animals are smarter are really complex inferences based on data from children's stories, Disney movies, an occasional nature program on public television, fables and myths, literature, advertisements, and television shows like *Lassie*, *Rin Tin Tin*, *Flipper*, and *Mr. Ed*. Whenever we look at a member of another species, we are looking through a filter heavily fogged by a dense set of expectations and prejudices – our dim and clouded eye. If we try to understand how culture and individual experience determine our personal theories of animal intelligence, we will learn quite a bit about ourselves and what we bring to our relationships with other animals. The goal of this book is to uncloud our perceptions of the mental abilities of other animals,

---

[7] Humphrey, 1978.

to examine the basis for our beliefs about what animals know and think, and to reveal something about both animals and ourselves in the process.

There is real benefit in thinking clearly about the intelligence of animals. Just as we value intelligence in one another, we also value it in other animals. And because we strive to protect the things we value, we can use our perceptions of species' intelligence to make judgments about their welfare. When it comes to deciding which species will end up in our laps and which will end up on our plates, animal mentality figures prominently. One reason we are usually nicer to smarter animals is because we believe that species with more brain power are more sensitive to their environment, and so are more vulnerable to pain, including emotional pain such as loneliness. What do we really know about the relationship between intelligence, awareness, and emotion in animals? The short answer is, not much. And yet every day individuals, committees, institutions, legislators, and private companies make decisions about how to treat animals, often based on ideas no more sophisticated than the Great Chain of Being. Any scientifically valid information that can be brought to the table would contribute to the difficult task of deciding the fates of animals. Throughout this book, I try to provide an objective analysis of what we do and do not know about animal intelligence. I also try to bring forward misconceptions and unfounded assumptions about the mental ability of animals that contribute to the way we feel about and, consequently, act toward them. In chapter 9, we'll directly address the question of how intelligence relates to feeling and suffering in animals – something we know very little about – and ask what the answers might mean for our relationships with other species. And in the final chapter, we'll further explore the maddening and artful human tendencies that have shaped (and clouded) our perceptions of the animal mind. We'll see how thinking carefully about animal intelligence can help us use our own intelligence more wisely.

Chapter 2

The Interspecies Cognitive Olympics

> Since psychologists measure intelligence, you would expect
> them to know what intelligence is, but as a matter of fact
> they are much more ready with their tests than with their
> definition.
>
> R. S. Woodworth, 1929[1]

Anyone who has digested a sizable chunk of the volumes written
about the definition of intelligence might be tempted (as I nearly
am) to turn the problem over to college sophomores grappling
with other unsolvable existential dilemmas. Nevertheless we
must enter the minefield of defining intelligence, if only to see
why people have studied animal minds in the way that they have
and why the results of those studies muddy the water as often
as clear it. Bear in mind too that as arcane as some aspects of
the definitional arguments may be, some exquisite discoveries of
animal behavior and cognition have been made in their honor.

Common usage seems like a good place to begin. In casual
parlance, intelligence means the ability to figure things out, to
adapt quickly and appropriately, and to use past experience and
current information to get the mental job done right. When
someone says, 'Hannah is very intelligent,' we know something
fairly concrete about what to expect from Hannah as a teammate
in a game of Pictionary or when lost together in an unfamiliar city.
Similarly, dog aficionados confidently rank dog breeds according
to intelligence.[2] Owners will then have certain expectations about

---

[1] Woodworth, 1929, p. 61.
[2] Coren, 1994; Hart and Hart, 1988; American Kennel Club website.

a dog's behavior. Those near the top of the list will presumably be trainable and responsive while those nearer the bottom will be more valued, perhaps, for their glossy coats and winsome expressions than for their intellect. In the most general sense, then, we all believe we know what intelligence is and how it is manifested in behavior. Indeed, psychologists have surveyed people's ideas about what intelligence is and have found that people generally agree on both what defines an intelligent person and on the general concept of intelligence.[3] In a nutshell, people think being smart means solving problems well, being good with words, and, to a smaller degree, being good with people. Happily, this 'folk definition' of intelligence gibes well with what most experts on the subject believe.

The Tortoise and the Hare-brain

So what's so tough about defining intelligence if everyone agrees? Plenty. If someone is an ace problem solver, a verbal virtuoso, and charming to boot, no swords will be drawn. But can we agree on the level of intelligence of someone who nimbly solves abstract reasoning problems, but trips over her own tongue and steps on other's toes? Or the socially adept person with the golden tongue who can't master a spatial, mathematical, or abstract puzzle without having a nervous breakdown? Who's smarter? As long as intellect is tracked along a single dimension, definitional problems are limited to figuring out what that one dimension is. As soon as another dimension is added, however, the trouble begins. The point of contention is not that intelligence is multifaceted; pretty much everyone agrees that people perform somewhat differently on different kinds of intelligence tests or test items. The brightest might have intellectual blind spots, and generally poor performers may shine in a particular domain; the texture of our intellectual landscape is uneven, if not rugged. The question is whether, despite some unevenness in performance,

---

[3] Sternberg, Conway, Ketron and Bernstein, 1981.

a pervasive unitary factor – a mental foundation of a particular strength – nevertheless exists. In 1927, Charles Spearman called the unitary factor 'g'.[4] It referred to the 'general mental energy' used for reasoning, comprehension, and hypothesis testing – what we commonly think of as hallmarks of intelligence. Proponents of 'g' argue that because intellectual performances within an individual have more in common than not, it makes sense to talk about intelligence as if it is primarily one thing. If someone is quick with numbers, good at puzzles, and always knows from which Shakespearean play a quote is drawn, it's not so much that they have unusual mathematical ability, strong spatial skills, and a flawless memory – they're just damn smart. Gainsayers argue that 'g' is illusory, that there is no single powerful factor that underlies intellectual performance. Sure, some people do well on all the tests and some blow them all, but that says more about the tests than it does about the cognitive processes that underlie intelligent behavior.[5]

Think of intellectual functioning as an Olympic event. If being smart is like being able to run fast, if it is a single, nearly unidimensional ability, then a simple footrace over a measured distance should readily separate the hares from the tortoises intellectually. Even doubling the length of the course or altering its terrain should not change the results drastically, assuming the group you are testing is fairly diverse. The equivalent intellectual race would be an intelligence test with only one kind of response. For example, reaction time, the time it takes to, say, hit a button after a light flash, has been proposed as an index of intelligence. Quick equals smart. That is about as uncomplicated an assessment of intelligence as one can imagine; it assumes that no matter what kind of mental task is at hand, speed of processing information accounts for much of the difference between Albert Einstein and Curly of the Three Stooges. The very first statistical studies of human intelligence, made by Sir Francis Galton in the 1880s, were this type of sensory and

[4] Spearman, 1927.
[5] Neisser et al, 1996; Gardner, 1983; Herrnstein and Murray, 1994.

motor test.[6] Speedier processing of sensory information and execution of movements were presumably correlated with more efficient internal (neural) mechanisms and, hence, intelligence. Such theories quickly fell out of favor but are again gaining credence as our understanding of neural functioning soars.[7] As we will learn, much of the history of animal intelligence testing has focused on the development of a single item test, designed to tap into a single intellectual resource. The idea of one simple intellectual commodity, divvied out unequally among species, is attractive for a variety of theoretical and methodological reasons.

If, however, being smart is less like running fast and more like being athletic, then asking contestants in the Cognitive Olympics to run only a 1,000-meter race might not be the fairest test. There is undoubtedly more to being a star athlete than being fleet of foot; all-around athletes are also coordinated and strong. The Olympic test for general athletic ability is the decathlon, consisting of ten disparate events, including running, shot put, pole-vaulting, and high-jumping. A decathlete inevitably performs better in some events than others, just as people (and animals) perform better on some intellectual tasks than others. The question is whether there is an underlying ability (call it 'athleticism') common to the ten decathlon events that determines performance across the events. If there is, then adding another event, such as swimming, which also depends heavily on athleticism, shouldn't alter which athlete walks away with the gold. Proponents of 'g' argue that while there is some variation in how people finish in different kinds of Cognitive Olympic events, people with lots of mental muscle and cognitive coordination tend to perform well regardless of the details of the task. If you do well on the Weschler vocabulary test, you'll probably also score high on Miller's analogies. In fact, a given person's scores on the different subtests that make up standard intelligence tests do correlate highly, though not perfectly; overall scores can be

[6] Watson, 1978, p. 330.
[7] Vernon, 1987; Reed and Jensen, 1992, 1993.

estimated using only the scores from a subtest or two. 'G' advocates believe that differences between people in intelligent behavior of any kind are due to having either more or less of the smart stuff. The main reason to offer variety in the problems that make up an intelligence test is to make performances more reliable; no single type of test (analogous to the footrace) will yield a dependable result.

Opponents of the idea of general intelligence say that if performance is fairly uniform across tasks it is mostly because the tasks are very similar, not because there is a universal process supporting performance. They argue that if intelligence tests are to be true intellectual decathlons, the events need to be more diverse and our assessments of performance more complex. Intelligence measures should include, for example, measures of musical ability, body/kinesthetic ability, and practical or adaptive intelligence – how well you hunt for a new job or how adeptly you deflect telemarketers. Intelligence, in this view, is not a unitary entity but rather a confederation of separable abilities. People are therefore intelligent in unique, complex ways; there is no general mental energy that can be rated with a single number, like the horsepower of a motorcycle. This idea of compartmentalization in human intelligence is directly relevant to questions of comparative animal intelligence and adaptive specialization: how can we reconcile the idea of adaptation to a specialized niche with the idea of an all-purpose mental device?

Measuring Up

The dilemma currently on the table is this: intelligence, whether in people or in animals, whether a general ability or a bundle of specific ones, cannot be measured directly. If we were only interested in a person's ability to add a row of numbers or in a cat's ability to find its way out of a box, we'd be home free. But what we are searching for is not instantiated in any one measure, at least not one that anyone has yet discovered. The fact that 1,020 experts in psychology, education, sociology, and genetics agree overwhelmingly on the elements of intelligence[8] is little consolation when it comes to the thankless job of choosing a test item for a child or designing an experimental arena for a fish. Talk is cheap.

The Weschler Adult Intelligence Scale is the current gold standard for human intelligence testing. In the spirit of the decathlon, it consists of eleven subtests grouped into verbal and performance (nonverbal) sections. During testing, people may be asked to recall a list of numbers (first forward, then backward), complete a series of pictures, do some arithmetic, and create a copy of an abstract design using blocks. Like the Stanford-Binet test and other psychometric intelligence tests, it has been designed to distinguish between people that come from the same population, variously defined. The more homogeneous the group, the more confident we can be that differences in test scores reflect differences in intelligence, and not some other factor, such as language skills, motivation, and the like. The tests are standardized on large populations, then 'normed' so that a score of 100 is the average score, with two-thirds of the scores falling between 85 and 115. In this way, an individual's score can be used (for better or for worse) for comparison with others of the same age, academic experience, cultural experience, and so on.

What happens if we apply the same idea to the study of comparative animal intelligence? For the sake of argument, let's skip over the issue of whether general intelligence is a concept worth clinging to, and accept, as many psychologists and other professionals have done, the utility of general intelligence tests. Would it be possible to design a beastly equivalent of the Weschler Intelligence scale? Remembering that these psychometric tests are designed to reveal differences between individuals drawn from the same population, the logical place to start would be with an I.Q. test for a restricted population, such as a particular

[8] Snyderman and Rothman, 1987.

species. Surprisingly little such work has been conducted. In 1993, Anderson developed a quadrathlon for lab rats, comprised of the following problems: a test of reaction to novelty (greater preference for novel objects means greater intelligence), a response flexibility test (finding a detour route to a goodie), and the speed and accuracy of solving a maze that had been learned only in pieces. As with humans on the Weschler intelligence scale, rats' scores on one problem were predictive of their scores on the other problems, and the statistical analysis suggested that a single factor (rat 'g'?) accounted best for the data. For example, a rat that ignored the soda can in the novelty test also tended to be sluggish in figuring out the way around a blocked path. And the physiological data backed up the idea that the tests were on the right track: high-scoring rats had heavier brains.[9]

So what? Well, the results might be useful if one wanted to institute an educational tracking system for laboratory rodents, or perhaps to suggest which rats should be encouraged to enroll in more challenging studies in the future. But if the goal is to develop methods for comparing intellectual performance across species, it might be sensible to apply the Andersen battery to several other species and see how they measure up. Because this is only a hypothetical experiment, we may select freely from Noah's ark without any practical concern. How about a mole, because it's a rodent and about rat-sized, and a hummingbird, because it is not? Let's start the mole in the detour problem, which uses a box with three chambers in a row. The first chamber is the start box, where the animal gets set down. Through a small opening the animal may enter the choice box, from which it may scurry through another opening into the goal box. Andersen used a Froot Loop (a doughnut-shaped kid's cereal) as a reward in the goal box, so we will too. The idea is that during training the mole will proceed from the start box to the choice box and into the goal box, where it enjoys its Froot Loop. After some practice, we will introduce the detour. The floor of the choice box has been tilted

[9] Anderson, 1993; Crinella and Yu, 1995.

so that in order to get to the goal box, the mole has to climb up over an edge, then down a slope into the opening to the goal box. The mole gets a demerit if it goes under the inclined floor at any time. On the first training trial, the mole squishes itself up into a corner of the start box, trying hopelessly to find dark, damp soil – the only environment in which it is comfortable. We decide to turn down the lights to make it more comfortable (and now we have trouble seeing the mole!). After several trials, the mole finally begins moving around and eventually completes its training. Now for the acid test. We incline the floor of the choice box and let the mole go. Like the rat, the mole sniffs around the inclined plane the first time, going under, reaching over, and then finally makes it up and over the wall. But unlike the rat, the mole continues to nose around and under the inclined floor the second time it goes through – and every other time – because without feeling it, he doesn't know its there! We tally up error after error and conclude the apparatus needs an overhaul.

But first we test the hummingbird in the maze problem this time. The maze consists of eight arms radiating out from a central hub, with a Froot Loop at the far end of each arm. Given our experience with the mole, we think about how the bird might respond in the apparatus. We decide to enclose the maze in wire mesh so the bird can't fly out. It takes a long time for the hummingbird to get used to being in the covered maze, but finally it calms down. We never get through the training phase, though, because every time the hummingbird encounters a Froot Loop, it slips it onto the end of its beak and tosses it away with a flick of its head. We realize we need to build little nectar dispensers at the end of each arm. Back to the drawing board.

That's Not Fair!

Of course, thinking sensibly about the natural history of the experimental animal would have avoided the vast majority of such problems. The essential dilemma, however, remains: how can we be sure that the testing situation we design – the rewards, the physical structure, the sensory requirements, and the response requirements – are equivalent for all the animals being tested? How do we know a rat likes Froot Loops as much as a hummingbird likes sugar solution? Even after we turned down the lights, was the mole as comfortable in the testing box as the rats had been? How would we know? If we are designing mental hurdles for a variety of species to jump over, we must ensure that any animal with sufficient intellectual propulsion can clear them. Most succinctly: the tests have to be fair. If the mole scores lower than the rat, it must be because the mole cannot solve the problem as well, not because it is more nervous, less motivated, or more prone to accidentally give the wrong response even when it knows the right one.

The same issue has plagued the history of human intelligence testing. After nearly a hundred years of psychometric testing, we are still not confident that we can administer an intelligence test that is fair to people living in different parts of the same city.[10] Granted, substantial progress has been made over the testing practices imposed on a variety of groups in the United States, notably immigrants, early in the last century. At the time, tests were not administered in the native tongue and required reading. Therefore, knowledge of English (particularly the American vernacular) and years of schooling were confounded with intellectual performance. The results were nevertheless used to bolster claims of racial and class differences in intelligence and fueled the fires of the eugenics movement. Interestingly, some of the early comparative psychologists were also prominent in the field of human mental testing.[11] Most notably, Robert Yerkes, for whom the U.S.'s twelve Regional Primate Centers are named, was a staunch believer in the genetic basis of I.Q. differences. Yerkes helped Louis Terman develop the Army's I.Q. tests, used with questionable justification on these immigrant populations.[12]

[10] Herrnstein and Murray, 1994; Devlin, Fienberg, Resnick, and Roeder, 1997.
[11] Kalat, 1983.
[12] Gould, 1983.

Although Yerkes is best known for his studies of primates, like many of his contemporaries, he sampled broadly through the animal kingdom for subjects for intelligence testing. In 1912, Yerkes published a paper titled 'The Intelligence of Earthworms', in which he describes maze learning in this unlikely subject;[13] he also studied frogs and mice. Edward Thorndike, who later became an educator, deduced general laws of learning from his observations of the attempts of cats, dogs, monkeys, and chicks to escape puzzle boxes and navigate mazes.[14] W. S. Hunter designed the delayed response task to test mental abilities in a veritable menagerie: dogs, rats, cats, raccoons, and children of different ages were put through their paces.[15] The task involved three doors, each with a light above it. One light was flashed at the beginning of a trial, indicating which door hid the prize. The subjects could observe the light from behind a barrier. After a delay, the barrier was lifted and the animal was free to choose a door. Hunter wanted to see how long a delay each species could tolerate before forgetting which light had been on. As was typical of this era, Hunter did his best to make the playing field level for his contestants, such as choosing rewards that seemed to motivate each and tailoring the size of the apparatus to match the size of the contestant. Here are the final scores, indicating how long the delay between the light and the choice could be before resorting to guesswork: rats (5 seconds), cats (18 seconds), raccoons (25 seconds), dogs (3 minutes), 15-month old child (20 seconds), 2.5-year-old child (50 seconds – behind the dog!). A five-year-old child could span a delay of five minutes or more. As intriguing as this scorecard may be, there is no way to know, in Hunter's studies or the others, whether any of the differences in performance had anything to do with intelligence. How could Hunter succeed in equating the testing conditions for these sundry subjects? The cats might have been too hungry to learn better, the color of the lights might have distracted the

[13] Yerkes, 1912.
[14] Thorndike, 1911.
[15] Hunter, 1913.

dogs, and the raccoons may have wanted to wash their reward before eating it!

If at First You Don't Succeed . . .

Hunter, Yerkes, Thorndike, and their contemporaries lacked a rigorous approach to making the tests fair. In the 1960s, a comparative psychologist named Jeff Bitterman introduced the idea of systematic variation.[16] Say you are training a lizard to slink to the left if a light is red and slink to the right if a light is green. After many trials, he's still not getting it and you begin to suspect he's an underachiever. How do you find out what might be limiting his performance? Start with the reward. Systematically vary the amount of the reward you give him for each correct response and see if it changes his score, either up or down. If it doesn't, consider changing the stimulus you're asking him to respond to. In a proscribed, methodical fashion, vary the intensity, hue, position, and size of the stimuli. Still no lizard light bulb glowing? Then vary the environmental conditions (temperature, ambient lighting, mood music, and so on) – up and down, back and forth, in and out – and see whether any changes or combination of changes makes the slightest difference in the lizard's ability to get it right. Sound tedious? You bet. And it's worse than that. You finally finished those 246 experiments, having exhausted your supply of lizards, and are now convinced that there are no conditions under which the lizard could possibly ever learn the discrimination problem; you present the results proudly at a professional meeting; at the close of your talk, each of your six dozen colleagues has thought of some other variable you might consider systematically varying or, worse, someone presents a paper showing that lizards *can* learn the task . . . Indeed, there are papers published in this area that almost read: 'I tried really, really hard to get *Ursus horribilis* to play chess. I really did.'

---

[16] Bitterman, 1960, 1965.

A Level Playing Field

The problem is that it is impossible to prove that an animal cannot clear some intellectual hurdle because the very next change you make in your procedures might be one that supports the correct performance.[17] No test can be perfectly fair or be assured of bringing out the best in everyone. The question is, really, when is a test fair enough? A test that was custom-designed to match an individual animal (or person's) needs, propensities, and evolutionary or cultural history would be least likely to be spoiled by extraneous factors and would be the cleanest test of intellectual resources. But that test would be nearly useless for comparing with other animals because it is idiosyncratic, almost guaranteed to be unfair to others. Each concession we make to optimize the conditions for one species threatens to put other contenders at a disadvantage. We must accept that there will always be a tension between the desire to compare species under impartial circumstances and the desire to draw some sort of a conclusion about which is the sharpest knife in the drawer. How to balance this tension is what most of the controversy in intelligence testing in animals is about.

As we will see in greater detail in later chapters, psychologists have resolved this dilemma (or failed to) in different ways. One tactic, favored by the behaviorists and their descendants, has been to test animals in extremely sparse environments, epitomized by the minimalist Skinner box. The development of the Skinner box was not aimed at animal intelligence per se; as I will discuss in chapter 5, the behaviorist obsession with rat and pigeon learning between the 1940s and the 1960s largely supplanted the more ecumenical comparative intelligence studies of the early 1900s. The methodology has nevertheless been applied widely since then to all sorts of questions of animal cognition. In a Skinner box (or 'operant chamber,' a term with

[17] Kamil and Yoerg, 1982.

a certain dark mystique) there is only one toy to play with: a lever (for rats and such) or a peckable key (for pigeons and the like). As with reaction time measures of intelligence for humans, the simplicity of the task eliminates most of the noisy variables that make drawing the line from intelligent performances to 'intelligence' so arduous. Unfortunately, the simplicity of the task also makes it questionable whether anything remotely intelligent is being measured at all. Some experts in both human and animal intelligence testing argue that more permissive testing environments, tests that encourage creativity, spontaneity, and invention, are the only way to get an accurate reading on intelligence. If a kid wants to make mud pies instead of doing block designs, then the test administrator should put the blocks away and evaluate the pies for architectural complexity. As we shall see, the same logic has been applied to designing tests for animals.

Even the most frugal test environment doesn't guarantee uniformity. A colleague of mine had to train a large number of rats to press levers in Skinner boxes as part of his dissertation work. The old-fashioned way to do this is a personal training session with each rat. First you hook up a push button to the rat chow delivery gadget. Then you watch the rat through a one-way mirror. When he moves near the lever, you push the button to give him a bit of food. You do this a few times until he is spending most of his time near the lever. Next you wait until he touches the lever to drop him a treat. Pretty soon he's touching the lever, having associated this act with the reward. In this way, you gradually shape his behavior toward what you want. It's not very difficult to do, but it does take time, especially if you have fifty rats to train. Luckily for my friend, a new, speedy way of training lever-pressing had recently been discovered: the autoshaper. The operant chamber is equipped with a retractable lever. It turns out that if you repeatedly stick the lever into the box, then deliver food, the rat will learn to press the lever automatically.[18] It's not very sensible,

---

[18] Brown and Jenkins, 1968.

because if the rat didn't press the lever he'd get a free lunch anyway; but somehow the lever's association with the food makes the rat press it, and once that happens the rat's in control and gets fed for every lever press. It's a little like the tale about the rooster thinking his crowing made the sun rise. One evening my friend deposited a hungry rat in each of twenty boxes outfitted with autoshaping programs. When he returned in the morning, he looked at the printouts from the rats' workouts. As expected, all the rats had learned to press the bar regularly. But one rat (there is always one) had a suspiciously low rate of bar pressing. My friend went to this rat's box and peeked inside. It didn't take long to see why the rate of lever pressing was so low. The rat would turn facing the back wall of the box, rear up on its hind legs, then fall over backward, hitting the lever with the back of its head. It would then gather itself and collect its reward. The rat did this again and again and again. Apparently, the rat had stumbled (literally!) onto this original solution to the problem and it stuck.

Another way to get around the problem of comparing performance in disparate species is to study species that aren't so disparate. There are excellent theoretical reasons, based on evolutionary principles, for entering species into the Interspecies Cognitive Olympics based on phylogenetic relatedness.[19] From a methodological point of view, selecting closely related species is also eminently sensible. If, for example, you want to learn about problem solving in ducks, you don't have to worry about customizing the apparatus, the reward, the stimuli, etc. The closely related species will waddle through the test in essentially the same manner, see the world in similar ways, and be happy with the same rewards. Or will they? After all, if you are staging Cognitive Olympics for duck species, then you probably have some reason to think some ducks are denser than others, at least in some respects, or why bother? There can be substantial differences in morphology, behavior, and cognition between even closely related species; the evolutionary pressure to divvy up the

---

[19] Hodos and Campbell, 1969.

world into those species-sized pieces called niches helps promote this. Still, the difference between a mallard and a merganser is more manageable, experimentally, than the difference between a mallard and a moose. We cannot eliminate the obstacles of equal opportunity testing by using sister species, but we can mitigate them.

Following Your Instincts

At the shallow edge of a narrow brook, a male stickleback puts the finishing touches on his pièce de résistance – a twig and grass nest anchored to a root jutting from the bank. He swims away from the nest, darting along the border of his modest territory, on the lookout for willing females. As he curves around the edge of a boulder, he meets head-on with an intruder, another male like him with a fire-engine red belly. When the resident stickleback sees the red of the intruder (which female sticklebacks lack) he charges at the other fish, giving chase until the intruder is far beyond the margins of his territory. Flush with the satisfaction of a macho job well done, our stickleback continues his territorial patrol.

It turns out that, during breeding season, male sticklebacks will attack most anything that vaguely resembles another male stickleback. But they get really hot under the collar at stickleback models that have red on the lower half, even if the shape is all wrong.[20] There is an apocryphal story about a stickleback kept in an aquarium near a window in Britain that went ballistic every time a red postal van pulled up to the curb. Now, this is just the sort of push-button, hardwired behavior you'd expect from a pea-brained animal – in this case, a very small pea. The inflexibility of the behavior is reminiscent of the wagtail that insisted on improving the reproductive success of another species. The stimulus (the red belly or the begging chicks) is an irresistible call of duty. Indeed, some of the most impressive feats

[20] Tinbergen, 1951.

of animals – web building by spiders, migratory navigation by butterflies, singing and nest-building by birds, colony organization by bees and termites, homing by spawning salmon, food storing by squirrels – seem to have more to do with instinct than intelligence. Whether we are talking about people or animals, the word 'intelligence' is usually reserved for actions that are more malleable and creative than simply following the letter of your genetic code. Of course, you don't need a very deep understanding of evolution to understand that programmed behavioral responses reveal exquisite adaptation; these are tools that have served these species very well. Still, they'll need more to make it into Harvard.

But is the distinction between instinctual and intelligent behavior valid? Can we easily draw a line between the hardwired, push-button, see-red-get-angry world of instinct and the elastic, scholastic world of intelligence? In a word, no. First, let's bring human beings down a notch. Smart as we are, we are not immune to having our reflexive buttons pushed. How different is the male stickleback from the human male who gets a thrill from images of women in *Playboy*? The man is about as likely to achieve his adaptive endpoint (reproduction) with an image on a piece of paper as the stickleback is to win the argument with the mail van. Granted, the man presumably knows the difference between a photo and the real McCoy, but how do we know the stickleback does not? If a cabbage white butterfly foraging on blue flowers alights on my blue notebook, all we can say is that she seems to be drawn to blue. Whether she can tell the difference between a flower and a notebook requires further study. The point is that biologically important stimuli yank everyone around: the mother responding to her baby's cries, the rabbit freezing when a shadow passes overhead, the dog challenging his owner's rank, the sparrow attacking its image reflected in a window. Those facts do not obviate intelligence. I told my five-year-old daughter that a naturalist once said birds didn't need to be smart because they could just fly away. She replied, 'That doesn't make sense. Birds are smart because they do fly away!' As an ex-pigeon chaser, she knew the score.

If you concede that people's base urges may be somewhat automatic, what about our higher functions? Let's go right to the top to language, that pinnacle of human intellectual invention, the trump card we play whenever another species is shown to have mastered another cognitive trick that used to be exclusively our province. For decades, language has been touted as the ultimate cultural product, the culmination of our general propensity to play with symbols. But the current dominant view of what language is about is found in Steven Pinker's *The Language Instinct*.[21] Yes, an instinct. Pinker and many other experts believe the evidence overwhelmingly supports the idea that the capacity for language and its basic structure are bred in the bone. The gift of language, and some of the elemental tools for its deployment, is in the tapestry of neural connections in our brains. Humans have a fundamental innate readiness to become chatterboxes in the same way as dippers will become divers. Although the difference between instinctual responses and intelligent behavior may seem straightforward, the distinction has, for the most part, only clouded our understanding of why animals and people do what they do. The journey from genetic code to behavior can be circuitous and capricious, whether that code belongs to a fish or a fisherman. We have to be very careful in slicing the fat of instinct away from the bone of intelligence, lest we have nothing left to sink our teeth into. Hingston, a naturalist and a major in the Marine Corps, wrote this in 1939:

> [Instinct] is the mainspring of the insect's life, the force that governs its routine actions, the psychic sea in which it lives. But running through it, illuminating it, breaking all over it, like ripples on a great ocean, are endless little gleams of reason.[22]

If you were to invent a punishment for someone, would you sentence him or her to the task of defining intelligence or of

[21] Pinker, 1994.
[22] Hingston, 1929, p. 150.

measuring it? For me, it's a toss-up. Defining intelligence is frustrating because although a testable definition may elude us, we feel we know intelligence when we see it. The concept is so familiar to us, so much at our disposal because we know – at least we *think* we know – that we've cornered the market on smarts. All definitional problems are tricky anyway, resulting in the feeling that a great deal of mental energy has been expended and nothing more has been understood. In this sense, the measurement issues, thorny as they are, are almost a relief. Even if the test is not perfect, it produces something concrete to start arguing about: data. There's my data and your data and their data, and somehow we have to reconcile the differences and reassure ourselves that the similarities are real. The pleasure of experimental design and measurement is a reprieve from the language-bound nature of the definitional problem, in the same way that nailing two things together is a reprieve from studying a blueprint. Then again, failure in the real world is more tangible than giving a wishy-washy definition. When Bitterman was trying to find what motivates a crab to learn, he tried the usual things, food (which they can go without for months), heat and light (which had no effect), and, finally, shock, which Bitterman said 'proved quite disorienting, often causing the animal to drop most of its limbs.'[23]

In order to think intelligently about animal intelligence, we need to keep the arguments about definitions and measurement in our heads at all times. Every experiment, every anecdote, every story about animals, every TV program about animal minds, every theory about how animals think, know, and feel comprises these core issues, whether they are openly discussed or not. And even among scientists, the positions taken are not solely the consequences of rational impartial consideration of a set of untarnished facts. There is no way to approach the question of animal intelligence without having a stance on these quicksand topics, although sometimes we'll have to dig to see what it is.

[23] Bitterman, 1960, p. 709.

Chapter 3

Angels to Insects

Vast chain of being! Which from God began,
Natures aethereal, human, angel, man,
Beast, bird, fish, insect, what no eye can see,
No glass can reach; from Infinite to thee,
From thee to nothing. – On superior pow'rs
Were we to press, inferior might on ours;
Or in the full creation leave a void,
Where, one step broken, the great scale's destroy'd;
From nature's chain whatever link you strike,
Tenth, or ten thousandth, breaks the chain alike.

A. Pope, 1773[1]

Mind Games

In the 1940s through the 1960s, reputable primatologists from all over the United States were engaging in a curious pastime: shopping for cartfuls of small objects at the local five-and-ten. Back at the lab, they unpacked all the thimbles, rubber balls, Matchbox cars, spools of thread, rubber tub stoppers, wooden blocks, fake flowers, paperweights, jumbo erasers, metal protractors, jars of lip gloss, cigarette lighters, clip-on earrings, poker chips, rubber ducks, and wooden nickels and summoned the monkey.

The monkey sits in a chair in front of a tray that has two shallow wells carved in its surface. Two objects have been placed over the wells, one on the right, one on the left. A peanut has been secreted under one object. The monkey, being a curious fellow and knowing that these games typically lead to treats, picks up the paper doll on the right. A peanut! He slips the peanut into his mouth and tosses the doll onto the table, turning his attention to the pink hair bow

[1] Pope, 1733/1975, p. 478.

on the left. The monkey picks it up: nothing there. The monkey thinks about keeping the bow, mouths it a moment, then puts it down. The tray disappears, only to reemerge a minute later with the same two objects, this time with the bow on the right. The monkey chooses the bow: no peanut. Slightly perturbed, he starts to swipe at the paper doll with the back of his hand, but the tray retracts. On the third trial, the bow is on the right again. The monkey gives it a passing glance and picks up the doll and the peanut in one smooth movement.

The monkey gets twenty bow-and-doll trials, with the doll as the winning ticket. He almost always chose the doll, and reaped the reward, after about the fifteenth trial. The twenty-first trial is different: the objects are a miniature cowboy hat on the left and a business card on the right. It's a different problem, and the monkey is at a loss. He likes the hat and picks it first. No peanut. The tray disappears. Now what might the monkey have learned in the twenty bow-and-doll trials that might give him a leg up on next trial of the hat-and-card problem (Trial 2 of the new problem)? Here is a partial list: 1) The experimenter is just as stingy today as yesterday – he only gives me one peanut each time; 2) Even though I personally prefer the left, the doll was a cash cow no matter what side it was on; 3) If it isn't here, it's there; ergo, although I really like the hat, I should probably pick the card next time.

This game is called 'learning set.'[2] Each pair of novel objects, presented in consecutive trials, is called a problem. The idea is to give the monkey a bunch of trials with each problem. In the first trial of a new problem, there is no way for the monkey to know which object is correct. But after having solved lots of these problems, say twenty trials each of sixty object pairs, the monkey might catch on to the rule for getting the goods on the second trial of a new problem: if the one I chose on Trial 1 was right, stick with it. If not, pick the other one. Learning set is sometimes called 'learning to learn,' because the animal isn't

[2] Harlow, 1949.

35

just learning something rote like: 'If it's green go here; if it's red go there.' Instead, if the animal is bright enough, it learns a procedure for mastering the solution to any novel combination of weird junk items that it might see next. A common measure of improvement during learning set is the percentage of correct choices on Trial 2 of new problems as a function of how many total problems the animal has endured. If the animal was catching on, you'd expect it to be right on Trial 2 about 50 per cent of the time for the first thirty pairs of objects (just guessing), and then show a steady increase through 200, 400, or even 1,000 pairs of objects. A smart cookie would be at nearly 100 per cent right on Trial 2 long before then.

Learning set experiments seem to be, on the face of it, good tests of intelligence. First, 'learning to learn' represents the kind of flexible problem solving that most people would locate squarely in the center of a definition of intelligence. Second, unlike plain old conditioning experiments (of the press-lever-and-get-food type), the learning set task is sufficiently complex and open-ended to actually differentiate between species. Finally, the task appears to be reasonably fair to different species. If a cat couldn't help choose the toy mouse even though it was wrong or if the monkey went bananas over the cowboy hat, it wouldn't really matter, since so many different objects were eventually used to assess learning ability. The apparatus itself could be adapted to the physical whims of various species. For all these reasons, learning set became a popular tool with comparative psychologists.

Lo and behold, the first decade of results from learning set research appeared to separate the wheat from the chaff intellectually. Among primates, humans (of course), chimpanzees and rhesus macaques (Old World monkeys) were the star performers. New World monkeys, such as spider monkeys, cinnamon ringtails, and squirrel monkeys, lagged behind, while marmosets were least impressive. But the marmosets put the cats to shame. Cats were on par with raccoons, both of which outstripped the rodents tested: rats and squirrels. Chickens and pigeons were also tested in learning set experiments and were found wanting.[3] In a comparative psychology textbook printed in 1960, one of the authors summed it up: 'Facility in the formation of learning sets has proven to be one of the most sensitive tests yet devised for measuring problem-solving ability in different species. No other test has so consistently and so meaningfully arranged the species.'[4] Harry Harlow, who pioneered the technique, said: 'By and large the phylogenetic data demonstrate that learning set formation is closely related to evolutionary position, as conventionally described.'[5]

But what did the textbook authors mean by 'meaningfully arranged'? Our best guess is that the learning set data aligned nicely with some preexisting ordering of the species. What is that stable order that gives these experimental results meaning? As I discussed briefly in the first chapter, western society has a long historical bias toward assuming that in any intellectual contest, the ordering of animals will conform to the ranking revealed in the learning set data – that is, the Chain of Being. The 'evolutionary position' to which Harlow refers is the rung of the ladder on which a species stands. That there were no surprises (e.g., the raccoons did not break rank and learn faster than the monkeys) is held up as evidence that the learning set task itself is sensitive and valid – the 'evolutionary position' is assumed to be the stable point. In this chapter, we will examine species relationships more closely and see whether that evolutionary ladder rests on stable ground. But first we need to come to grips with the ideas that have shaped how we view the natural order.

The Good, the Bad, and the Stupid

The Great Chain of Being was forged on the anvil of metaphysics. Plato's stab at accounting for the Real World began with the idea

[3] Miles and Meyer, 1956; Miles, 1957; Shell and Riopelle, 1958; Shell and Riopelle, 1957; Warren, 1966, 1973; Warren and Baron, 1956; Zeigler, 1961; Plotnick and Tallarico, 1966.
[4] Riopelle, 1960, p. 224.
[5] Harlow, 1959, p. 508.

of the Good, an ultimate being devoid of envy, great at making things, and lonely. That combination of traits in the Good resulted in the appearance of everything that exists or ever has existed (although the Good, being self-sufficiently perfect, had no need of anything else). Nothing that exists, of course, could be as perfect as the absolutely flawless Good; in every rock, tree, bug, beast, and babe are defects. Along came Aristotle, who liked tidy boxes for things. He imposed organization on Plato's set of imperfect existences. As an observer of nature, Aristotle saw, on the one hand, that animals, plants, and other natural objects could be classified, that the world was sortable. On the other hand, he also noted that all things graded into other things – the universal overlappingness of the real world, as Lovejoy called it.[6] He saw that animals of one stripe blended into those of another; there were fish that breached the air, birds that soared the seas, and mammals that dabbled everywhere. He read species and group boundaries clearly enough, but could not ignore the variety inside the fuzzy lines.

Because people have a tendency to simplify ideas, Aristotle has been associated since medieval times primarily with the continuity idea, rather than the classifying idea. While it is certainly true that Aristotle injected the idea of continuity into Western thought, it is also true that he didn't stress it as much as people, especially in the late eighteenth century, came to claim. As Lovejoy explains:

> That all organisms can be arranged in one ascending sequence
> of forms, he [Aristotle] did not, indeed, hold. He saw clearly –
> what it required, certainly, no great perspicacity to see – that
> living beings differ from one another in many kinds of ways –
> in habitat, in external form, in anatomical structure, in presence
> or absence or degree of development of particular organs and
> functions, in sensibility and intelligence; he apparently saw
> also that there is no regular correlation between these modes
> of diversity, that a creature which may be considered superior

[6] Lovejoy, 1936.

to another in respect to one type of character may be inferior to it in respect to another.[7]

For Aristotle, then, humans were not necessarily on the top of the heap each and every time. It all depended on what feature served as the basis of comparison.

Nevertheless, by the late eighteenth century, the themes of imperfection and continuity had been fused to produce a hierarchy of things in the world, removed from the ideal Good (now 'God') by imperceptibly varying amount of defect, like a gray scale with infinite resolution: 'All the different classes of beings which taken together make up the universe are, in the ideas of God who knows distinctly their essential gradations, only so many ordinates of a single curve so closely united that it would be impossible to place others between any two of them.'[8] Aristotle's allowance that many different hierarchies of species were possible had been lost. The Great Chain of Being had become a Scale. Of the earthbound beings, humans were the most perfect, regardless of the dimension along which one might measure – including, of course, intelligence.

Upward Mobility

One final architectural detail remained to be added that would convert the Scale into a Ladder – the idea of progress. It wasn't enough for some philosophers that man should rest comfortably on the topmost step, only a glance away from the lowest angel. All creatures, from the lowly dregs to those superior beings within spitting distance of the Creator Himself, have been striving since their inception to move up a rung or two. Nature was no longer static. Rather, creation was, by one scheme or another, a process, specifically a process whereby the creation of the lowly preceded the creation of the ever more perfect. It is by these nineteenth-century inventions that we arrive at the idea of man as being the pinnacle of earthly creation. Given our position on

[7] Lovejoy, 1936, p. 56.
[8] Leibniz, in Lovejoy, 1936, p. 144.

39

the ladder, humans can strive to be good in this life in the hopes of getting bumped up in the next. The hope of rubbing shoulders with the angels was destined to be more alive in some people than in others, however; one disturbing consequence of the dogged adherence to the notion of continuity was that all the rungs on the ladder must, perforce, be filled, even those between humans and chimpanzees:

> Animal life rises from this low beginning in the shell-fish, through innumerable species of insects, fishes, birds, and beasts, to the confines of reason, where, in the dog, the monkey and chimpanzee, it unites so closely with the lowest degree of that quality in man, that they cannot easily be distinguished from each other. From this lowest degree in the brutal Hottentot, reason, with the assistance of learning and science, advances, through the various states of human understanding, which rise above each other, till in a Bacon or a Newton it attains the summit. [9]

Luckily, promotions are available to all:

> Man – who will then have been transported to another dwelling place, more suitable to the superiority of his faculties – will leave to the monkey or the elephant that primacy which he, at present, holds among the animals of the planet. In this universal restoration of animals, there may be found a Leibniz or a Newton among the monkeys or the elephants, a Perrault or a Vauban among the beavers.[10]

The transmutation of the Chain into a climbable Ladder is clear. The wedding of religious philosophers with naturalists assured the primacy of man, whatever the forecast for the monkey and elephant. Moreover, the stage had been set for imbuing human characteristics, particularly human intelligence and morality, with

[9] Jenyns, in Lovejoy, 1936, p.197.
[10] Bonnet, in Lovejoy, 1936, p. 286.

the extraordinary significance they have since had. If humans are the epitome of creation perfected, then whatever we have in spades must be the right stuff to have.

Tree of Life

Darwin complicated this rather simple linear arrangement of life. Certainly his notions of evolution were in step with the gradual progress implied by a completely inhabited ladder to perfection. Where Darwin differed from the religious naturalists was in where, how, and in what direction change might occur. Sure, some species eke out decent livings thanks to improvements on earlier models (greater efficiency, better organization, more complexity), but others have done equally well, or better, by slipping down a few notches to an earlier version or – and here is the biggie – jumping off the ladder entirely into an unexploited niche. Over time, through the impartial magic of natural selection, animals could gain features, lose features, and even use old features for new purposes. We can know that the creatures around today had evolved from other creatures, but without painstaking analysis, technological advances and decades of argument, it wasn't (and isn't) always obvious who begat whom and when. The Ladder had become a tree, and a tangled one at that.

Or had it? If the *scala naturae*, as the Ladder has been called, had truly been supplanted by Darwin's evolutionary tree, then why would that 1960s textbook refer to a quasi-evolutionary series (such as human – Old World monkey – New World monkey – cat – rat) as 'meaningfully arranged'? The idea of a quasi-evolutionary series is to use living species as proxies for extinct species as a means of retracing the evolutionary steps to a particular feature – a body design, a behavior, or a cognitive ability. But such quasi-evolutionary series only work if the relevant part of the evolutionary tree can be drawn with some confidence, and if the species chosen are not highly specialized.[11] For example,

[11] Hodos and Campbell, 1969.

the monkey's uncle that gave rise to its New World cousins is in a different branch of the tree than are the ancestors of the Old World monkeys to which we seem to be related. The New World monkeys hanging around by their tails today cannot, therefore, be used as stand-ins for our ancestors. Just because an animal happens to be a primate doesn't mean its behavior is relevant to ours; many primate species are specialized to do their own thing, which isn't necessarily at all like ours. Primitive carnivores, like cats and raccoons, were never ancestors to any modern monkey and nothing recognizable as a rat ever evolved into a carnivore. Comparing monkeys to cats to rats is a futile exercise if the goal is figuring out the evolutionary origins of some primate feature. Within mammals, nearly everyone jumped off the main trunk of the tree during the Paleocene (60 million years ago), developing independently evolving branches ever since. If the learning set data are indeed 'meaningfully arranged,' it's not because they mirror the real evolutionary history of intelligence.

Given that *The Origin of Species* was published in 1859, it would seem that everyone has had plenty of time to abandon the Ladder metaphor and adopt the Tree. Surely one would expect scientists, even by the 1950s, to have recognized the implications of Darwinian evolution and resisted behaving as though monkeys are simply humans that, without the benefit of a few million years of gene juggling, lack manners and some extra forebrain. Whatever you might personally feel about rats, it should have been abundantly clear that, no matter how much time might go by, rats weren't going to mutate into sophisticated carnivores. Still, many, if not most, of the prominent behavioral scientists of the mid-1900s accepted, either implicitly or explicitly, that a clean linear ranking of species was possible and that this ranking was related to 'phylogenetic status.' Reviews of the evolution of learning or intelligence were comprised of descriptions of performance in mazes, Skinner boxes, and other contraptions by various species, sometimes including invertebrates, sometimes not, but always presented in order of ascension of the *scala naturae*.[12] Mental abilities, or simply a greater quantity of a unitary ability, were added on in each 'higher' species, like options in a successively fancier line of cars. Presumably, one could replace the mental engine of a rat for one with more horsepower and drive away with the mind of a dog. In this sense, the Ladder of Being was consonant with the concept of general intelligence, of a single brand of smart stuff that was doled out according to vertical position. The complexity of the branching genealogy of the animal world, along with the recognition that species could, over evolutionary time, become stupider as well as smarter, was somehow forgotten.

No Missing Links

Perhaps we shouldn't be surprised that an idea that had persisted for more than 2,000 years would not be relinquished overnight, especially since it sat humans on the highest earthly rung. A primary link connecting the Chain of Being with biological evolution was, as we have seen, continuity. While it is true that a species may differ from those swinging from above or crawling below on the distant branches of the Tree, species on the same twig, or on a nearby limb may resemble one another closely in body and mind. The fact of genetic inheritance gives us justification for believing that kissing cousins will have a more similar intellect than distant relations. Darwin was wild about the idea of mental continuity. The hard sell of the theory of evolution via natural selection was, of course, that noble English people could have knuckle walkers as relations. To ease the distance between brutes and gents, Darwin played up the emotional depth, intellectual zeal, and moral fiber of animals. Elizabeth Knoll, in an essay entitled 'Dogs, Darwinism and English Sensibilities,'[13] showed in these quotes from Darwin how he simultaneously yanked up on one rung of the ladder and pressed down on another:

[12] Grindley, 1950; Washburn, 1936; Bitterman, 1965; Harlow, 1958.
[13] Knoll, 1997.

No one supposes that one of the lower animals reflects whence he comes or whither he goes – what is death or what is life, and so forth. But can we feel sure that an old dog with an excellent memory and some power of imagination, as shewn in his dreams, never reflects on his past pleasures in the chase? And this would be a form of self-consciousness . . . On the other hand . . . how little can the hard-worked wife of a degraded Australian savage, who uses hardly any abstract words and cannot count above four, exert her self-consciousness, or reflect on the nature of her own existence.[14]

Darwin had hung the skeleton of an ape in every closet in the civilized world. The least he could do for the Victorians was try to convince them that their nonhuman relatives were not as embarrassing as they had supposed. In *The Descent of Man*, Darwin presented evidence that he believed demonstrated that 'there is no fundamental difference between man and the higher [*sic*] mammals in their mental faculties'[15] and that differences in intelligence among species in general were differences 'of degree and not of kind.' In doing so, he sparked the search for the common threads of intellect throughout the animal kingdom, which was the beginning of the field of comparative psychology.

The tension between the branching tree model of mental evolu-tion and that of the Ladder of Being was nowhere more evident than in the writing of Romanes, a naturalist and contemporary of Darwin. While Romanes certainly accepted that evolutionary lineages diverged again and again, his thoughts were dominated by the temptation to rank species linearly. Romanes also believed that ontogeny recapitulates phylogeny: 'the development of an individual human mind follows the order of mental evolution in the animal kingdom.'[16] Not only did modern animal species show continuous, gradual evolution of mental ability, but also each individual, in the course of growing up, replayed the entire

[14] Darwin, 1874/1998, p. 86.
[15] Darwin, 1874/1998, p. 67.
[16] Romanes, 1888, p. 5.

history of cognitive, emotional, and moral development of the animal world as a whole. A child, as it develops, climbs up the *scala naturae*, accumulating mental abilities for birthday presents, not resting until reaching the rightful position at the top. A three-week-old infant, Romanes claimed, had the acumen of a larval insect, or an earthworm – which is to say, not much. By ten weeks of age, that baby was the cognitive and moral equivalent of a blowfly or a beetle. Snakes would have a hard time outwitting a four-month-old but by fifteen months of age, the child could hold his own against apes and dogs, thus realizing his evolutionary potential. Romanes's scheme serves to show how deeply ingrained was the idea of a progression of intellectual abilities and reinforces the gradual, sometimes glacial pace of the evolution of human belief.

More modern examples of the same outdated thinking are not hard to find. In 1993, Eddy, Gallup, and Povinelli asked people to judge both the cognitive abilities of thirty species of animals and their degree of similarity to humans.[17] There was a strong correlation between presumed similarity and presumed smarts: the less similar to humans, the less intelligent the animal was thought to be. That general result is not very remarkable, but the details of the rankings are. First, the similarity judgments did not conform perfectly to the Ladder of Being. For example, both chickens and robins were placed in the same similarity group as crocodiles and snakes, but two other birds, eagles and parrots, made it into the next higher category dominated by nonprimate mammals. Why is an eagle perceived to be more comparable to a person than a robin is? We'll tackle that question in the next chapter. For now, the most salient point was that the authors themselves fell heavily into the false phylogenetic series trap. The similarity ranking and judgments of cognitive ability of each of the thirty species were dumped into one of nine phylogenetic boxes (invertebrates, fish, reptiles, etc.). The data were then analyzed as if these phylogenetic groups represented an orderly series of

[17] Eddy, Gallup, and Povinelli, 1993.

degrees of remoteness from humans! In reality, crocodiles, whose data were placed within the reptile group, are more closely related to birds than to the other reptile representatives in the study. Also, because it's impossible to say whether modern birds are more closely related to any given mammal than are modern reptiles, the bird group data didn't have to be inserted in the graph between that of the mammals and reptiles. There is no justification for arranging the data so that it looks as if lay people's judgments about animals match up perfectly with phylogeny (that is, true phylogeny, not a 'phylogenetic scale'). It is indeed ironic that in attempting to illustrate how people tend to see certain kinds of animals as being more or less related to humans, the scientists themselves succumb to the same ancient bias that arrays species in single file behind us.

A contemporary primatologist, Frans de Waal, calls the use of continuity to make inferences about mentality 'evolutionary parsimony'. He argues that it is more prudent to assume that close relatives have the same mental abilities (and emotions and awareness) than to assume that they do not.[18] Say a chimpanzee and a person both look intently in a box that had previously held a prized object and then both scratch their heads when the box turns out to be empty. Evolutionary parsimony says that whatever images, feelings, and machinations are moving through the person's head are probably also there in the chimp, unless there's contradictory evidence. A lobster, observed engaging in the same behavioral sequence, would not be awarded the same cognitive status by default, because of its phylogenetic distance from the human. The idea is hardly new: Margaret Washburn sang a similar tune in 1917:

When a being whose structure resembles ours receives the same stimulus that affects us and moves in the same way as a result, he has an inner experience which resembles our own . . . We may extend this inference to the lower animals, with proper

[18] de Waal, 1991.

46

safeguards, just as far as they present resemblances in structure and behavior to ourselves.[19]

When it comes to getting the benefit of the doubt about your mental life, it helps to have relatives in high places.

A caveat about mental continuity and evolutionary parsimony. The possibility of specialization throws a monkey wrench into the gradual, cumulative continuum of abilities that evolutionary continuity implies. Sometimes the apple falls pretty far from the tree and we can reasonably expect qualitative differences in behavior between closely related species. Some experts on phylogenetic trees think there are lots of discontinuities, that species sometimes jump, rather than amble, as new offshoots form, leaving chasms rather than slender gaps between sister species. Even more disturbing, there are no patents on species innovations: what looks like similarity due to ancestry could instead be due to independent evolutionary events. Life is rife with copycat adaptations. But not to worry. It doesn't really matter from a scientific point of view whether the chimp is awarded provisional human mental status or not. It's only an assumption that may or may not lead to a testable hypothesis. Without definitive experiments demonstrating the phenomena at stake (smarts, intentions, consciousness, etc.) no one's mind should be changed on the strength of hunches about continuity.

Jay Is for Genius?

In 1971, Hunter and Kamil tested blue jays for the ability to acquire learning set.[20] Outstripping the performance of their bird-brained relatives, the chicken and the pigeon, the blue jays chose the right object on Trial 2 about 80 percent of the time after plowing through 300 pairs of objects. (Remember that 50 percent correct is what you'd expect by chance alone.) This score was the same as what rhesus monkeys had achieved! But did blue jays and

[19] Washburn, 1917, p. 24.
[20] Hunter and Kamil, 1971.

47

monkeys solve the problem in the same way? Other researchers had determined that the strategy that the monkeys used was something akin to a 'win-stay, lose-shift' strategy. If the object chosen on Trial 1 hid the treat, then stay with it on Trial 2. If that object was the loser, shift to the other object on Trial 2. But how could anyone know what strategy an animal was using? How can we look inside the animal's head and know what lurks within?

Say you give a monkey a simple discrimination reversal problem. There's a red light and a green light. If the monkey chooses red, it gets a reward. If it chooses green, it gets nothing. After many such trials the monkey is reliably choosing red. Then you reverse the game: now green pays off and red doesn't. It takes a few trials for the monkey to catch on to the switch, but it does, at which point you again reverse the payoffs. It's not hard to see that responding to the reversals on this discrimination problem is very similar to learning a new problem on the learning set task. Both are easily mastered using the win-stay, lose-shift strategy. It stands to reason that a monkey that was a veteran of discrimination reversal learning might acquire a learning set more rapidly than a monkey without that training, even though, in one case, the colors just switch back and forth and, in the other, there are new objects each time.

Both rhesus monkeys and chimpanzees are better students of object discrimination learning set if they have already taken a course in discrimination reversal learning. That is, they show positive transfer from one task to the other. Squirrel monkeys, those New World monkeys supposedly an intellectual notch below the Old World group, did not show any benefit of prior training on reversal learning. Neither did cats. Pigeons, who never got the learning set in the first place, did not even show any savings when transferred from one simple discrimination problem to another: switching back and forth between red and green did not help them learn to cope with switching between vertical and horizontal stripes.[21] Blue jays, however, were helped greatly in

[21] Ricciardi and Treichler, 1970; Schusterman, 1962, 1964; Warren, 1966; Durlach and Mackintosh, 1986.

acquiring learning set if they had already learned discrimination reversal. Not only that, but a careful analysis of the details of the jays' performance shows that, as far as anyone can tell, the jays were solving the problem exactly as the chimpanzees and rhesus monkeys were.

So the Ladder collapses. And it wasn't just a fluke. Other birds in the blue jay family (the corvids), such as rooks and crows, also form learning sets without much difficulty.[22] How do we account for this pattern of results, now that they are not quite so 'meaningfully arranged'? One possibility is that the common ancestor of the corvids and the Old World primates had the ability (however we characterize it) and it was simply passed along to both groups. But then we'd have to propose that New World monkeys and cats and pigeons and chickens and who knows what else lost that ability somewhere along the branches. It's sobering to note that the common ancestor of birds and mammals probably had the cognitive capacity of a leaf blower. The more likely scenario is that the blue jay developed the know-how independently – a copycat ability. In evolutionary-speak we say that the rhesus monkey and the blue jay show 'convergence' – they developed the same ability in parallel, not through common heredity. Whether that ability is best characterized narrowly (as the ability to form learning set) or broadly (as general intelligence) is up for grabs.

Evolutionary Trend-setting

The case of the blue jay is not isolated. Other species have twisted the links of the Chain of Being, causing animal psychologists to finally begin acknowledging the complexity of mental evolution and the weakness of our techniques for examining it. But having said that, *all* that, there is one more reason why the *scala naturae*, or some version of it, has persisted. Evolutionary biologists call the process 'anagenesis,' which means 'upward' evolution, the progressively greater complexity and efficiency attained during

---

[22] Mackintosh, 1988.

evolution.[23] Anagenesis transcends phylogenetic relationships, in that two species in diverse lineages (blue jays and rhesus monkeys, for example), might be at the same anagenetic level, but have arrived there by different historical pathways. (Some biologists that study species relationships reject the entire notion of anagenesis simply because, in largely ignoring which species arose from which others, it is purely descriptive. They say that anagenesis is not a biological process, but only a process of some biologists.) Certain anagenetic trends seem quite clear, such as the increase in brain size during human evolution, because the changes are within a closely related group and the anagenetic trend happens to correspond to the true historical one (the phylogeny). Sometimes, though, the prevailing trend is spread across several different branches. For example, the first mammals were quite petite. The group rapidly diverged into primates, bats, anteaters, rodents, carnivores, etc, spreading into every available niche like so many Internet companies. After the split, some species in each group had a growth spurt. This would be an anagenetic trend that had nothing to do with position on the tree, except that, as you move away from the diversion point (along whatever branch), those mammals get beefier.

Is increased intelligence an anagenetic trend? In the broadest and perhaps trivial sense, the answer must be yes, in that no one was solving brainteasers in the primordial soup. Beyond that, it depends on where you look and how good the information about phylogeny is: in order to say anything about whether animals are getting smarter, you have to know how smart their ancestors were. Again, good information on this point is scarce, and there is no justification for using living species as stand-ins for extinct lineages just because they happen to be standing on the limb above. Let's say we wanted to look at problem solving in a family of fish species whose evolutionary relationships are clear. If, based on paleontology and evidence of relatedness, we are confident that some members of the family had retained the more ancient designs

[23] Gottlieb, 1984; Yarczower and Hazlett, 1977; Yarczower and Yarczower, 1979; Demarest, 1983.

(are more 'primitive'), while others had innovated and, perhaps, upgraded, then we are on fairly firm footing for comparing living species and making tentative conclusions about the direction of a trend in cognitive ability. We might say that an anagenetic trend toward great brainpower exists in this family, then go on to look for it in other fish families for which we have decent historical data. We might find little Ladders of Intellect in a number of places. On the other hand, if we insist on painting with a bigger brush, comparing teleost fishes (most of the fish you'd be familiar with) to amphibians and reptiles, and reporting the results as an anagenetic trend, we'd be in hot water. Teleosts evolved collaterally to the line that gave rise to the frogs, newts, snakes, lizards, and their friends. The modern teleost fish is nothing like its common denominator with the other groups, so a comparison of the fish's behavior with the others is futile.

In a sense, the early brand of comparative psychologists that used quasi-evolutionary series to draw conclusions about the evolution of intelligence were attempting to discover anagenetic trends where they had no business looking for them.[24] And it wasn't just the psychologists who were committing these sins. Sloppy anthropocentric evolutionary thinking was not unusual even among evolutionary specialists of the era:

> In human phylogeny, the typical characteristics of anagenesis are exemplified perfectly well: increased complexity and rationalization, improved plasticity of structures and functions, independence of the surroundings and autonomy. After all, it was a brain victory that brought man into the ruling position of the world.[25]

The branch that led to human evolution was viewed as the main trunk of the tree along which the only important events of mental evolution had ever occurred. The monkey-cat-rat Cognitive

[24] Hodos and Campbell, 1969; Campbell and Hodos, 1991.
[25] Rensch, 1959, p. 305.

Olympics served to reinforce a view of mental evolution that should have been down for the count long before. Campbell and Hodos warn that some psychologists are now shaking the barely settled dust off the Great Chain of Being, arguing that it has been legitimized by anagenetic theory. Anagenesis, though, is no theory.[26] Anagenesis is a description of evolutionary design fashions that may or may not have hit every part of the tree. Therefore, a random selection of points along the branches (a carnivore here, a rodent there) will not reveal the trends, if they even exist. The study of anagenesis will not account for why intellectual abilities vary throughout the animal kingdom.

Nepotism and Continuity

One of the residues of a longstanding belief such as the Great Chain of Being is that people forget to think about the world differently. In the case of animal intelligence, the assumption that complex intellectual ability was the exclusive right of a few select mammals discouraged scientists from looking elsewhere for signs of intelligent life. The romantic musings of Darwin and Romanes, who read deep emotion and lofty thought into the lowliest of creatures, were never taken seriously by the experimentalists that succeeded them. The principle of continuity, which linked the Chain and held up the Tree, initially gave comparative psychology both energy and credibility, but it was only briefly that the full spectrum of animal life came under empirical scrutiny. Suitable methods for studying animal intelligence never had a chance to be developed. By the 1930s, very few comparative psychologists, other than primatologists, spoke at all about the mental ties that evolution had wrought between people and animals and, indeed, among the varieties of animals themselves.

One consequence of the abandonment of true comparative psychology was a lack of attention to the fascinating behaviors of animals other than primates. Primatology, with its close affiliation

---

[26] Campbell and Hodos, 1991.

with anthropology, was set on a course different from that of mainstream comparative psychology, despite a common ground that included our questions about animal cognition and intelligence. Primatologists typically publish in their own journals, attend their own meetings, and compile their own edited volumes. Until quite recently, there was little cross talk between the primate people and the rest-of-the-species people, largely because of the privileged position other primates were assumed to have next to the Primary Primate – the continuity issue again. Of course it's completely understandable: other primates often are more like us than other creatures are. But that thinking, taken to the extreme, is what got us into trouble with the learning set data. That primates are similar to us is, at best, a working hypothesis. We have to give other species that ended up ascending the same tree by a different route a chance to show their stuff.

Consider this. As an example of a situation in which evolutionary parsimony should be applied, de Waal relates the story of a chimpanzee named Georgia.[27] When visitors arrive at the colony, Georgia fills her mouth up with water, and then resumes her normal activity. As soon as the visitors are within range, Georgia sprays them, and then falls to the ground in hysterics. Even personnel who are familiar with this game may fall prey to it anyway due to Georgia's subtlety. De Waal wants to be free to talk about Georgia's behavior in the same way that he would talk about a person doing the same thing; after all, the genetic relationship is quite close. He would like to do this without being scolded for being anthropomorphic by his colleagues who don't work with primates. De Waal notes that spontaneous ambush has never been reported in a rat (that darling species of the hard-headed experimentalists), though chimps have been caught at it many times. It's the spontaneity that makes the behavior seem so intelligent.

In an article about the pitfalls of anthropomorphism, Robert Mitchell points out that although De Waal is probably right

[27] de Waal, 1997.

about rats, lots of nonprimate species are known to ambush spontaneously, including coyotes, wolves, and bears.[28] Indeed, some aspects of stalking, as exemplified by members of the cat family, qualify as ambush. Maybe these other mammals belong in the same basket with the chimp and the human. Or maybe you are reassessing whether the ambush story really says anything unique about the chimp now that the behavior seems more widespread. But what about this: small male cuttlefish (relatives of the octopus) sometimes change their appearance to resemble females. They retract the webs on their arms (a male trait), and change their body color and patterns to a more feminine look. These cross-dressing males follow male-female pairs until the male leaves to fight another male rival, at which point the small male changes back into male regalia and courts the female. If the larger male comes back before the deed is done, the small male adopts his disguise once again.[29] Or how about this: females of one type of firefly (*Photuris*) mimic the signals of females of another species of firefly. The signal they are copying is one that is used to let males know that tonight's the night: it's a sexual signal. The *Photuris* female flashes alluringly until a male of the other species begins to approach. The *Photuris* female then descends from the top of grass stems down into thicker vegetation and dims her flashes, presumably because *Photuris* is noticeably bigger and the male would get suspicious. When the male is within reach, *Photuris* attacks and eats him.[30]

Somehow we need to make sense of all these stories connected by the thread of ambush and disguise. If we are going to have different types of explanations for each story, there had better be a very good justification for it. Simple appeals to evolutionary continuity just won't cut it. Our nepotistic intuitions may tell us that the chimp must be doing something more complicated and interesting than the firefly. Why else would it have such a large brain? But what if I told you that the octopus has the biggest, fanciest nervous system of any invertebrate? We must

[28] Mitchell, 1997.
[29] Norman, Finn and Tregenza, 1999.
[30] Lloyd, 1986.

be very careful to state our biases clearly. If we do not, we run the risk of making grave errors in estimating how intelligent diverse species are. Simply put, we don't know enough to make sweeping generalizations about what behavior says about intelligence in any particular kind of animal. We do know that we have an overwhelming favoritism toward primates and to a few other select species. Before we can evaluate the data in hand we need to learn more about who is the teacher's pet and why.

Chapter 4

Appearances and Acquaintances

> They call him Flipper, Flipper
> Faster than lightning
> No one you see is smarter than he
> And we know Flipper, Flipper
> Lives in a world full of wonder
> Flying there under, under the sea.
>
> Theme song from the TV show *Flipper*

A handful of recent surveys has asked people to rank various species according to their intelligence, all with pretty much the same result.[1] For example, one study asked undergraduate psychology students (the white rat of the human race) how reasonable it was to say that a human child, a pet dog, pet cat, pet bird or pet fish could accomplish specific mental feats. The questions were about sensation and perception, pleasure, counting, sorting, imagining, memory, and other cognitive stunts. Here's a sample: 'Could the child (or dog, cat, bird, fish) know that a treat still existed if it was behind a barrier?' 'Could the child (or pet) pretend the treat was something to play with?' and 'Could the child (or pet) remember eating the treat yesterday?' The overall score for each species, as well as the species' score for each different mental ability, conformed to that now familiar ordering: primate, dog, cat, bird, and fish.[2] Surveys asking similar questions about slightly more exotic species delivered the same bottom line. In one study, chimps and dolphins shared the top rung, followed by dogs and cats. A couple of steps below these favorites were pigs, followed by pigeons, mice, and

---

[1] Davis and Cheeke, 1998; Eddy, Gallup and Povinelli, 1993; Rasmussen, Rajecki and Craft, 1993; Herzog and Galvin, 1997.
[2] Rasmussen, Rajecki and Craft, 1993.

rats. Snakes, turtles, frogs, and bats clumped together beneath them, with goldfish, ants, worms, and spiders lurking at the bottom.[3]

We could dismiss these findings by simply saying that these unsuspecting college sophomores are holding on to the Great Chain of Being, probably without even knowing what it is. Through cultural osmosis, they have absorbed the status quo of 2,000 years. A detailed analysis suggests, however, that more than just an implicit Ladder of Being determined the rankings revealed by these studies.

Like what? First, on a strict *scala naturae*, the dolphin is out of order since it is not a primate: we need to account for its lofty position. Second, if we skip over the primates, dogs and cats are our closest intellectual kin, at least according to these surveys. These pets were believed to be twice as likely to master the cognitive hurdles as elephants. In every study, you could drive a herd of elephants through the gap between the perceived intelligence of dogs and cats and that of other (nonprimate) mammals. Because nearly every home in the Western world has willingly housed either a cat or a dog, we should entertain the possibility that familiarity is tipping the scales. Finally, we need to figure out why a mammal such as the bat has been granted no more perspicacity than a frog. Yes, some combination of the Great Chain of Being and an acceptance of evolutionary continuity are behind these rankings, but other influences, in our cultural history and, possibly, in our species' own evolutionary history, may be in play.

Friends and Relations

It was by no accident that Darwin strove most emphatically to connect the mentality and emotionality of people with that of dogs, rather than, say, doves or horses.[4] Neither his theory of evolution, nor any general understanding of biology, demanded that he preferentially underline our similarity to dogs over other

[3] Herzog and Galvin, 1997.
[4] Knoll, 1997.

species. But politically and emotionally, the choice was inevitable for an English gentleman who had set himself the task of making the idea of evolutionary continuity palatable:

> I agree with Agassiz that dogs possess something very like a conscience. They certainly possess some power of self-command . . . Dogs have long been accepted as the very type of fidelity and obedience. [5]

The characteristics of loyalty and obedience, coupled with an expressive face and body, can account for why dogs are such popular and valued pets. Depending on the breed and the individual, dogs can be noble, charming, affectionate, and reliable. No one else is as likely to be so utterly delighted to see you at the end of each day. But while every dog owner should rightly appreciate these and other endearing traits in their pet, nothing says that the intelligence of an ape is part of the package deal. Maybe dogs are as bright as chimps and maybe they aren't. (They probably aren't.) But it is precisely the familiarity and the emotional ties to the family dog that impel us to promote it to genius level. We apply the same secret rules to our fellow humans: the old in-group, out-group story. People in your in-group are those that are similar to you, either because they look like you, belong to the same clubs, or enjoy the same activities, or, and this is the kicker, because they are simply around more often.[6] In-group members are seen as better looking, nicer, and more intelligent than members of out-groups (that is, someone else's in-group). And all you have to do to gain membership to *my* in-group is move next door!

Pets, partly because of their proximity to their owners, are definitely in. Most people consider pets to be family members and attitudes toward pets are similar as those toward children, whether or not there are real children in the family.[7] An analysis

[5] Darwin, 1874/1998, p. 78.
[6] Zajonc, 1968.
[7] Berryman, Howells and Lloyd-Evans, 1985.

of photographs of people with their pets revealed a big change since the nineteenth century in how the animals were positioned relative to their owners. Pets used to be photographed at the feet of people, or among children. More recent portraits almost always showed the pet with one person, usually in a conversational pose.[8] The intensity of our relationships with pets causes us, quite naturally, to imbue them with high-level mental abilities, whether they have earned those extra I.Q. points or not. We like them so we think well of them.

Lloyd Morgan, a comparative psychologist at the turn of the last century, spent a lot of time observing dogs. On one occasion, he gave his dog a stick and watched what the dog did when it encountered a narrow gap in a vertical railing. The dog never could learn to tip its head, orienting the stick vertically to allow the stick, and the dog, to pass through.

> Two of my friends criticized these results, and said that they only showed how stupid *my* dog was. *Their* dogs would have acted very differently. I suggested that the question could easily be put to the test of experiment. The behaviour of the dog was in each case – the one a very intelligent Yorkshire terrier, the other an English terrier – similar to that above described. The owner of the latter was somewhat annoyed, used forcible language, and told the dog that he could do it perfectly well if he tried.[9]

Despite his poor performance, the English terrier had earned his owner's loyalty, and the positive regard that came with it. Consider the relative ranking of the cat and the cheetah in a survey of the perceived intelligence of a motley array of species. On a ten-point scale, the cheetah's score was a full point below that of the cat.[10] Considering their close phylogenetic relationship and the lack of any data at all on cheetah intelligence, the difference

[8] Katcher, 1989.
[9] Morgan, 1900, p. 143.
[10] Eddy, Gallup and Povinelli, 1993.

most likely represents a familiarity bonus for the house cat. And that's after you factor in the rankings of people who *hate* cats!

When we open our doors and our hearts to a person or a pet, our bond with them skews our perceptions; love makes us all a bit blind. Barbara Woodhouse, a well-known dog trainer, claims that 'by being constantly with their owners, by listening to conversation, and by connecting certain sounds with certain actions, the dog can and does understand about 400 words, more if it is a well-loved, extremely intelligent dog.'[11] While Woodhouse may be an excellent trainer, she is no linguist: this claim is pure dogwash. Some dogs respond reliably to commands, verbal or manual, but there is no evidence that any dog has a vocabulary of this size. With her obvious affinity for dogs, it's understandable that Woodhouse would believe that nearly every dog has better verbal skills than the average three-year-old child, but that doesn't mean the claim is accurate. As much as we love our pets – our family members – we must try not to play favorites when we are attempting an impartial debate on the nature of animal intelligence.

Woolly Thinking

It's easy to be mislead when you think you already know who's got the brains. Richard Byrne, who is usually a primatologist, spent some time studying shepherds, sheep, and sheep dogs.[12] Border collies, those quick little black and white jobs, are born sheep hasslers. Without any training whatsoever, a border collie will run this way and that, crouching, sitting down, moving a herd of one hundred sheep around like a twitching school of fish. Of course, the bunching tendency of the sheep helps keep things orderly. Shepherds train the dogs by attaching a different whistle to each type of maneuver the dog makes. Simply through this association, the whistles are eventually transformed into commands to move the sheep here and there. The dog is

[11] Woodhouse, 1994.
[12] Byrne, 1995, p. 35–36.

the flexible learner, permitting its innate chasing patterns to fall under the control of the shepherd, playing the role of the pack leader. The sheep are, well, sheep, getting pushed around willy-nilly by a smart, hairy little tyrant with sharp teeth, under the mysterious control of someone with an even bigger brain.

Not quite. Byrne found that Gujarati shepherds in India whistle just like their British counterparts. The big difference is that the Indian sheep dogs are often asleep on the job during the whistling. It turns out that the Indian sheep respond to the whistles directly, without the necessity of a pushy dog acting as a translator. The sheep seem to regard the shepherd as a herd leader. The dogs are not completely superfluous; they earn their keep by maintaining a watchful eye for predators. As Byrne notes, the expressive qualities of their faces tells us why we assume that dogs are more intelligent and responsive than sheep. However, just because the lights don't seem to be on doesn't mean nobody's home. Sheep are smart enough to develop long-term relationships based on individual recognition, even forming alliances.[13] They may all look the same to you but not, apparently, to one another.

You Ought to be in Pictures

Living with animals isn't the only means by which they become familiar and, hence, judged more favorably. Airtime counts, too. *Flipper* did more for the perceived intellect of porpoises than all of the rigorous cetacean research that preceded and followed the show simply because Flipper was so likeable. He always looked as if he had an amiable, toothy grin on his face and his chatter sounded like laughter. And wasn't he always ready to help Sandy and Bud when they were in a fix? Of course, scientific information about the huge brains and social nature of dolphins and porpoises augmented the positive effect of their sunny personalities, sending them to the top of the charts. A survey of children's attitudes toward animals conducted by the BBC in 1988 during a broadcast

[13] Rowell and Rowell, 1993.

when *Flipper* was a current show revealed that the dolphin was the number one favorite animal. Dogs had slipped to number two.[14]

Television and movie producers realize, of course, that taking advantage of species preferences that are already established in their target audience is much less risky than trying to convince them to love something strange. Lassie and Benji were shoo-ins, as were all 101 of those Dalmatians. These doggie stars are portrayed as faithful, lovable, and smart as the dickens. But if Hollywood ever encroaches on certain areas of the Brazilian rainforest, the casting will have to change. The Bororo Indians of central Brazil keep only red macaws as pets, although dogs, chickens, and pigs hang around. The macaws belong only to the women, are considered sentient, and are at the core of the spiritual life of this tribe.[15] One can readily predict how the Bororos would rank the intelligence of macaws relative to dogs and chickens. Other primitive cultures plucked wild species from the back forty to live with them as near equals. We in Western society are a long way from that. As civilizations became more urbanized, direct contact with most species was lost. The wild became the barnyard and the species mutated into more congenial forms. By 1900, the barnyard had become the backyard. The vast majority of families no longer had working farms and retained only a species or two, in companionship, rather than in service.[16] In our shrink-wrapped, drive-through modern world, pets are just about the only animals most people ever get a chance to know well. Consequently, popularized animals in Western cultures are almost always common pets, although there have been a few notable exceptions. *Tales of the Riverbank* was a popular television show created in Canada during the 1960s. The main characters were a hamster and a white mouse, but the wise creature from which they sought advice was a bullfrog. In Australia and Britain, children of the 1960s and 1970s watched the adventures of Skippy the Bush Kangaroo, an extremely intelligent marsupial. Here is

[14] Paterson, 1990.
[15] Shephard, 1996, p. 108.
[16] Russow, 1989.

the characterization of an exchange between Skippy and his human friend, Sonny, taken from a nostalgia website:

Sonny: (looking worried) What is it, Skip?
Skippy: *A funny clicking sound like someone tutting*
Sonny: What kind of accident, Skip?
Skippy: *The tutting sound again.*
Sonny: Better run and tell dad to get help, Skip.
Skippy: *Yet more tutting!*
Sonny: Oh, all right then, Skip. You go and get the helicopter. I'll wait here.

Even disregarding telepathic kangaroos, talking horses ('the famous Mr. Ed'), and mice with pet cats (Stuart Little), most popular media are poor sources of accurate information about species' abilities, cognitive or otherwise. But in our court of public opinion, it hardly matters. Once we see an animal interacting in a positive way with people, or acting *like* people, we start considering provisional membership to our in-group and the boost in intelligence that such membership carries. Whether an animal becomes familiar because of real virtue or simply favorable PR from Disney, our feelings about them will have been changed. And it is that change in feelings, that step toward kinship, which compels us to see them as intellectual brethren.

Love in a Blind

People who study animals for a living are not immune from this effect. In fact, animal behaviorists must constantly struggle to see their subjects clearly and dispassionately, despite the heavy doses of familiarity that prolonged exposure to a particular species inevitably brings. I have special sympathy for primatologists in this regard: they must work hard against the prejudicial effects of both familiarity and similarity, which encourages anthropomorphism. Some well-known primatologists have been criticized for the ease with which they assume apes and monkeys have a special kind of intelligence or mentality. Mitchell provides an interesting example relating to chimpanzees that seem to recognize themselves in mirrors, given sufficient time in front of one.[17] Almost a hundred years ago, a psychologist named Cooley developed an idea about self-concept in people, arguing that our self-concept results from other people's appraisals of us: what we think of ourselves is an objectified view made up of others' judgments. Gallup and his colleagues who pioneered the mirror work in chimpanzees argued that if recognizing your image in a mirror reflects the possession of a self-concept and if Cooley was right about the process, then mirror self-recognition would only happen if the chimps were housed together. How else could they get the appraisals from other chimps from which to fashion a self-concept? As it turns out, chimps raised alone never act as though they recognize themselves in a mirror. The primatologists then concluded that chimps must have a self-concept of the kind Cooley described.

The problem with this conclusion is that there is no evidence that the chimps raised socially were using each other's appraisals to cobble together a 'self'. When we look in a mirror, we know that we are seeing the skin around a 'self'. The apparent similarity between the chimps and people helps draw the parallels even without the right data. Soon, the chimp researchers began to use mirror self-recognition as evidence that chimpanzees knew about the minds of *other* chimps. (Remember Cooley's idea was that the 'self' was originally constructed from the opinions of others, not the other way around.) As a final step in drawing the line sharply between the mental haves and have-nots, all of the fuzzy logic and broad assumptions based on primate kinship led to denying 'selfhood' to any species that couldn't recognize itself in a mirror – all of them apart from most chimps and orangutans and one gorilla. About this type of biased interpretation, Mitchell wrote: 'What I think happens when scientists interpret animal behavior is that they are looking for evidence to support a

17 Mitchell, 1997.

story (often presented bare-bones as a theory), but unfortunately sometimes the story is so convincing that evidence is unnecessary to convince.'[18]

Social Gaffes

If you are very close to a particular animal there is yet another way in which you may be putting more inside its head than there is room for. This idea, like others I have already mentioned, is borrowed from social psychology: if we are considering pets as family members, then we probably apply some of the same tacit rules in our interactions with pets as with people. One of the many illogical stunts that people pull in relationships is called the 'fundamental attribution error': we tend to attribute our own behavior to external, situational causes but interpret other people's behavior as caused internally by persistent traits.[19] So, if the voice mail tree of a large company infuriates *me*, it's because the system is poorly designed and inefficient. If the same thing infuriates *you*, it's because you are impatient and overly sensitive. Almost everyone commits this error routinely. And in a way it makes sense. You are much more likely to have inside information about the situational details that help determine the choices you make and the kind of behavior you exhibit. Other people trying to figure out what makes you tick won't be as clued in. For them, putting most of the causes inside you and forming them into stable, predictable traits gets around the problem of lack of information about external prompts. People are biased to see behavior, when it is not their own, as driven by forces within.

If pets are people, too, then we are probably committing the fundamental attribution error when we account for why the dog made a mess of the carpet or why the cat panics when the dishwasher goes on. Internal causes are, by their very nature, more psychological than external causes. Moving behavioral

[18] Mitchell, 1997, p. 158.
[19] Gilbert and Malone, 1995.

triggers inside the skull automatically grants everyone – pets and people – an organized inner world that is more responsible for their behavior than the push and pull of the environment. Of course, the traits we attribute to animals need not be flattering. Thinking that an animal is stupid is an internal attribution. But because of the effects of familiarity, that in-group bonus, chances are that attributions made by people to their pets will be more complimentary than critical. Also, when we decide that we like someone (or some animal) we attribute saintly acts to persistent personality traits but tend to excuse beastly acts as driven by external causes! (If your kid does well on a test, it's because he is smart; if he doesn't it's because the test was too hard or he's coming down with a cold or he doesn't like his teacher . . .) It's not hard to see, then, how with the help of these ubiquitous psychological propensities a favored animal could end up seeming quite a bit more thoughtful, more complex, and more intelligent than it may really be.

I recently had my consciousness raised on just this point: last week we got a dog, my very first. She's great! Cassi is a Rhodesian ridgeback and at nine months is weighing in at over eighty pounds. I took her over to our neighbors' the other day for a play date with their dog, one of those sharp little Australian sheep dogs. Cassi, it turns out, is a social cream puff, at least in comparison to their dog, who was circling her at top speed as if she were a sheep, barking like a banshee, and jumping up to try to nip Cassi's nose which, given their relative size, was just out of reach. I was relating the encounter to my husband and said something like, 'Cassi just took it. She was probably figuring that if she put up with the hysterics, the other dog would eventually chill out and then she could make friends with her.' He received this excessively rich explanation with a patient sigh and a small smirk. 'Did Cassi eventually extract an apology from her new friend?' Even after I digested my large slice of humble pie, I would be less than honest if I said that I never again thought of Cassi's mental life as more complex than a daytime drama. It's only human, but now I know better than to talk about it.

The Importance of Being Adorable

Unless you have spent the last few years at the bottom of a mine shaft, you are probably familiar with the Japanese cartoon phenomenon of Pokémon. Among the hundreds of characters that comprise the Pokémon collection, one has emerged as the mascot and sentimental favorite: Pikachu. Pikachu has a tubby bright yellow body, an oversized round head topped with long black ears. Its eyes are dark and huge, his mouth is a tiny pink porthole, and his nose is nonexistent. If it weren't for his long lightning bolt tail, he'd look exactly like the result of a genetic engineering accident involving both rabbit and canary DNA. He is undeniably and deliberately cute. In scientific jargon, Pikachu is a heavily neotenized creature. Neoteny, as a biological term, refers to the retention of juvenile features into adulthood. Humans are a neotenized species because we show traits as adults that are present only in the young of our primate ancestors. Here are some of our babyish Pikachu-like traits that we never outgrow: round head, lack of body hair, flat face, small teeth. Behaviorally, we also show neoteny, as evidenced by our long childhood. With considerable narcissism, we also prefer neoteny in other species. Think of neoteny as an in-group marker. Pikachu is only the most recent example of our love for neoteny. Nearly all cartoon characters exhibit similar traits. Stephen Jay Gould has analyzed the increasing neoteny of that ubiquitous Disney symbol, Mickey Mouse.[20] Not only is Mickey strongly human in his behavior and appearance (talking, wearing clothes, walking upright), he has also become more neotenized over the last sixty years. Charlie Brown's dog Snoopy, Bambi, Furby, and a great many toy animals have exaggerated juvenile features. Neoteny sells.

Our love for neoteny is not limited to fake animals on our toy shelves and at Disneyland; we also prefer those characteristics in our pets. Humans have bred neotenized features into many

[20] Gould, 1980, p. 95–107.

pet species, but particularly into certain species of dogs. The chihuahua with its dainty body, bulbous head, and giant dark eyes is the ultimate neotenized animal, but several other dog species approximate this body plan one way or another. There are no floppy-eared wild dogs or wolves. Neotenized behaviors, including docility and tractability, have also been selected as favorable traits over the history of dog domestication. As the dog expert Stanley Coren points out, some breeds of large dog (Newfoundlands, Saint Bernards, and Great Danes) have such low activity levels that they are called 'mat dogs'; left to their vegetative selves, these dogs would lie immobile on a mat in front of the hearth all day long.[21] Other domesticated animals, such as pigs and cows (but notably not the cat) also have become more babyish under selection by humans.[22] What is the effect of all this cuteness? We have been designed by evolution to nurture and protect our babies. Motherly love is the most essential of biological mandates, especially given our species' extremely helpless newborn period and prolonged dependency. Just as the stickleback attacks when it sees anything fishy with a red belly, we are irresistibly charmed by anything that resembles a baby, either in looks or behavior.[23] That outsized head, those giant unblinking eyes, those stubby little legs, that button of a nose, that soft skin – whether it's your kitten or your infant daughter, your response is probably the same: 'Aaaahhhh . . .' The push-button appeal of neotenized animals is reflected in our choices of pets and in the prevalence of animals in advertising and entertainment. Juvenile features, and our emotional responses to them, can also weigh heavily in ethical situations. The extremely appealing faces of young harp seals undeniably augmented the public outrage over their clubbing. Would we have cared as much if they had been young manatees, which look like overinflated Jimmy Durantes? Conservationists have long been frustrated at the difficulties in rallying public support for species that fail to

[21] Coren, 1994.
[22] Lawrence, 1989.
[23] Lorenz, 1981, p.164.

reach cuteness criteria. A survey of preferences for zoo animals (including one conducted in 1960 by Desmond Morris) showed that the Top Ten were all 'humanoid', having the neotenized features of large eyes, rounded faces and cuddly body.[24]

Who's smarter, a German shepherd or a Pekingese? A ferret or a rabbit? A tiger or a piglet? Most people would choose the first of each pair, based at least in part on appearance. The same physical and behavioral features that elicit protective impulses from us also tell us that the brain behind that cute face may be a porkpie short of a picnic. After all, neoteny implies innocence, and innocence isn't typically associated with brilliance. It's maturity that brings wisdom. Remember, too, that I.Q. tests for people are age-normed, meaning that lower standards apply to lower ages. We expect the developing mind to be a bit dull. Have you ever heard anyone say: 'Why, your baby looks very clever!'?

Another reason that people might automatically rank the intelligence of a ferret above that of a rabbit may be that we recognize an implicit relationship between an animal's body design and its lifestyle. The eyes of predators, such as wolves, hyenas, tigers, and foxes, usually are smaller (even beady) and oriented forward down the muzzle, which is typically elongated. The eyes of their prey, in contrast, tend to be larger and oriented to the side, where they can get a full view of whoever might be considering putting them on the menu. One theory of the evolution of intelligence is that smarts are related to dining habits: it doesn't take a genius to munch grass for hours on end; it does take one to find and catch a nimble grass-muncher. Hunting, especially when performed in a group, appears to require complex problem-solving ability. Observers of lions, for example, have noted that during complicated maneuvers such as driving prey to an ambush, lions often appear to monitor the movements of the other lions.[25] For their part, the professional prey species, predominantly herbivores, certainly need to be vigilant. The issue of whether avoiding becoming the victim of a hunt requires the

[24] Paterson, 1990.
[25] Stander, 1992.

same cognitive acrobatics as required for hunting has not been settled. But we are talking about our *perception* of the relative intelligence of the hunter and the hunted. Prey species have some behavioral habits that do not inspire confidence in their mental abilities. Looking like 'a deer caught in the headlights' refers to a frozen posture and wide-eyed stare characteristic of an antipredator response common to many herbivores. As adaptive as such strategies undoubtedly are, at least in the presence of good brakes, they nevertheless contribute to our dim view of the 'dumb bunny' and his grazing friends.

Pig Out

In practice it will be very difficult to tease apart the effects of similarity, familiarity, sentimentality, and neoteny on our judgments of comparative intelligence. It's relatively easy to make up a story about what influences our perceptions of any given animal, but harder to be sure that the story is accurate. Take the dolphin. We could say that the media portrayals of dolphins have always been favorable, and that its plight in the nets of tuna fishermen also makes it a sentimental favorite. We may also know from nature programs of its large brain and clever use of sonar communication. On the similarity dimension, it's not on the privileged primate branch, but at least it's a mammal (though a suspiciously fishy sort). The dolphin's large head, smooth skin, and appealing face make it a candidate for an intelligence downgrade based on neotenization, but that could be balanced by our knowledge of that it has to be bright enough to catch fish. Depending on how you load each of these factors in your equation, the dolphin could end up anywhere in the intelligence lineup.

For some species, such as the pig, the situation is even more complex. During the Middle Ages, all sorts of creatures were convicted of criminal behavior and tried by the courts.[26] A plague

[26] Mason, 1988.

of caterpillars was nearly excommunicated by the Catholic church for destroying crops but was ultimately released due to the efforts of an advocate. Weevils were brought up on charges of helping themselves to some tasty vines, but were also spared by the nimble wits of their lawyer. He asserted that the weevils, like all God's creatures, had been put onto the earth to be fruitful and multiply: how could the weevils honor that dictum without a bit of sustenance? While several species of larger animals also were prosecuted for wrongdoings during this era, a preponderance of the accounts involve the unlawful activity of pigs. In 1386 a sow was convicted of the murder of a child and was led to the public execution dressed in man's clothes. Another pig was accused of having eaten a child. Because the crime occurred on a Friday, the pig received a two-count indictment: one for murder and one for breaking the religious ban on eating meat. In the fifteenth century in France, the boarding costs at the royal prison charged the same rate for a pig as for a man.

Before pigs became domesticated, they were revered for their intelligence and respected for their power.[27] They were, for example, sacred to the goddess Artemis. The status of pigs, however, plummeted during the Middle Ages. During this time, the wild boar, lean and wily, was penned and transformed into an organic garbage disposal. No other mammal has been more consistently denigrated since. Elizabeth Lawrence, in an article about animal symbolism, provides a comprehensive account of the slanderous attitudes that are commonly held about pigs. Aesthetically, we don't like pigs because of their mud-wallowing habits, their little eyes, and their aggressive feeding habits. Because of their omnivorous diet, pigs, like humans, tend to put on a few pounds when given ample food but little exercise. Muddy pigs not only appear unclean, but also were officially declared so in the Book of Leviticus, adding a religious taboo against the consumption of their flesh to the growing list of reasons to revile pigs. The numerous slights in the Bible have served to establish firmly the

---

[27] Lawrence, 1993.

pig's repulsive character in the history of Western thought. The best known of these slurs is the admonition not to cast pearls before swine. Direct associations between pigs and the Devil himself pepper the text, thereby linking pigs with the ultimate out-group. Lawrence also notes that a pig is conspicuously absent from the otherwise inclusive barnyard clan at the nativity. And let's not forget that fetal pig with the latex veins awaiting your amateur autopsy.

One theory of pig unpopularity centers on the nature of our relationship with pigs. The pig is the only domesticated animal that is raised solely for butchering. You can't milk it and it doesn't lay eggs, but its ribs taste delicious with barbeque sauce. The point of having a barnyard pig is to eat it (or to sell it for someone else to eat). What makes things a bit uncomfortable for us is that the pig's diet, at least traditionally, came directly from the family table and the pigpen was usually close to the house, for convenience. Like the family dog, the family pig ate scraps. Edward Leach, an anthropologist, hypothesizes that there is shame associated with feeding an animal from your table just so you can put it back on the table, roasted with an apple stuck in its mouth.[28] That shame becomes attached to the pig itself. We revile the pig, he argues, because we can't otherwise rationalize how we treat it. It's fat, it's dirty, it's stupid, it's greedy – it's bacon.

In recent surveys, people have rated the pig's intelligence as on a par with that of a cow – that is, pretty dumb for a mammal. And while the media has portrayed pigs more positively than as being instruments of Satan, their mental acuity has rarely been emphasized. By and large, pigs are displayed as bubble-gum pink innocents, always starting out as a darling little (neotenized) piglet. One of the most famous pigs, Wilbur of *Charlotte's Web*, escapes slaughter because of the sympathies of a little girl and a literate spider.[29] He grows up to be sweet, thoughtful, and emotional, but hardly brilliant. The movie *Babe* begins with an orphaned piglet that gets adopted by a border collie, thus

[28] Leach, 1975.
[29] White, 1952.

beginning its life believing it is the premium pet – a dog. Everyone adores Piglet of *Winnie the Pooh* fame because he is tiny, clean, steadfast, and endearing.[30] The Warner Brothers version, Porky Pig, is well meaning but gullible, voluble, neurotic, and foolish.

People who study and work with pigs consider them unusually intelligent creatures. Though not the most convenient of laboratory animals due to their size and boisterous personality, pigs have proved tractable research subjects. Pig hunters also have great respect for the intelligence of their quarry; wild pigs are furtive, wary, fast, and not easily outsmarted. Most pig hunters are lucky to catch sight of one in a season, let alone get a bead on one. Another group of pig enthusiasts took hold in 1985 when the first pot-bellied pig was imported into the United States. Though most people would still balk at the idea of a pig for a pet, thousands have invited them into their homes. Most have been as impressed with their trainability and cleverness as with the rate at which a diminutive piglet can be transformed into a 300-pound porker!

In two notable instances, pigs have realized their intellectual potential in popular media. In George Orwell's political satire, *Animal Farm*, pigs first incite a revolution and then become the despotic rulers of the barnyard. Gradually they become more and more like their human oppressors – dressing in clothes, walking upright, sleeping in beds – all with the help of the dogs, who act as their thugs. Indeed, Orwell presents his own ranking of the intelligence of domestic animals by indicating their capacity for literacy:

> As for the pigs, they could already read and write perfectly. The dogs learned to read fairly well, but were not interested in reading anything except the Seven Commandments. Muriel, the goat, could read somewhat better than the dogs, and sometimes used to read to the others in the evening . . . Benjamin [the donkey] could read as well as any pig, but never exercised

[30] Milne, 1996.

his faculty . . . Clover [a horse] learnt the whole alphabet but could not put the words together. Boxer [another horse] could not get beyond the letter D . . . On several occasions, indeed, he did learn E, F, G, H, but by the time he knew them, it was always discovered that he had forgotten A, B, C and D . . . None of the other animals on the farm could get further than the letter A. It was also found that the stupider animals, such as the sheep, hens, and ducks, were unable to learn the Seven Commandments by heart.[31]

Orwell's pigs, however, use their intellect harshly by subjugating the other animals. It seems that in the popular imagination, pigs cannot be at once intelligent and sympathetic. The only exception to this rule that I have rooted out is Arnold Ziffel. Arnold was the beloved son of Fred and Doris Ziffel, neighbors of characters played by Eddie Albert and Eva Gabor on the 1960s hit TV show *Green Acres*. Arnold was a son who happened to be a pig. He was always clean and polite. He even went to college. There is an urban legend that at the end of the show's final episode, the rest of the cast invited Arnold to a barbeque – as the pièce de résistance. In today's world, it just doesn't pay to be a good, smart pig.

The complicated story of our attitudes toward pigs reveals the sizable gap between what we think we know about an animal and what we really do know, or what we might know if we let go of our preconceptions (our pig-headedness, if you will) long enough to take a good hard look.

Eating Crow

For animals we believe we know very well, like dogs and cats, we must carefully reexamine how our emotions and expectations have framed our perspective on the intelligence of their behavior. Have you ever had an outsider capture a truth about your family simply because they could stand back far enough to see it clearly? Pretend to be a stranger to your dog, and to

[31] Orwell, 1946, p. 39–40.

dogs in general, and see if it changes your opinion of what transpires between its ears. For animals that are neither friends nor strangers, like pigs, we should be more humble about our lack of direct knowledge of their abilities and try not to let fables, legends, and ancient tradition determine our appraisal. I'm no pig-lover, but there is a measure of poetic justice that the butt of every barnyard joke may turn out to be the Einstein of the bunch. Sometimes our dislike for certain animals causes us to deliver left-handed compliments about their cognitive capacities, demeaning them while we acknowledge their intelligence. Why are foxes clever rather than just plain smart? Why are coyotes wily rather than elegantly intelligent? Are we trying too hard to separate these wild canids, which don't give a damn if we never throw them a stick or scratch their ears, from our best friend the dog? Why are crows and ravens thought to misuse their intelligence, like street-smart teenagers, unlike the dolphin, which uses its intelligence amiably to whistle to its friends and synchronize graceful leaps into the air? Is it because of all the bad press that crows have gotten in fables and myths? Or is it that a crow looks like an angry calligraphy stroke in flight and like a cocky black-eyed thief up close? Crows barely beat out lizards and skunks in a recent animal popularity contest.[32] Are we really so shallow that our emotional response to an animal's appearance or way of life is what determines how bright we think they are?

The take-home message is that familiarity, similarity with humans, the innocence of neoteny, and the look of the about-to-be-lunch are not, as far as we know, definitive shortcuts to deciding who is smarter than who, although there may be a measure of truth in each idea. Swallowed whole, each of these factors can distort our capacity to perceive clearly how animals really behave. Yes, every schoolboy knows that there is no such thing as perfect objectivity. Better, however, to know your predispositions and biases than to get tangled in them and miss the facts.

[32] Kellert, 1989.

Chapter 5

You Can Lead a Horse to Water,
But You Can't Make It Think

> For as men of the utmost scientific skill have failed to prove
> good observers in the field of spiritualistic phenomena, so
> biologists and psychologists before the pet terrier or hunted
> fox become like Samson shorn. They, too, have looked for
> the intelligent and unusual and neglected the stupid and
> normal.
>
> E. Thorndike, 1898[1]

In the nascent years of the 1900s, John Broadus Watson transformed psychology from a weak sister of philosophy into an
innovative, comprehensive stand-alone discipline modeled on
engineering and physics.[2] Until then, the chief activity in experimental psychology had been the dissection of the conscious
thoughts of professional introspectionists. To Watson, looking
inside one's head to understand the psyche was a quaint parlor
game appropriate to the backward 1800s; he instead championed
a real science for a bold new century, governed by a rigid philosophy that eschewed references to the mind, placing the full burden
of the explanation of behavior in the environment. Watson's
tightly controlled experiments with animals purportedly showed
that behavior was tidy and lawful and reducible to little reflex
pieces, which, when linked together, comprised the glorious
range of all behavior in all species through all time.

If Watson had been a pioneer, B. F. Skinner, who appeared on
the scene in the 1930s, was a messiah. Skinner explained how
behavior came under the control of reward and punishment,
and how new behaviors could be sculpted from the raw material

[1] Thorndike, 1898/1998, p. 1126.
[2] Watson, 1914.

of old behavior; shapeless twitches and incidental movements could, by the hand of nature (or a clever experimenter), become dances, speeches, or embraces. Skinner had a utopian vision of a world in which, through behavioral engineering based on conditioning principles, the environment could be perfectly tuned to elicit the best from everyone.[3] Bonded by a common vision that encompassed not just science, but life, Skinnerians didn't just agree with behaviorist principles, they believed in them.

Science Marches On

Behaviorism held psychology in a headlock for decades; one would be at pains to exaggerate just how little oxygen was permitted to reach the brains of the discipline as a consequence. Behaviorism was born in the United States in the early 1900s, but really took hold in the 1920s and 1930s, when new psychology departments were sprouting in universities across the country. Energetic and cocky behaviorists filled the ranks. Psychology departments expanded further after World War II and, again, because behaviorism was still dominant, most psychology departments ended up with a very strong behaviorist contingent. Behaviorists bred more behaviorists, perhaps with slightly different stripes, but behaviorists nonetheless. Through the 1970s, most psychology majors in the United States, including those destined to become psychoanalysts, would have been rigorously schooled in conditioning principles and most would have learned to teach a rat to press a bar for food. Until quite recently, if you wanted to be an experimental psychologist – that is, if you wanted to conduct a scientific study of human and animal behavior – you would have been asked to toe the behaviorist line.

Interestingly, behaviorism never secured the vise grip on psychological thought in other countries that it did in the United States. Europeans in particular were more accepting of genetic influences on behavior: you were who you were born to be and

[3] Skinner, 1948, 1974.

pretty much stayed that way. There was something about the idealism inherent in the behaviorist philosophy that appealed to Americans; anyone, from any background, could become whatever they wanted, assuming the conditions were right. As products of our environment and our environment only, the possibilities were limitless. The brain, and the behavior under its control, was like the American West: inexhaustible, rich with prospect, malleable, and ripe for the picking. American faith in the overwhelming importance of personal environmental history in determining behavior is still very strong. Consider our rush to automatically assign victim status based on unfortunate developmental circumstances, even going so far as to rationalize and excuse violent crimes when environmental conditions are less than optimal; for instance, if Johnny ate too much sugar, 'The Twinkie Defense' might be cited. We were a nation of behaviorists before the first rat pressed an operant lever.

As a phenomenon of the era of streamlining, Behaviorism is best known for what it rejected. It rejected the mind, of course, and all the thoughts, feelings, consciousness, desires, motives, and beliefs that filled it up. Between the ears was a black box – a Pandora's box – filled with destructive mental entities that would lure pragmatic scientists away from the real business of behavior. Better to keep it shut. Behaviorism rejected the study of complex behavior in natural circumstances. The goal of psychology was to predict and control behavior, and how could you do that with the animal running around and you chasing after it? Consider this statement from one of the leading experimentalists of the century: 'One of the most persistently baffling problems which confronts modern psychologists is the finding of an adequate explanation for the phenomena of maze learning.'[4] How nearsighted was the rest of the world worrying about trivial issues like psychopathology and child development! But for Hull and his colleagues, complex behaviors (and the deeper issues that accompany them) were made up of smaller

[4] Hull, 1932, p. 40.

units chained together; once you understood how the individual components were developed and maintained in a rarified setting like a laboratory maze, the mystery of complex behavior would be solved. A true psychology, including an understanding of human nature, would be found in the alleyways of a rat maze.

Behaviorism also rejected the study of different kinds of animals. Rats, pigeons, monkeys, and humans all respond to reinforcement schedules the same way, so why bother filling the lab with exotic species? Behavior and the principles that govern it are generic. How else could Skinner have justified titling a book about bar pressing in rats *Behavior of Organisms*?[5] Get rid of all the terms and theories that can't be nailed down, the behaviorists said, and start with what we can know for sure, what we can see, and what we can measure. The behaviorists were dead certain that a few general principles of learning, and therefore of behavior, would emerge. They took the flabby, undisciplined, quasi-scientific study of psychology and sent it to boot camp. When it was released, it couldn't write poetry or sing a lullaby, but it sure could march!

Equality Under the Laws of Learning

Within the behaviorist worldview, the solution to the problem of animal intelligence was a snap. Intelligence is the same as learning because all behavior is learned, including the behaviors we label as intelligent. Learning proceeds the same way in every animal. As Watson put it: '[I]n passing from the unicellular organisms to man, no new principle is needed'.[6] In reviewing species selection for experiments on learning and intelligence during the early history of psychology, Bitterman remarked:

> As a working hypothesis, the proposition that learning is essentially the same in all animals led to the study of many animals. As an article of faith, it led, by the principle of least effort, to concentration on one.[7]

[5] Skinner, 1938.
[6] Watson, 1914, p. 318.
[7] Bitterman, 1960, p. 705.

The Chosen Species was the white rat. Some minor species differences in learning did crop up but were attributed to variation in sensory and perceptual abilities, factors which were dismissed as uninteresting and irrelevant. To the behaviorists, the species differences wrought by the relentless hammer of natural selection presented only engineering problems in the design of testing situations and did not impinge on how learning – or intelligence – was conceived: '[O]nce you have allowed for differences in the ways in which [different species] make contact with the environment, and in the ways in which they act on the environment, what remains of their behavior shows astonishingly similar properties.'[8] The 'article of faith' that intelligence equaled learning, and that learning was both universal and indistinguishable among species, nearly hamstrung comparative psychology before it could take a step.

While the behaviorist doctrine may appear extreme and unsupportable in today's world, it was in total harmony with other contemporary ideas. A simple, one-size-fits-all account of learning fit in beautifully with the dogma of the human I.Q. testers of the time, who believed fervently in the idea of general intelligence and in the validity of a single test to measure it. Of course, the idea of orderly quantitative differences along a single dimension (such as the number of learned associations that an animal could make) was also consonant with our old friend, the Great Chain of Being.

Darwin's Legacy to Behaviorism

Behaviorist bashing is a popular sport these days, now that cognitive psychology is in the ascendancy and mentalistic terms are as thick in the air as mosquitoes in Alaska in June. It's easy to make behaviorism sound foolish – I do it all the time. Every popular book about animal behavior or animal thinking talks about the Behaviorist era as if a mass hypnotic event had frozen

[8] Skinner 1956, p. 230.

solid every sensible mind in the United States. Cognitive science is touted as the prince who delivered the kiss to the pale, immobile form of the princess, Psychology, laid out on the cold slab of behaviorism. She awakens with all her mental states in overdrive (Thinking! Feeling! Conscious!), with only an occasional reflexive twinge to remind her of her Skinnerian captor.

But if we want to point a finger of blame for the withering of a comparative study of animal intelligence, behaviorism is something of a straw man. The behaviorists' view of animal intelligence did not come out of left field. Rather, it was an inevitable successor to the half-baked 'evolutionary' comparisons that were attempted, beginning in Darwin's time, in the guise of demonstrating mental continuity. Throughout history, people have had no trouble seeing how animals differed from one another, and especially how they differed from us. Evolutionary divergence, by whatever mechanism, was obvious, even to the most naïve observer of nature. The key idea that distinguished Darwinian evolution from natural theology was that new species were derived from old ones, that relatedness was the pervasive feature of life. Darwin helped redirect the emphasis away from species differences, preaching the kinship of shared history and tracing for us our familial connections along the evolutionary tree.

Consider the case of the Galápagos finches. In this classic story of island speciation, finch pioneers to a birdless island became the ancestors to a bewildering variety of finches, new species with custom-built morphology and behavior, each adept at exploiting a different niche. On any given island there might be finches that look or behave like woodpeckers, like thick-billed sparrows, or even like vampires. (Some finches suck blood from seabirds.) Legend has it that Darwin stood at the stern of the Beagle as the sun set over the islands, composing the first draft of *The Origin of Species* in his head, with samples of the thirteen disparate finch species spread out on a cloth at his feet. The legend is, however, a myth, as the historian Frank Sulloway and others have discovered.[9] Although Darwin saw and collected the finches, he thought they were only varieties, not separate species; he did not immediately recognize their powerful relevance to evolutionary divergence because, as Jonathan Weiner put it, 'Darwin in the Galápagos did not have Darwin's shoulders to stand on.'[10] In writing *Origin*, Darwin relied almost exclusively on evidence from artificial selection, such as that conducted by pigeon fanciers.[11]

Fifteen years passed between the publication of *The Origin of Species* and *The Descent of Man*. During that time Darwin was battling the old-guard naturalists who refused to buy into the theory of natural selection, at least as it involved humans inheriting anything from a hairy ape. *The Descent of Man* was a treatise on our intellectual, moral, and biological affinity to primates and other mammalian ancestors drifting back in time over millions of years. Similarity born of evolutionary continuity was the note that Darwin struck again and again: he was selling the gospel of brotherhood. Imagine that, instead of emphasizing evolutionary continuity, Darwin and his interpreters had stressed *discontinuities* in behavioral and intellectual evolution. Darwin might have featured the story of the Galápagos finches in his chapter on mental evolution in *The Descent of Man*. If Darwin had been motivated to examine psychological differences, he might have speculated that each of the finch species' behavioral specializations might have been accompanied by a tailor-made set of learning abilities, perhaps resulting in better problem solving in some variants than others. He could have used the story of the finches to make a more general point about how we might then expect to find analogous mental differences, driven by disparity in environmental demands, among, say, humans and their primate ancestors. But those arguments would have served a different political and social purpose.

The level playing field on which the behaviorists placed their

[9] Sulloway, 1982; Wiener, 1994.
[10] Weiner, 1994, p. 23.
[11] Darwin, 1859.

rats to learn had been constructed at the turn of the twentieth century, when the theory of evolution by natural selection was advanced, though not, it seems, completely understood. Thorndike's work with a small handful of species, for example, was taken as a strong indication that all species differences were merely quantitative, that all animals had It (problem-solving ability, learning ability, 'g'); it was just that some had more of It than others.

> There is, as we pass from the early vertebrates down to man, a progress in the evolution of the general associative process . . . It may be that the evolution of intellect has no breaks, that its progress is continuous from its first appearance to its present condition.[12]

Species were stripped of the environments for which evolution had so studiously adapted them and, instead, were set to tasks designed to reveal a core ability, which was assumed, not proposed, to exist. The similarities between species, including humans as one example, were always emphasized over the differences. Similarities were the novelty. This happy recognition of family resemblances among disparate species cast even glaring differences into obscurity, leading to outrageous statements by ostensibly clear thinkers. To wit:

> If Amoeba were a large animal, so as to come within the every-day experience of human beings, its behaviour would at once call forth the attribution to it of states of pleasure and pain, of hunger, desire, and the like, on precisely the same basis as we attribute these things to the dog.[13]

Thorndike, Hobhouse, Watson, and others listened to the synopsis of evolution by natural selection that downplayed divergence and then searched for and found the common thread of behavioral universality to which they had been discreetly directed.

[12] Thorndike, 1911, pp. 285–287.
[13] Jennings, 1904, p.336.

Perception Is Everything

Not everyone jumped on the behaviorist bandwagon. Indeed, in Germany in the early 1900s, a whole new branch of psychology was under development. Instead of analyzing behavior by decomposing it into reflexive bits as behaviorism mandated, Gestalt psychology embraced the inner world, focusing on holistic perceptual experiences as the real determinants of behavior. One of the seminal thinkers in Gestalt psychology, Wolfgang Kohler, spent most of World War I in the Canary Islands, staging demonstrations of Gestalt phenomena in chickens and chimpanzees. In his best-known chicken trick, Kohler presented chicks with grain on two shades of gray paper, but only permitted them to take grains from the darker side. If they pecked at the lighter paper, Kohler shooed them away. As any behaviorist would predict, the chicks quickly learned to only peck at grains on the darker paper, where they might have a little peace. Kohler then offered grain on two shades of gray paper again, one the same darker shade that had been rewarded previously, the other darker still. If these were behaviorist chicks, Kohler reasoned, they should prefer the exact shade that had been the winner last time – the lighter one in this case. They were, however, Gestalt chicks. Ignoring the absolute color of the paper, they pecked the darker paper again, even though pecks on that color had never been rewarded.[14] Kohler interpreted these results as demonstrating that perception, and therefore knowledge, is organized by the animal into natural units (*Gestalten*, or configurations), which are acted upon as such. Instead of laboring to reduce the world into stimulus-response bites, animals could also deal with the whole enchilada.

The repercussions of this philosophy for views of animal intelligence were more obvious in Kohler's work with chimpanzees. Kohler's experimental setups resembled Skinner boxes about as

[14] Watson, 1978, p. 477.

much as Outward Bound resembles West Point. He gave chimps an out-of-reach target, usually some bananas, and an array of sticks, boxes, and such that might prove useful in obtaining the goods. He then sat back and observed how the chimps solved the problem, if they did. In one case, the sticks were too short to be used as a rake to retrieve bananas on the far side of a fence. The chimp put the smaller end of one into the larger end of another, forming an elongated stick. This act looked to Kohler like a lucky break for the chimp, a trial-and-error accident like the way Thorndike's cats got out of the puzzle boxes. But once the sticks were joined, the chimp, with a delighted look of 'Aha!' on his face, knew just what to do. To Kohler, such solutions appeared as coherent wholes, as 'insightful', rather than assembled laboriously from trial-and error sequences:

> We can, from our own experience, distinguish sharply between the kind of conduct which, from the very beginning, arises from a consideration of the characteristics of a situation, and one that does not. Only in the former case do we speak of insight, and only that behaviour of animals definitely appears to us intelligent which takes account from the beginning of the lie of the land, and proceeds to deal with it in a smooth, continuous course.[15]

Intelligence, in his view, was an internal organizational process by which understanding a problem occurs. Being smart means being able to arrange your mind to figure something out. The trouble with the behaviorists, Kohler complained, was that none of the problems they set for their animals could possibly be solved with intelligence. As Bertrand Russell put it, 'Sir Isaac Newton himself could not have got out of the Hampton Court maze by any method except trial and error.'[16] If experimenters would only give animals opportunities to use the broader reaches

[15] Kohler, quoted in Russell, 1927, p. 30.
[16] Russell, 1927, p.30.

of their intellect, Kohler argued, they would.[17] In other words, if you took the rat out of the box, it might think out of the box. This idea was prophetic of the cognitive revolution around the corner.

On one side of the Atlantic, then, were the exacting behaviorists, training psychology to become a strict, natural science. Rats, and later pigeons, were put through their paces in confined circumstances, and their behavior was found to conform most obediently to a few simple laws of learning. On the other side of the pond, were the existential Gestalt psychologists, willing to postulate a vivid intellectual and mental life for humans, apes, and perhaps a few select others. They believed in their methodology as fervently as the behaviorists believed in theirs and were unhappy to have their science denounced as medieval speculation by the brash American upstarts. William McDougall, an Oxford social psychologist, had this to say:

> The commandments of natural science must, of course, be obeyed. But the behaviorists forget to mention one such commandment, in fact, the one which should be given first rank. If in a given field we make certain observations, and particularly, if we make them all the time, such observations must be accepted under all circumstances, whatever may happen elsewhere. Otherwise, why should activities in this field be honored in the name of empirical science? The behaviorists, however, not only fail to mention the commandment, they disobey it consistently. What is the reason for this strange conduct? There can only be one reason: In this fashion they are enabled to choose such facts as fit their particular philosophy, and to ignore all those which do not fit. Now there is something that clearly does not fit. Watch a rat in a maze. The most outstanding characteristic of his behavior is *striving*. Always the creature is after something, or tries to get away from something else. It is, of course, the same with man, including the behaviorist who, for a certain purpose, selects

[17] Kohler, 1930.

some empirical data and refuses to recognize others. Striving is the very essence of mental life. Really, behaviorists ought to learn about the more elementary facts of life before they advertise their junior-size science.[18]

Intellectual Knockoffs

Like the American buffalo who once blackened the prairies with their numbers, the behaviorists were reduced to a small tender herd. A few members of the Conditioning Cult continue, to the present day, to do battle with the Mentalist Infidels, those cognitive psychologists who descended, in part, from the Gestalt clan. In particular, Robert Epstein, a direct intellectual descendant of B. F. Skinner himself, has made a career out of irritating cognitive psychologists. Epstein instituted the Columban Simulation Project,[19] the chief aim of which is to demonstrate that pigeons (*Columba livia*) can do many of the psychologically complicated, cognitively laden stunts that apes and people do, given the right training. Just as psychology thought it had gotten rid of that party-pooper behaviorism, Epstein stages a comeback.

To the chagrin of cognoscenti, two of Epstein's papers were published in the most prestigious science journals in the world, the American *Science* and the British *Nature*.[20] The *Nature* paper was titled '"Insight" in the pigeon: Antecedents and determinants of an intelligent performance.' The paper was, in essence, a behaviorist spoof on Koehler's classic experiment with chimps, some boxes, and an out-of-reach banana. The Tenerife chimps in Koehler's study were each placed in a large enclosure with boxes strewn around and a banana hanging from the ceiling. Of course the first thing the chimp tried when it noticed the banana was to jump up and grab it, but the banana was too high. The chimp would then typically look around and, spotting the

[18] As paraphrased by Kohler, 1953, p. 422.
[19] Epstein, 1981.
[20] Epstein, Lanza and Skinner, 1981; Epstein, Kirshnit, Lanza and Rubin, 1984.

boxes, move them under the banana, climb on top, and secure the prize. Sometimes three or four boxes would have to be stacked to make the grab. Some chimps solved the problem right away, others not for hours or even days. Whatever the speed of the solution, however, the A-ha!-ness of the experience was apparent to Koehler.

The pigeons in Epstein's lab were trained in a dollhouse version of the chimp situation. The Skinner box had a toy banana attached to the ceiling and a tiny box. (The toy banana proves that behaviorists *can* have a sense of humor, despite all contravening evidence.) Epstein and his colleagues trained the pigeons, using standard shaping procedures, to peck the toy banana in order to get a few nibbles of grain. Soon the pigeons were enthusiastically pecking at the banana. The banana was then raised and the pigeons were trained to step up onto the miniature box to reach the banana for a peck. In separate training sessions, the little box was placed on the floor of the Skinner box and the pigeons were shaped to push the box toward a green dot on the floor. The banana was absent during these box-pushing trials.

On the day of reckoning, a pigeon was placed in the Skinner box with the dangling banana and the box, but no green dot as a target for pushing. Here is Epstein's account of what transpired:

> The test situation is a new one for the bird, so at first there may be very little behavior and then what appears to be competition between the climbing and pushing repertoires (stimuli are present which control both repertoires). The bird manages to look 'puzzled': It looks back and forth from banana to box, stretches toward the banana, motions toward the box, and so on. At some point the bird starts to push the box . . . it very clearly starts to push the box toward the banana. This, it now appears, is a matter of generalization, though not based on physical similarity but rather on the fact that behavior with respect to both the green spot and the banana had been

reinforced. A bird trained to push the box toward the green spot but not to peck the banana or climb on the box did not push the box toward the banana when the banana was placed out of reach in the chamber . . . Once the bird has pushed the box in the neighborhood of the banana, it has arranged for itself a new stimulus – box under banana – which is the occasion upon which the second repertoire, climbing onto the box and pecking the banana, had been reinforced.[21]

And so the pigeon, having moved the box to a comfortable position, steps up and makes the banana peck that gets him the grain.

The initial gut reaction most people have to this demonstration is to dismiss the pigeon's performance as a predictable result of directed training, a paltry circus act in comparison to the chimpanzee's elegant, spontaneous solution. It's like comparing a paint-by-number painting to an original Rembrandt. The behaviorists' inability to distinguish the two would seem to be sufficient to account for their near extinction. Except, Epstein and his colleagues *do* realize there is a difference between what the pigeon did and what the chimp did. In the case of the pigeon, the cause of the behavior, the reinforcement history, is clear: the right sequence of behaviors was followed reliably by a hopper full of grain. In the case of the chimpanzee, the same reward-driven process was responsible, only no one was around to take data while the chimps were learning about boxes and pushing and reaching and so on. According to behaviorist dogma, the chimps must have been reinforced, in some implicit way, for the behaviors that they showed 'spontaneously' on the day of the test. Behavior just doesn't spring up out of nowhere. The only spontaneous event that Epstein saw was the novel combination of the trained pushing and climbing sequences, or the 'automatic chaining' as he calls it. If the pigeon's insightful performance can be accounted for by conditioning principles, why not the

[21] Epstein, 1986, p. 97.

chimpanzee's? Here's another thing to think about: if you were a naïve observer peeking into the Skinner box on the last day of testing, wouldn't the pigeon look mighty clever?

Mirror, Mirror on the Wall, Who's the Smartest of Them All?

Why doesn't your dog use a mirror to remove a bit of meat from between his teeth or to straighten out an ear that has flopped the wrong way? Gordon Gallup, a primatologist, thinks it's because dogs lack the same level of self-concept that many apes are blessed with.[22] In the mirror test that Gallup and others use to determine who gains membership to this exclusive club, the animal – say a chimpanzee – is first given extensive exposure to mirrors. While under anesthesia, the chimp's body is painted in a few places, some that it can see directly and others that are only visible with the aid of the mirror. When the chimp wakes up, the researchers count the number of times the chimp touches the spots, in front of the mirror and otherwise. As mentioned in the previous chapter, vanity of this sort has only been demonstrated in chimpanzees, orangutans, and a single gorilla. And humans, of course. Most monkeys can learn to use mirrors to find things that are otherwise hidden, but, of the species tested, none perform like the apes during the vanity test. Gallup argues that these tests are prima facie evidence for a self-concept, that what the animals see in the mirror is an 'I'. That self-concept becomes, according to Gallup and others, the cornerstone for all sorts of mental gymnastics, including thinking about the mental life of others.

How could an ardent behaviorist like Epstein resist? Using a Skinner box (of course) and some pigeons (what else?), Epstein and his colleagues attempted to demystify the vanity test.[23] A pigeon was trained to peck a blue stick-on dot placed on different parts of its body. Next, a mirror was inserted in the

[22] Gallup, 1970, 1987; Povinelli, 1987.
[23] Epstein, Lanza and Skinner, 1981.

box and the pigeon received food for pecking at blue dots that appeared on the walls and floor. Then blue dots were flashed briefly behind the pigeon while it was looking at the mirror. The pigeon was reinforced for turning around and pecking the spot where the blue dot had been a moment ago. The pigeon was then fitted with a bib around its neck and a dot was placed, out of view, on its breast below the bib. The researchers watched the pigeon with the mirror in place and with the mirror absent. Each pigeon made about ten pecks toward the dot when the dot could be seen using the mirror, and none when the mirror wasn't there. Epstein delights in noting that the rate of mark-directed responses was higher in pigeons than in chimps!

To a behaviorist, the game is up. Because behavior is king, if you get the same behavior in a chimp and a pigeon, all the mysteries have been solved. Just as in the 'insight' experiment, the chimps' reinforcement history in front of the mirror, though lost to observation, was nevertheless responsible for its clever performance, in exactly the same way as was demonstrated explicitly for the pigeon. The weakness in this argument is that it may be possible to get the same behavior, the same final performance, through different means. You can still call yourself a behaviorist and believe that different reinforcement histories might end up delivering the same behavioral bottom line. Just for starters, the absence of coaching in the case of the chimpanzee resulted in a much leaner schedule of reward than what the pigeons got, whatever that intangible reward might have been in the chimpanzees' more naturalistic setting. If we could somehow know the exact reinforcement history that led to mark-directed behavior in the chimpanzee, or to mirror use in people, how similar would it have to be to that of the pigeon in order to be judged as 'the same'? The reinforcement histories *could* have been similar and they could have been as different as a chimp and a pigeon.

If you are willing to ditch behaviorism and join the throng in peering into that black box in the head, there are all sorts of mechanisms that might differ between the pigeon and the chimp internally, but leave their behavior during the critical test the same. Imagine taking two pictures of the same scene, one with a traditional camera and one with a digital camera. From scrutinizing the photos, you might not be able to tell that there were different machines involved, operating on somewhat different principles. If you were clever, you could probably think up ways to get each camera to spill its guts, so to speak. But with only a single pair of photos in your hand, you would be hard-pressed to know if you have true mechanical equivalence or only similarity in performance.

Behaviorists, by allowing only the photos as admissible evidence, are destined to be snowed under by apparent similarity. Consider what Epstein has to say about the difference between primates and pigeons in the mirror test:

> The only impressive thing about chimpanzees and children is that they can acquire the second repertoire [that relating to mirror use] – albeit quite slowly – without explicit training. This is a matter of sensitivity to contingencies. *That* is how man and the great apes differ from other organisms, which should surprise no one.[24]

The behavior of primates in front of mirrors is so 'sensitive to the contingencies' (able to be shaped by reward) that a trainer is superfluous. The pigeons, and presumably other species that fail the vanity test after passive mirror exposure alone, need a leg up. Epstein almost succeeds in making this difference sound trivial. To my mind, it is huge. If someone spends 400 hours teaching me to play a simple piano sonata and I can finally eke out a reasonable performance, is what I did comparable to what a few gifted people could do: play it just as well after hearing it only once? Here's another example. One of Kohler's chimps had been permitted to watch other chimps solve the

[24] Epstein, 1986, p. 105.

boxes-under-the-elevated-banana problem. When it was his turn, this chimp just never caught on.

> He tried it with the very primitive method of jumping from ground level under the fruit . . . or he climbed on the box just where it stood and, looking at the objective, made repeated preparations to jump . . . he climbed again on the box just where it was, mustered all his strength, ran as fast as he could toward the fruit, and jumped from the floor. As though the advantage of standing on the box would be transferred to this place by sheer speed![25]

The chimp did push boxes around, but never under the banana. Kohler saw this as 'a failure of processes of organization'. Having observed similar unimpressive behavior by this individual in other settings, the chimp was, to paraphrase Kohler, a few bricks short of a load. Imagine that Kohler had invited Skinner over to Tenerife to shape this chimp's behavior, just as the pigeon's was shaped, and that soon this chimp was stacking and grabbing with the best of them. What exactly would have been demonstrated? That all chimps are equal under the laws of learning?

We have no idea what part of the chimpanzees' performance in the vanity test might be a product of good, old-fashioned conditioning. No one has asked the question. (Except for Epstein, Lanza, and Skinner, for whom the answer was a foregone conclusion.) In fact, there is no agreement whatsoever on what mark-directed responses during the mirror test mean, despite the numerous such tests conducted since the original. Radical behaviorists, neobehaviorists, philosophers, cognitive psychologists, Cartesian introspectionists, primatologists (pigeon apologists and otherwise), cognitive neuroscientists, and unrepentant mentalists each have a different take on the data in hand. There is no reason why conditioning couldn't be part of a more cognitive or even mentalistic story of mirror recognition, although few

[25] Kohler, 1930/1971, p. 181.

cognitive types and even fewer behaviorists would give their blessing to such an unholy marriage.

A Poor Imitation

The behaviorists were very right about some things and very wrong about others. They were right that most species that have been studied seem to respond to the contingencies of reinforcement (the consequences of their actions) in similar ways. They were correct in asserting that if you could gain control over these contingencies, you could gain control over the behavior of the animal. Barbara Woodhouse, for all of her talk about dog telepathy, linguistic competence, and soulfulness, makes heavy use of conditioning principles in her training instruction, as do most dog trainers. Animal acts at circuses and zoos couldn't function without them. Many widely accepted child-rearing practices are built on reinforcement theory. The behaviorists, however, turned out to be very wrong about one important detail: we cannot make sense of behavior divorced from the behaving animal. The clean, obvious world of performance bears an uneasy relationship to its messier, more obscure origins inside the animal. If Epstein is right about those 'sensitivities to contingencies', they must reside inside the animal. To say that a child learns the relationship between her movements and their mirror reflection more easily than does a pigeon is to say something about the child and about the pigeon, not just their behavior. That difference in learning represents a proclivity that may be carried from situation to situation, perhaps from birth, perhaps for the individual's entire life. Recognizing that animals may differ in ways that matter, despite superficial behavioral similarity produced by the hands of nature or by the whims of an experimenter, opens up another world of explanation.

Interestingly, the same issue has surfaced in a wing of cognitive science, artificial intelligence. One of the great founders of the field, Alan Turing, said that machines could be deemed intelligent if they passed what has since been dubbed the 'Turing

Test'.[26] A computer and a regular, silicon-deficient but neuron-rich person occupy separate rooms from which they communicate with an investigator via teletype. The investigator's job is to query the contestants and figure out which room houses the person. Turing's goal was to circumvent all the difficult discussions about the nature of intelligence and let behavior provide the intellectual barometer. If the investigator can't distinguish the output of a person from that of a machine, the machine earns the badge of intelligence. Sound familiar? It should – it's a radical behaviorist position. What is illuminating is how cognitive science has answered this challenge. While there is some dissent, most researchers and philosophers agree that the Turing test is, as Paul Churchland says, 'not a very deep idea'.[27] Jerry Fodor makes this analogy:

> Try to get an experimental paper accepted in a journal on the following ground: I have got an argument that says that Pluto does not have any rings, namely I looked at it with this telescope and I could not see them. What the editor of the journal will tell you is that that shows one of two things. Either Pluto does not have any rings, or your telescope is not sensitive enough to see them. Similarly for the Turing Test: If a machine can pass the Turing Test, that shows either that the machine is intelligent or that the judge did not ask the right questions.[28]

Finding the right questions to ask of a machine – or an animal – is precisely what the quest for a valid psychology of intelligence is all about. The pigeon simulations leave too many reasonable, scientifically legitimate questions unanswered. We leave the table hungry.

The behaviorists insisted that causes for behavior are positioned outside the animal, never internally. They took everyone

[26] Turing, 1950.
[27] Churchland, 1995, p. 44.
[28] Fodor, 1995, p. 88.

to task for thinking crookedly and talking loosely about animal behavior, and punished us all for our failure as scientists by creating the most boring set of ideas ever unleashed upon a discipline. Cognitive scientists may like to take credit for dealing the fatal blows to behaviorism on the playing fields of mind and behavior, but I believe the real story is less like David and Goliath and more like *Waiting for Godot*. Behaviorism is a closed system whose principles, goals, and basic ingredients are codified and unassailable. While it must have been thrilling to help write the new religion, the novitiates who came later were left only the task of filling in the gaps. It was mostly a clean-up operation, hardly the sort of enterprise likely to hold the attention of generations of bright, young, creative psychologists. Gradually, they were lured away by the fancy new toys of cognitive science (the computer and the possibility of artificial intelligence), by nature (the fathomless complexity of the natural world and the joy of getting your feet wet), by philosophy (the release from the taboo of speculation about inner worlds), and by the freedom of chasing across that last new frontier – the mind.

Chapter 6

Unpacking the Black Box

> Yet a feeling remains that there is something deeply wrong with
> all such discussions (as this one) of other minds; nothing ever
> seems to get settled in them. From the finest minds, on all
> sides, emerge thoughts and methods of low quality and little
> power . . . So, because this is still a formative period for our
> ideas about mind, I suggest we must remain especially sensitive
> to the empirical power that each new idea may give us to pursue
> the subject further.

M. Minsky, 1980[1]

Behavior in Cognito

Like television, fast food, and rock and roll, cognitive psychology
emerged on the scene in the 1950s, a stepchild of the post war
technology boom. This glitzy, gutsy approach to the study of
mind and behavior, unfazed at the prospect of plummeting into
the mind shaft, was worthy of the brave new world. Models of
information flow were lifted from communications engineering.
Theories of computation and information processing were appropriated from the computer sciences. Concepts about organization
imposed from within were borrowed from Gestalt psychology and
from Jean Piaget, the French developmental psychologist. Taken
together, the ideas comprised a rational scaffolding for a scientific
examination of the mind, one that would not commit the errors
of behaviorism, namely, outlawing everything worth knowing.
Psychologists also saw that the neurosciences were finally making
headway in the exploration of the brain: why shouldn't a science
of the mind tag along or, indeed, lead the way?

Of course, if behaviorism had succeeded in providing adequate

[1] Minksy, 1980, p. 440.

explanations for why people and animals do what they do, then a radical new approach would not have turned many heads, much less sparked what some have characterized as a revolution. Revolution takes hold only when the populace is starving, in this case for juicy ideas. A series of findings from the mid-1900s convinced most people that behaviorism had come up short in explaining learning and, by inference, intelligence. Most of these were demonstrations of behaviorally silent learning, cases in which an animal didn't change its behavior but had, it turned out, learned something anyway. Like an actor prepping behind the scenes, the learning was taking place offstage, in the mind, where behaviorists dared not, or would not, tread. Here's a simple example.[2] A rat hears a tone and sees a light flash at the same time. This happens several times. Next, the light flashes, and shortly afterward the rat gets a little shock to its foot. What happens when the tone is presented? Well, the rat acts frightened. The behaviorists had no way to deal with this result because when the tone-light combination was originally presented, nothing happened to the rat, and its behavior, the only currency of interest, remained unaffected. According to the behaviorists, there was no reason for the rat to learn anything about the light or the tone, since they had no consequences. Backstage, however, the rat had filed away the link between the tone and the light – just in case. Sure enough, the light turned out to be a harbinger of unpleasant tidings. The only thing the rat knew about the tone was its suspicious affiliation with the light, so the rat tarred the tone with the same brush and was afraid. It turns out that rats, and other animals, are learning surreptitiously all the time, whether they are getting reinforced for it or not. No theory based only on behavior and environmental history could have pointed the way to this discovery.

If behavior resisted portraiture in pure stimulus-response terms, then cognitive scientists had to venture under the skin for the right sort of explanation. The problem of intelligent behavior was redefined, in the hands of cognitive psychology,

[2] Rizley and Rescorla, 1972.

as the problem of intelligent *process*. As for the role of behavior, it's déjà vu all over again: just as Romanes had proposed in 1883, the goal of studies of animal intelligence became, once again, to use behavioral 'ambassadors' to learn about internal mechanisms.[3] External stimuli are still essential to cognitive psychology; they are the input to the cognitive processes, the grist for the mill, the food for thought. However, it is the workings of the machine that consumes stimuli and spits out behavior that matters most.

> The task of the cognitive psychologist is a highly inferential one. The cognitive psychologist must proceed from observations of humans [or animals] performing intellectual tasks to conclusions about the abstract mechanisms underlying behavior. Developing a theory in cognitive psychology is much like developing a model for the working of the engine of a strange new vehicle by driving the vehicle, being unable to open it up to inspect the engine itself.[4]

The central idea of cognitive psychology is that our access to the world is mediated. We can never know the world as it actually is, as opposed to how it seems to us after our minds have finished fiddling with it. Information from the environment is like a musical score sitting on a stand: the mind is the instrument that gives it life and the only meaning that we ever know. Like an invisible, ubiquitous tour guide to the world, the mind draws attention to points of interest, jumps to conclusions, and glosses over the small stuff. It can make 3-D images pop in or out, help you hear your name amidst noisy banter, and turn yesterday's heated argument into just another blip on the screen of married life. And just like a successful laundry detergent, your mind can make colors brighter or whites whiter. While you go about your business, your mind is working overtime, dissolving the memory of your old phone number, polishing the associations you'll experience the next time you smell freshly cut grass, and compiling the data you'll

[3] Romanes, 1883/1977, p.1.
[4] Anderson, 1980, p. 17.

need on New Year's Eve when you ask yourself whether this year was better than the previous one. During every moment information whizzes by the senses and enters the mind; where does it go? How is it categorized, stored, reshuffled, compared, forgotten, translated, embellished, hidden, distorted, linked, and, eventually, used to *do* something (or to decide not to)? And, most critically for our purposes, what aspects of the operation of this Rube Goldberg creation speak to intelligence?

Mindfields

Our ability to answer the question of how intelligence manifests itself in the structure and function of the animal mind will be limited by two things: the precision with which we can define intelligence and the depth and accuracy of our knowledge of animal cognition. We did our best earlier on (chapter 2) to define intelligence, and no miracles have taken place between then and now to lift the fog that remains. The core idea of intelligence is, and has nearly always been, problem-solving and learning ability. The task for a cognitive theory of animal intelligence is to nail the facts of mental processing onto a framework of what we believe constitutes intelligence. An animal is smart because it has the mental equipment necessary to make snappy comebacks during its repartee with the world. But how do we discover what this equipment is? Some camps of cognitive science view the study of the mind as primarily an engineering problem: what must the mental flowchart be if the stimulus input looks like this and the behavioral output looks like that? Action-specific modules (for memory, for categorization, for counting, etc.) divvy up the job, passing information back and forth, perhaps sending out a behavioral emissary, perhaps not. Some researchers and philosophers demand that these mechanisms be consistent with what we know about the brain. Although playing the game on a functional level, they believe that cognitive theory must be reconciled with the tangible neural truth. A minority takes the Cartesian view that brain design is irrelevant to mind design.

(Perhaps, then, evolution could have provided us with only a mind and allocated the space on top of our shoulders for something we really need – like some extra limbs.) Yet others reject the idea of cognitive compartmentalization all together, embracing instead a more holistic, network-based idea of mental activity, each mental byte as necessary and insufficient as a single termite. This is merely the tip of the iceberg of divergent thinking about thinking. There is little consensus on the right method for unpacking the black box, particularly as we move from relatively easier problems (like what happens in short-term memory) to thornier ones (like how Kohler's apes solved the banana problem).

When we stood aside to show behaviorism the door, we let in all the problems of a science of these slippery, shadowy mental phenomena. Given that the theory and methodology of cognitive science has about as much order as the average teenager's room, we might soon find ourselves longing for the shipshape barracks of radical behaviorism. I'm reminded of the old joke about a man searching under a streetlight. A passerby asks what he has lost. 'My watch.' 'Where did you lose it?' 'Over there,' says the man, indicating a dark portion of the street, 'but the light is better here.' Behavior and external stimuli are in a sunny clearing compared to the dim recesses of the mind, but most psychologists have voted to go spelunking anyway. Cognitive scientists of all stripes agree that a detailed description of mental design is the only way forward on the trail to understanding intelligence, both as behavior and as a property of an intelligent brain.

Experimenting with Nature

Remember the confused male wagtail that fed the dipper chicks? Imagine that I had only described to you his behavior when taking care of his own brood, in the way that natural selection had approved. You would be impressed with the skill with which he allocated food evenly to the young in the nest, metering the frequency of visits to the time of day and the chicks' hunger level, and even monitoring the size of the prey he carried to them, matching his foraging to the dynamic dietary requirements of his brood. Without the insight gained from the natural experiment induced by the dipper nest way station, we might have been tempted to ascribe considerably more thoughtfulness to his behavior. Because the wagtail persisted in feeding alien chicks, even to the detriment of his own flesh-and-blood, we have to wonder just how much of his brain was engaged in this enterprise to begin with. (Jeffrey Masson and Susan McCarthy, authors of *When Elephants Weep*,[5] would inevitably suggest that the wagtail's behavior revealed nothing less than compassion for the plight of dipper chicks, that moral duty to fellow creatures won the day over the selfishness of Darwinian demands.) The point is not, of course, that wagtails are stupid. Rather, the mechanisms behind the wagtail's behavior had accepted input that was too general to guard against getting duped by another's species young. As a consequence of this weird incident, we know something now about the wagtail's internal processing that would otherwise have been obscured by the efficient operation of a process receiving standard input. Exceptional events often expose the more general rule.

Nature only rarely permits experiments to occur on the proving ground of the real world. If we want to explore animal cognition and intelligence, we have to create the situations that will get animals to spill their mental guts. Wilsson wondered what inspired beavers to build a dam.[6] An architectural vision? The proximity of top-grade lumber? No, it turned out to be the sound of running water, which sounds so aversive to beavers that they will work like, well, beavers to stanch the flow and shut off the noise. When Wilsson's loudspeakers played a tape of burbling water, the beavers hastily covered up the offending boxes with mud. Such simple manipulations can give us clues about what enters into an animal's decision to do one thing or another, but more detailed, deft experimentation is required to get a complete picture of how motivation, sensation, perception, and higher cognitive functions contribute to nimble problem-solving.

[5] Masson and McCarthy, 1995.
[6] Wilsson, 1971.

The Haves and the Have-nots

Given that we can't specify exactly what it means to have intelligent mental processes, we'll have to be satisfied with agreeing that certain features would probably be useful to most creatures that wanted to do some serious cogitating. At the top of the list would be having a capacious memory, with the information accessible in various formats, properly linked to other potentially relevant bits of knowledge. A differentiated memory – for skills, for events, for facts – with varying expiration dates would keep things tidy. A solid grip on cause and effect would also seem basic, while hypothesis testing might be reserved for the higher-end models. Being able to sort the world and respond to general properties, in addition to the specifics, would also be handy, so let's add serial order and pattern recognition, categorization, and concept formation. Some numerical skills might be a bonus ('Weren't there *three* pups here a minute ago?'), and being able to read the emotions of others might lead to a happier and longer life. This is a minimal list; many other cognitive abilities could be tacked on.

One of the dominant approaches to animal cognition has been to figure out which animals have these components of intelligent processing and which do not. The progress has been slow because, as we've learned, making a convincing argument that an animal isn't capable of some mental trick is difficult; we know more about what abilities certain species have than what they lack. This bias is accentuated by the sad fact that negative results rarely find the light of day in professional journals. Still, we know with some certainty that, for example, pigeons are pretty poor at learning abstract rules that could transfer from one situation to another (compared to corvids and primates), but are brilliant at rote memorizing.[7] Rats can use a flexible code to solve a maze with twelve rewards: they either remember which places they have already visited or which places they haven't yet visited,

[7] Mackintosh, 1988.

depending on which list is shorter.[8] Scrub jays can remember where they put their food caches, what is in them, and which type of food was hidden when.[9] Dolphins, but not human infants and apes, get the point of pointing to something.[10] Alex, the famous African gray parrot, can keep track of up to six objects, categorize things by shape, color, and size, use the labels 'same' and 'different' correctly, and reprimand a trainer for handing over something other than what was asked for.[11] I could, but won't, go on for pages.

Such a laundry list of the mental abilities (or disabilities) of particular species nudges us only slighter closer to our goal of understanding the nuts and bolts of intelligent cognitive processing. In addition to knowing which elemental abilities have been installed in each species' mind, we need to know how they are interconnected, how narrowly or broadly they can be applied, how information is shunted through the system, how sense is made of competing demands, time constraints, and random noise. A particular skill revealed in a laboratory task is only one piece of a much larger puzzle, an intricate complex of abilities that evolved under circumstances we only dimly understand. As Irene Pepperberg noted about Alex's numerical skills:

> The value of such work lies . . . in its use as a step toward determining the extent of animal cognitive competence, that is, whether the observed abilities can be developed into more complex capacities, such as labeling larger quantities and understanding addition and subtraction. In such a manner numerical competence may indeed become a comparative indicator of general intelligence.[12]

And, further, numerical competence could be linked to other competencies, allowing Alex, and other mathematically inclined

[8] Cook, Brown and Riley, 1985.
[9] Clayton and Dickinson, 1999.
[10] Herman, Abichandani, Elhajj, Herman, Sanchez and Pack, 1999.
[11] Pepperberg, 1987, 1990, 1994.
[12] Pepperberg, 1994, p.42.

animals to boost performance on tasks that are not obviously math tests. This is, as Pepperburg alludes, the logic behind the idea of general intelligence, that distinct abilities are components of a system that, considered as a whole, exhibits a certain level of intelligence. If Alex can count, then perhaps the cognitive mechanisms that support counting and other related math skills are integral to his intellectual abilities in general.

A related complication in interpreting the results of even the best-controlled experiments is that the subjects haven't a clue which compartment of their black box is being queried at any particular time. We may design the test to target one ability or the other, but the animal approaches the test blindly, not having read the grant proposal. Researchers are increasingly aware that just because we see an experiment as a test of X doesn't ensure the animals do. From the animal's point of view, a test of theory of mind may be a conditioning experiment; a test of cognitive mapping may be an encounter with visual images that need to be matched with familiar views of the environment.[13]

I would go one step further and argue that while a test may be more or less accurately aimed at an isolated ability, it is the entire beast, not an excised portion, that answers back. The animal does, and must, throw its whole mental machinery at the problem, most broadly defined as 'What is happening to me right now and what I might need to do about it.' Rats running on a radial maze have been instructing scientists on just this point for over twenty years. A radial maze has arms (usually eight or twelve) radiating from a central hub, each baited with a bit of food. The maze was designed as a memory test, so the rat's job is to clear the maze of food without visiting an arm twice by remembering where it's been. Rats require little training for this task – they are naturals. To find out how the rat solves the maze, experimenters have tried to stop the rat from using one type of cue or another, both to find out if it is using some lazy trick instead of its memory (like leaving a Hansel and Gretel crumb trail) and to figure out what exactly it

[13] Shettleworth, 1998, p. 574.

is remembering. So, to rule out the use of odor trails, they take the rat off, rotate the maze ninety degrees, then let the rat finish the job. No problem. Take away distant landmarks to navigate by and the rat does fine. Take away close landmarks, the same results. Make the rat run another radial maze after the first few choices and it can still come back and remember which arms were baited in the first maze. Make the rat blind, it finds its way anyway.[14] A rat in a radial maze experiment is like James Bond in a chase scene: there is always one more stunt left. After literally hundreds of radial maze experiments, the answer to the question of how the rat solves the maze, in the undoctored condition, is that it is 'multiply-determined', i.e., that we don't really know. This cognitive detouring is part of what we mean by intelligence, but at present, our explanations – our cognitive theories – do not do justice to how the rat's mind works when it chooses its path along the maze.

We know quite a bit about how the rat represents the world to itself and what it does with that information. Arguably, we know more about it than almost any other area of animal cognition; the study of many other cognitive components is still at the have and have-not stage. Don't get me wrong. It's not that studies of particular animal competencies are off-track – clearly, this is where we need to begin – but we are further away than it may seem from anything resembling a coherent methodology or a comprehensive theoretical framework for studying the animal mind. Many elegant studies have opened our eyes to the ways in which an animal's cognitive functions relate to its intelligent behavior. But we should be careful not to mistake a few trees for a forest.

---

[14] Olton and Samuelson, 1976, Olton and Collison, 1979; Beatty and Shavalia, 1980; Zoladeck and Roberts, 1978.

Tall Stories

Many of the studies that point tantalizingly to cognitive dexterity in animals (often those most widely cited in popular books on animal thinking) were, however, one-off demonstrations or brief research programs. Alternative accounts that might have made the animals seem a bit slower on the uptake might have been acknowledged in the discussion section of published papers, but were somehow misplaced when the results were summarized in other contexts: Pigeons can manipulate images![15] Plovers intentionally deceive intruders with broken wing antics![16] Monkeys are aware of their own social ranking![17] Pigeons can report their internal states and feelings via symbols![18] Ravens have insight![19] Pigeons have abstract concepts![20] And every skeptic's favorite: Apes have language![21] Some of these claims and others unmentioned may yet turn out to be true but that moment has not arrived. Similar criticisms could, of course, be leveled at domains other than animal cognition. Certainly Epstein's experiments fell far short of settling the issue of what simulations of primate behavior by pigeons were all about. The main point is that while lifting the taboo on studies of the mind has undeniably resuscitated an area of research rendered moribund by the chokehold of Behaviorism, the black box remains very dimly lit. We cannot be satisfied with merely hinting at what animal cognition *might* be like or resort to labeling with casual language internal processes about which we know vanishingly little. As unsatisfying as it is, in over twenty-five years, to have taken only baby steps toward a solid understanding of animal cognition; it is better to be sure of the ground we have covered than to skip lightly over the sinkholes and fissures in the body of data on which our ideas about animal cognition rely. We cannot blithely substitute our wish for more

[15] Neiworth and Rilling, 1987.
[16] Ristau, 1991.
[17] Preuschoft, 1999.
[18] Lubinski and Thompson, 1993.
[19] Heinrich, 1995.
[20] Herrnstein, 1984.
[21] Gardner and Gardner, 1969; Gardner, Gardner, and Van Cantfort, 1989; Patterson, 1978.

complete answers – or more beguiling ones – for good science.

Studies of human cognition have perhaps fared better, both because language can greatly facilitate interrogations of mind design and because we already know, at least at a descriptive level, what people can do. We've been watching them closely for centuries. Animals, on the other hand, are more remote. For many of the species under study, detailed descriptive accounts of how they pass the time are lacking, or, if they exist, may be colored by preconceptions of cognitive complexity. Without an accurate picture of what the behaviors are, studies of the internal mechanisms that support those behaviors are destined only to contribute to the confusion. Using Anderson's analogy, if we can't even drive the car and see how it behaves, to what do we pin our assessments of the mechanics of the engine? We'll explore this issue further in the next chapter.

The Itsy-bitsy Spider

Portia, an Australian jumping spider, is an araneophagic aggressive mimic. What this means is that *Portia* hunts other spiders, and is not shy of using unsporting methods. Her catholic tastes require her to have a number of different arrows in her quiver. First, *Portia* doesn't look like your average jumping spider: *Portia* looks like a bit of debris. Unsuspecting prey spiders can be stalked in the open where *Portia*'s strange irregular gait makes it harder to detect. As Wilcox and Jackson describe: 'If the [spider] being stalked detects movement and turn to look at *Portia*, it normally peers at what appears to be no more than a piece of detritus and then turns and continues on its way, and to its doom.'[22] A very intriguing bit of evolutionary design, you might say, but hardly rocket science. OK, but follow *Portia* out onto the prey spider's web. When *Portia* pays certain spider species a web visit, they don't feel *Portia* walking on the silk because of *Portia*'s slow and choppy gait. Others prey species have wised up over evolutionary time. When they feel

---

[22] Wilcox and Jackson, 1998, p. 416.

Portia's characteristic step, they exhibit what the researchers call *'Portia* panic': they run like hell and fling themselves off the web. To foil such detection, *Portia* uses smokescreens. In the laboratory, *Portia* was more likely to move across a web during a gust of wind than during quiet moments. What's eerier still is that *Portia* doesn't have to wait for blustery weather to satisfy its appetite: *Portia* flexes sharply on the web, setting up reverberations that mask its footfalls. *Portia* can then advance toward the resident spider during the noise.

Sometimes *Portia* tires of those games and works on its acting skills instead. The spider drums a wide variety of different signals on the prey's web, each one potentially the species-specific signal of the resident. The resident spider, probably hoping it was a member of the opposite sex making a social call, responds to the signal it likes. When *Portia* receives the response, it continues to play the winning signal. As Wilcox and Jackson note, this is a beautiful example of trial-and-error learning. It even works in the laboratory, where researchers responded at random to one of *Portia*'s signals and observed that *Portia* started playing that tune more often. *Portia*'s finest hunting tactic, however, is directed at a spider that builds orb webs against tree trunks. This spider has its own formidable defenses. When an intruder enters the web, the orb-web spider flexes its legs so violently that the interloper is thrown off the web completely. So *Portia* finds a way around this, quite literally. Spying the orb-web spider's position, *Portia* climbs around the web, often up the tree, over branches and other obstacles, to a position above the web. This route can take *Portia* out of sight of the prey and may take an hour to negotiate. That means *Portia* has to remember where the goal is relative to the present position. When *Portia* arrives, it drops a line of silk down next to the other spider Miss Muffet-style, swings over, and dispatches it. All I can say is that I'm glad *Portia* is *small*.

Before this story came to light, no one would have thought to nominate a spider for a list of the Top Ten Intellectual Giants. *Portia*, and a cadre of other unlikely species, emerge as dark horses in the Interspecies Cognitive Olympics: the researchers themselves hadn't a clue these creatures were half as sharp as they are turning out to be.

When we began research on *Portia*, few thoughts would have seemed more foreign to us than that one day we would seriously be discussing cognition in a spider. Yet, over and over again, *Portia* has defied the popular image of spiders as simple animals with rigid behavior. [23]

In accepting these unexpected findings, there is something else we have to contend with: 'How it is that an animal with so little in the way of a brain can nevertheless do so much.'[24] With a poppy-seed-sized brain, *Portia* can learn by trial and error, tailor her predatory approaches to match the prey species' characteristics, and remember the location of and plot a path to a distant, obscured prey. If *Portia* can accomplish all that (and possibly more) with such limited physical resources, what does that say about the relationship between brain, mind, and behavior?

No Brain, No Gain

They don't teach allometry in first grade, which is why my daughter, Rebecca, identifies the blue whale as the smartest creature on earth. For her, big brain equals big I.Q. Unfortunately, it isn't that simple. The blue whale does have an enormous brain, but it also has an enormous body to go with it, and that body demands a whale-sized neural allotment for sensory and motor processing. Also, the design of larger animals results in a reproportioning of body parts: little animals usually have bigger heads for their body size than do large animals. We can correct for this using allometric scaling and get a rough idea of how much extra brain an animal seems to have over and above what it needs just for basic maintenance. Think of allometry as a cost-of-living analysis for incomes in different parts of world. What is left over after you subtract all non-luxury costs, which vary with locale, gives you an estimate of spending power – or, in case of intelligence, of the amount of brain tissue available for lofty thinking. There

[23] Wilcox and Jackson, 1998, p. 428.
[24] Wilcox and Jackson, 1998, p. 428.

are, as you might expect, countless ways of computing surplus brain volume and we can't get into the nuances of the techniques here. Most, however, agree on certain results. Within mammals, for instance, primates have the most brain to spare, with humans in particular having much more brain than our bodies alone have use for. No surprise there. Blue whales are actually a bit neurally underpowered, but Flipper, judging by his brain size, probably wrote his own show.[25]

Can we really get a fix on comparative intelligence simply by measuring brains? That would seem to be a rather ham-handed method considering all the complexities we have been laboring with in assessing intelligence across species. Nevertheless, sensible results have been obtained when brain measures are correlated with variables known to relate to intelligence. In normal humans, scores on an I.Q. test correlate with the size of various brain areas, as measured using MRI; people with higher scores had bigger brain structures involved in cognitive functioning (like the temporal lobe, hippocampus, and cerebral hemispheres), more gray matter (neurons and their connecty bits), and more room inside their skull in which to put all that brain.[26] In other primates, the size of the neocortex (the corrugated stuff on the outside layer) varies more than any other brain structure. Dunbar found that the larger the social group, the bigger the neocortex; presumably gossiping, friendship, backstabbing, and social climbing require extra processing capacity. (We'll get into that in chapter 8.) A similar analysis of relative brain weights was performed on birds from the corvid family – those learning set buffs. Corvids, as a group, are brainier than other birds. Parrots have large brains for their body size while the heads of pigeons and chickens are, by contrast, a little lighter than the average bird.[27] Sometimes brain-body weight ratios can put the spotlight on species or groups for whom behavioral data is meager; Ebbesson and Northcutt have shown that sharks and rays have ratios as

---

[25] Jerison, 1985; Stephan, Frahm and Baron, 1981.
[26] Andreasen, Flaum, Swayze, O'Leary, Alliger, Cohen, Ehrhardt, and Yuh, 1993.
[27] Portman, 1947.

much as 400 per cent higher than those of the average fish or amphibian, even after they adjusted for the relative density of bone and cartilage.N28 That puts sharks and rays in the same vicinity as birds and mammals. It makes you doubt whether sharks really 'mistake' a surfer for a seal on a crunchy cracker, doesn't it?

These rather gross analyses do reassure us that brains have something to do with being smart, but a finer-grained examination will resist such a simplistic, albeit sensible, correlation. For starters, great apes, which seem to outshine monkeys on certain cognitive tests, do not sport a proportionately larger neocortex. Richard Byrne suggests that those intellectual feats at which apes excel may rely on changes in neural function or organization, rather than being simply a matter of requiring more CPUs – the difference between a remodel of a house versus an addition.[29] Fair enough, but then how do we ever reject the null hypothesis that no differences in measured brain square footage means no difference in cognitive wherewithal? We are not able, as yet, to examine the details of neural organization and observe whether one brain has a circuitry more congenial to cleverness than another. We can compare how tightly the neurons are packed and how lavishly the neurons are interconnected, but these measures are many, many layers of inference away from the idea of intelligence. And if we are looking to large-scale brain anatomy to help us separate the intellectual wheat from the chaff, what of the diminutive *Portia*? Like most insects, *Portia* has limited neural resources, at least compared to any vertebrate. How, then, do we account for *Portia*'s perspicacity? The most renowned purveyor of the big-brain, big-I.Q. link, Harry Jerison, claims that

> [T]he 'intelligence' that corresponds to higher grades of encephali-zation [proportionately bigger brains] is one involving knowl-edge of reality, or, in terms of the earlier discussion, the quality of the reality created by the brain to account for the information that is received.[30]

[29] Byrne, 1995.
[30] Jerison, 1985, p. 30.

If that is true, then *Portia* has a very sparse reality, an assertion at odds with its demonstrated detouring abilities. Perhaps *Portia*, like a practical person on a tight budget, finds functional detours around the neuron shortage. It wouldn't be the first time evolution innovated on behalf of a species. Then again, given the operating cost of neural tissue, passing out chunks of cortex like candy at Christmas to certain vertebrates would have to be offset by sizable fitness benefits. So we are left for now in the unsatisfying position of knowing that we need a brain to be smart, but also knowing that it's not a simple matter of purchasing I.Q. points with neurons.

Buried in Thought

We have been talking about cognition in a detached, third-party way as a set of mechanisms designed to manage information on behalf of an adapted, behaving animal. In doing so, we have delicately avoided discussing the herd of elephants in the middle of the floor. I'd like to introduce one to you now: this elephant's name is Thinking. (You will meet some other elephants, notably Awareness, in a later chapter.) In discussing the various cognitive competencies that animals might and might not have, we have done a two-step around the issue of whether any of those competencies add up to animal thinking. Before we can come to grips with thinking and how it relates to intelligence, however, we need to distinguish two related terms that are often muddled: mental events and mental experiences.

Mental events are, simply, the actions of cognitive processes. They can reflect activity during straightforward conditioned reflexes, in perceptual or attentional mechanisms, or in complex linguistic processing. We don't need to worry about whether it is sensible to label as a mental event every tickle one neuron gives another: this is part of what cognitive neuroscience has been charged to discover. Suffice it to say that the term 'mental events' is meant to be sufficiently inclusive to cover all those cognitive operations that could be subsumed under the fuzzy umbrella of intelligence, plus many others. Mental experiences, on the other hand, are one type of mental event, namely those that have a subjective component. Mental experiences are the mental events that you know about without the help of scientists.

So, what kind of mental event is thinking? The kind that is also a mental experience, or the kind that is hidden from your mind's eye, or, because life is complicated, a little of each? People writing books about animal thinking have wildly divergent views on this point; I'll present a couple of examples. Richard Byrne, author of *The Thinking Ape*, gives a definition of thinking based on the ideas of the psychologist Kenneth Craik: thinking is 'mental simulation of intentional action,'[31] a definition that Byrne believes includes only some primates. But then, in further discussion, he opens the door to include other mental activities as being indicative of thought, namely problem solving, abstract generalization, and new uses of old tricks. Here Byrne seems to invoke levels of complexity of thinking, a hierarchy of thoughtfulness that culminates in the ability to think analytically about imagined circumstances ('What if . . . ?') and adjust behavior to the best hypothetical outcome. While there is considerable disagreement on the power of experiments to detect this ultimate cognitive ability, Byrne describes the ground rules of the game effectively. For Byrne, thinking ability runs on a parallel, if not identical, track to intelligence. But Byrne remains agnostic on the issue of whether thinking, as it pertains to animals, must have a subjective component – that is, whether animals *experience* thinking.

In his books *Animal Thinking* and *Animal Minds*, Donald Griffin muddles together his ideas about thinking and consciousness.[32] Griffin suspects an animal is thinking whenever its behavior is complex and proves adaptable to changing circumstances, but this is also his criterion for invoking conscious awareness. Thinking means conscious thinking and every creature with a dozen neurons to its credit does it. If we cleave off consciousness from Griffin's criteria, what is left over is a gee-whiz definition of

[31] Byrne, 1995, p. 150.
[32] Griffin, 1984, 1992.

thinking. In example after example, Griffin tells a story about some animal's complex adaptation to its environment and, sometimes, its flexible response to a perturbation, then states that conscious thinking 'is apparent', 'probably occurred', or, my personal favorite, 'would be useful' (as if evolution automatically provides animals with every attribute that could possibly give them a leg up. If evolution were that generous, animals might share not just our intelligence but also our technology; lions would be using laser-guided firearms to hunt gazelle and birds would have security systems for their nests.) According to Griffin, if the animal's behavior impresses you ('Gee whiz! I didn't know a bug could do that!'), whether or not you know the complexity of the mechanisms that control the behavior, it must be thinking. And, what's more, that animal *knows* it's thinking.

There are a dozen perspectives intermediate (and oblique) to Byrne's and Griffin's. Instead of attempting to reconcile the irreconcilable, let's turn away for a moment from animal minds and think about human thinking – *my* thinking. (On such a subjective topic, I'll assert that my phenomenology is about as valid as the next person's.) When I say, 'I thought about how to win friends and influence people during my run today,' or 'I thought about you a lot yesterday,' I mean *conscious* thinking, as in being aware of moving words, ideas, images, and formless entities around in my mind. I am also absolutely certain that I can make decisions, sort through information, and even be creative without doing anything that I would normally label 'thinking'. There are intelligent mental events going on behind the scenes, even when I am asleep, but they aren't what I think of as thinking. When I am thinking, I am aware of it, though perhaps not aware of each and every thought: I don't catch every word, or follow all the trains of thought – it can be pretty much of a blur – but, if you interrupted me, I could tell you in reasonable detail what it was all about. So unless my introspective account is evidence of psychopathology, thinking by people, in common parlance, means, or at least is accompanied by, conscious mulling over. The philosopher Daniel Dennett comes to a similar conclusion in *Kinds of Minds*, when he says that our mental life is distinguished by being 'reflectable-upon'.[33] Do we know that animals are not reflective? We'll tackle that question in a later chapter. For now, let's just agree that it would be inconsistent to attach the label "thinking" onto an animal's cognition without good evidence that the animal was cognizant of those cognitions, because that is what thinking means when applied to people.

But what about the content of the thinking? Byrne is not alone in defining thinking as the most complex, nonhabitual cognitive acrobatics of which the mind is capable – the zenith of intelligent mentation. My introspections don't give me a clear answer as to whether my conscious thinking is the best my mind has to offer. Certainly I do a lot of fancy mental work without giving it a moment's thought. For example, I'm sure I'm not the only parent on the planet who can read a children's book aloud while thinking (consciously, of course) about something else entirely. So maybe thinking is the smartest thing I do, maybe it isn't. (This morning I caught myself thinking about whether to have black or golden raisins in my breakfast yogurt. I didn't think about it for very long, you'll be reassured to know. It went something like this: 'Golden or black? Definitely golden.' If that sort of thinking is among the brightest of my cognitions, I'm in trouble.) By my definition, then, thinking may not have special relevance to questions of intelligence, mine or another animal's.

Pigeon-holing

Yet another definition of thinking points up a final complexity to ponder in the pursuit of a description of the animal mind. Marian Dawkins, author of *Through Our Eyes Only*, says an animal is thinking when it can manipulate an internal representation in response to some new twist in the environment, working out the appropriate, adaptive behavior. Like Griffin, she wants this kind of thinking to be evidence for consciousness, although she admits that the link is fairly weak.[34] Dawkins says that the demarcation

[33] Dennett, 1996.
[34] Dawkins, 1993, p. 97.

between the thinkers and the nonthinkers is the ability to 'work things out in the head' before committing behavior to environmental consequences. For Dawkins, thinking is the hallmark of intelligence; the nonthinkers have only fixed rules to guide behavior – they can't ad-lib. While this distinction seems sensible at face value, in practice it's harder to put animals squarely in one of these two boxes. As a negative example, Dawkins describes the behavior of foraging bees. The rate at which a receiver bee unloads the nectar from a forager is an indication of the quality of that food source relative to the other loads that have recently arrived; better nectar is unloaded faster. Foragers monitor the unloading rate and, before leaving for another foray, dance with vigor proportional to that rate, ensuring recruitment to a good source and abandonment of relatively poor ones. She contrasts such rule-governed behavior to the ability of pigeons to extrapolate movement of a rotating clock hand. Neiworth and Rilling trained pigeons to peck whenever the clock hand had moved at a constant speed, even when the hand disappeared for a while before reappearing. Pigeons learned to do this correctly, both with the start locations they were trained on, and with start points that were new.[35] Dawkins argues that this manipulation of an internal representation (e.g., the integration of movement speed information with the last seen clock hand position) means those pigeons were thinking.

Are the cogitations of the bee and the pigeon qualitatively different? The bee had to remember the rate at which it was unburdened, then adjust its dancing proportionately. The pigeon had to use an absolute timing mechanism (it takes this long for the hand to move that distance no matter where it starts), or make a rough computation of distance from speed. (The pigeons didn't have to know exactly where the hand would appear, just whether it was 45 degrees off target or not.) Can we say with assurance that the pigeon's performance was so much more mentally nimble than the bee's that it should be awarded a position on a higher cognitive pedestal? For the sake of argument, let's say the bee was following

[35] Neiworth and Rilling, 1987.

a rule but the pigeon was mentally improvising. Following rules is not necessarily a simple business; a complicated set of rules with probabilistic outcomes may require as much mental dexterity as a little 'thinking'. We simply do not know enough about the cognitive requirements of the behaviors we want to compare to make broad judgments about what is mental child's play and what is not.

More than one researcher has argued that more mentalistic or higher-level explanations (e.g., Dawkins's 'thinking', concept-learning, imagery, cognitive mapping) should be favored, on the grounds of parsimony, when the alternative is a lengthy, unwieldy string of associative connections. But without knowing the computational currency of each type of representation of information, how can we judge which is more frugal? How many conditioned associations equal one concept? And is the more economical method always better or necessarily selected for? Consider the uneven cognitive terrain of the pigeon. These birds are superb at discriminating between and remembering individual examples of almost anything. Vaughan and Greene showed pigeons slides of outdoor scenes, arbitrarily reinforcing half of the slides as 'correct'.[36] How many 'right' and 'wrong' slides do you think you could remember? The pigeons rapidly learned and remembered four sets of eighty slides each – for a whole year! Now contrast that capacity with how thick pigeons are in the concept-learning department. Only with belabored tutoring do pigeons ever show any glimmer of understanding that if, say, the job was to peck red (and not green) after seeing a red sample, then in the next test, upon seeing a square, the correct response is to peck the square (and not the circle). In theory, the pigeons could just remember one concept ('peck the SAME one') and rid their teensy minds of all the individual if-red-peck-red, if-square-peck-square, if-striped-peck-striped rules. But they don't. Blough showed pigeons two identical letters and one different one (two As and one K, or two Gs and one R), with the odd letter always

[36] Vaughan and Greene, 1983.

correct. Instead of learning to just pick the odd one, the pigeons learned twenty-six correct letters.[37] Where was that ability to 'work things out in the head' when they needed it? Given what we already know about how pigeons learn, it would be somewhat surprising if their performance in the clock experiment required a rich 'thinking' kind of explanation.

And as Blumberg and Wasserman note, automatically preferring the more mentalistic explanation may be 'confusing linguistic brevity with conceptual elegance.'[38] The bottom line is that we don't really know, at the level of cognitive machinery, how the bee adjusts its boogying or what the pigeon is doing, in its mind, when it watches the clock or commits to memory 320 slides. Consequently, we are as yet in no position to confidently rank their mental representations and cognitive operations according to complexity or sophistication. Once our knowledge of animal cognition looks a little less like Swiss cheese, and once we agree on the subjective status of thinking, we can perhaps readdress the question of who is thinking and who is not. In the meantime, the next time someone tells you an animal is thinking about something, ask for a diagram.

[37] Blough, 1985.
[38] Blumberg and Wasserman, 1995, p. 137.

Chapter 7

Is the Clark's Nutcracker an Idiot Savant?

What we count as intelligence, adaptability, and diversity are given generic shape by reality, not by us or our art.

P. Shepard, 1978[1]

The One and the Many

When she was just four years old, Nadia could draw horses better than could most adults. By the ripe old age of six, her drawings not only revealed a firm grasp of proportion, perspective, foreshortening, and movement, they also were expressive and boldly rendered. Nadia's style is reminiscent of Rembrandt's. Sadly, Nadia could not talk about her drawings, did not recognize her parents, and was generally uncommunicative. At school age, Nadia was diagnosed with autism and mild mental retardation with severe language deficit.[2]

Nadia's hauntingly precocious artistic ability placed her in a special class among the autistic: that of the idiot savant or, using current terminology, the autistic savant. (If the primary diagnosis is mental retardation without autism, a person with savant characteristics is called a retarded savant.) Like Raymond, the character portrayed by Dustin Hoffman in the movie *Rainman*, savants display an island of talent in a vast sea of disability. Raymond had a small archipelago of quirky skills; he could do calendar arithmetic, memorize phone books, and, of course, count cards at a casino. A savant named Robert also has a cluster of fantastic abilities. He can sketch homes in minute detail, play eleven musical instruments by ear, and do calendar

[1] Shepard, 1978, p. 14.
[2] Selfe, 1977; Treffert, 1988.

math. When Robert was asked, however, to link sixteen pictures of women with their birth dates, his mental retardation was readily apparent: he could not get any pairings right, even after three sessions.

What is so fascinating about savants is the isolation of these islands of talent from general intelligence, as measured on standard I.Q. tests. Retarded savants typically score between fifty and seventy points; their islands rise precipitously out of a depressed basin. Autistic savants can have I.Q.s over 140 – in the genius range – in this case the unusual ability is more like Kilimanjaro rising off the high plain. The salient point is that the savant ability (or abilities) is formidably inaccessible to other cognitive functions; some genetic or developmental event stranded that narrow cognitive ability like a storm leaving a shipwrecked sailor alone on a desert island. The ability to calculate that December 2, 1923 was a Tuesday is not linked to a broader mathematical skill, as the savant may not be able to add a short column of numbers. Similarly, the ability to play, without error, a musical piece after a single hearing is not necessarily indicative of exceptional musicality or superior memory, since savants with this knack may not be able to identify basic scale intervals or remember the names of the pieces they play so well. The peaks of the savant intellect are so sharp that we can still get an accurate read on general intellectual functioning by averaging over the rest of the landscape. This would be true even if we used an unconventional intelligence test that included measures of, say, musical ability. The gifts that savants have are small, tightly wrapped packages.

Imagine that there was a savant who had not two or three specific talents but a dozen. Would we then expect a boost in intelligence attributable to those abilities? What about forty specific talents? A hundred? The answer to this thought problem is at the core of our understanding of intelligence, whether in normal people, in people with brain disorders, or in animals. At the limit, an infinite number of specific outstanding talents should equal one very smart cookie. If Nadia were as brilliant at every intellectual task as she was at drawing, she wouldn't be even mildly retarded – she'd be a genius. Or would she? Let's think about it slightly differently. If we incrementally added distinct abilities to the intellectual profile of a retarded savant, at what point would that person begin to become more intelligent? This puzzle harkens back to our discussion of defining and measuring intelligence: is intelligence a unitary ability or a confederation of specific ones? Is intelligence in the peaks, or *between* them?

We'll approach this question by first asking how compartmentalized the mind (and brain) appears to be from the perspective of cognitive science, with data gathered primarily from people. We will then ask by what means and to what extent evolutionary processes have had a hand in shaping the architecture of the animal mind. By the close of the chapter, we should understand better why so many researchers studying animal cognition have been so reticent to speak of intelligence at all.

The Modular Squad

Until quite recently, the dominant metaphor for how the mind works was some version of boxes-in-the-head, a concept borrowed from engineering and computer science. Input streams in through the senses and gets shunted through a series of boxes, which sort and manipulate the information according to the prescribed function of each box. One box's output becomes the next box's input; processing operates in serial fashion, or in parallel; information cascades through the system. Milliseconds or years later, out pops behavior. Cognitive scientists who put their money on a modular model of the mind, like Jerry Fodor and Howard Gardner, believe each cognitive process is delimited in its ability to know what's going on in other boxes, or in the mind as a whole.[3] For them, cognition is like the concoction of a secret recipe, with each of several blinded cooks able only to contribute an ingredient or action for each step of the recipe –

[3] Fodor, 1983; Gardner, 1985.

each knowing little or nothing of what the others have done. Processing modules are autonomous and single-mindedly dedicated to particular types of input (visual, spatial, kinesthetic); if there is integration, it is circumscribed. At the extreme, this view holds that there is nothing general or centralized about the mind. There is no executive function. As Gardner puts it:

> If the modularists are on the right track, there is a disturbing possibility for psychology. Rather than being a single coherent discipline – as its leading figures have understandably wished – psychology may turn out to be more of a holding company. In such a vision, there will be separate studies of language, music, visual processing, and the like, without any pretense that they fit into one supradiscipline.[4]

Psychology as a field should, in this view, model itself on the modularist vision of the mind. I'd wager that Gardner's list of the 'modules' of psychology would not include the study of intelligence because, by most accounts, that discipline would cut across many of the others.

The savant phenomenon shows how, under aberrant circumstances, certain aspects of cognitive functioning may become extremely modular, stubbornly impervious to information that would normally have an influence and, importantly, function at a higher level than and without reference to many other relevant cognitive processes. Other clinical disorders that produce specific behavioral and cognitive deficits suggest that mental functioning can be localized; a good neurologist can identify the general vicinity of a stroke, for example, based on behavioral evidence alone. But how modular is the normal human mind, or other species' minds? We don't have a clean answer. There is reasonably strong evidence that many sensory, perceptual, and motor systems have a modular design. During the initial stages of visual perception, for example, information entering your brain from your ears has

[4] Gardner, 1985, p.133.

no influence; prior to the point at which sensory systems combine their information, the processing within a sensory modality is chugging along pretty much independently. The mind is not undifferentiated porridge or, as Steven Pinker eloquently said, the mind is 'not made of mental Spam'.[5]

As an all-encompassing feature of mind design, modularity has, however, run into problems on several fronts. From the perspective of the study of intelligence, the most significant of these is the problem of background knowledge, also called the commonsense problem. Although the evidence against this sometimes seems overwhelming, people routinely access a massive database of informational trinkets nearly every time they use their brains for something. No one really knows how much of this background knowledge each of us stores, but if the U.S. Treasury could be paid one dollar for each info-bit in the average person's memory, the national debt would certainly vanish. You access this database for almost every task except those that are very narrowly defined, like playing chess, which is why computers can be successfully programmed to beat people – even masters – at that game. Where even the fastest computers come up short is in answering questions like 'Do doctors wear underwear?'[6] Computers are dumbfounded by this question. People are not. It's unclear exactly how people answer questions like this, but they do, easily. Some cognitive scientists see the problem of background knowledge as essentially one of stuffing enough factoids into a computer. Believe it or not, there's a guy in Texas right now who's downloading the *Encyclopaedia Britannica*, fact by fact, into a computer. Eventually that computer will know things like 'Water is wet,' 'The Osmonds are Mormons,' 'Nickels can be made of wood,' and 'The English drive on the left.'[7] He and others figure that once that computer has that wealth of information, then it will develop the kind of elastic intelligence that people have and come considerably closer to passing the Turing test; it

[5] Pinker, 1997, p. 31.
[6] Searle, 1992.
[7] Lenat and Guha, 1990.

will assume, but not be entirely sure, that most doctors do wear underwear. Other cognitive scientists, including the philosopher John Searle, see this project as a lot of data entry for nothing, because in their view background knowledge isn't propositional, but comprised of skills, practices, and other murkier types of knowledge that we don't know how to program into a computer and never will.[8]

So people have a vast store of readily accessed information. For what purpose? Winning at trivia games? Yes, and for doing other things we think of as intelligent. Indeed, the efficient deployment of background knowledge may be central to intelligent behavior. As the philosopher John Haugeland said:

> It is absolutely essential, in order to have intelligence at all, for a system to have flexible nonbrittle commonsense that can handle unexpected situations in a fluid, natural way, bringing to bear whatever it happens to know.[9]

The problem with the boxes-in-the-head model, then, is that it is hard to see how the vast library of commonsense knowledge can ever penetrate each box doing its little subroutine. People, and perhaps some animals, demonstrate cognitive processing that is unconstrained by a strict flowchart in which each box delivers prespecified info-bits to the next box in line. One way to shake the system loose and to reconcile it with how we know people use their minds is to replace the boxes with a massively interconnected network of units. Information in such a connectionist network is not in the units, but *across* them, in a pattern of activity. Individual units participate in many patterns, like cities served by several airlines. This more diffuse model of cognitive processing has the advantage of allowing information of any sort to be in the loop and therefore capable of affecting behavioral outcomes. The connectionists don't believe

[8] Searle, 1992; Haugeland, 1995.
[9] Haugeland, 1995, p. 105.

the background knowledge problem has been solved, but they do think their networks are inherently more compatible with an eventual solution than any strictly modular approach.

Neither logic nor the available evidence demand that any modularity found in cognitive architecture during sensory, perceptual or motor integration be carried through the whole mind or be present at every level of organization. The way we effortlessly dip into our immense pool of background knowledge argues against an extreme modularist position, especially because such contextual information is known to affect even supposedly autonomous perceptual and motor processing: who hasn't 'seen' an animal lying dead in the road only to discover, while driving past, that it was only a piece of trash? Such perception may not be constructed out of whole cloth by experience and intrinsic knowledge, but they inform it. Grooming patterns in mice are highly stereotyped and immune to extramodular influence at fine levels, but are nevertheless more flexible at a grosser level. When a mouse sticks out its tongue to lick a paw, it does it the exact same way every time, no matter its age, sex, or experience. The way it flexes its wrist, extends a leg, and closes its eyes is precisely specified and genetically controlled. But when those grooming components are orchestrated into a little bathing routine, the score is written with more leeway; this mouse spends more effort on the belly than the tail, that mouse forgoes face washing when pressed for time, and this one used to do exactly seven licks to the right paw but now does exactly eight.[10] At one level, the behavior is rigidly modular, at another it's open to the effects of experience, environmental state, and, perhaps, whim. (Grooming and anointing routines in people show similar properties though are less constrained at all levels.[11] Spy on yourself after your next few showers and see if you always dry your body parts in the same order.) Among people who study human cognition, all but the most fervent modularists acknowledge that the mind cannot be a sea of independent islands with only a few bridges making

[10] Fentress, 1972; Berridge, Fentress, and Parr, 1987.
[11] Young and Thiessen, 1991.

precisely defined connections. In contrast, most researchers in animal cognition talk about cognitive modules as if that were the only possible variety of mind design. In doing so, they may be deciding the question of comparative intelligence before thoroughly studying it.

Brain Boxes

The argument about modularity is one of the oldest in psychology. Around the time that Darwin was penning *The Origin of Species*, some early brain scientists figured out that a hole in the head in a particular place reliably resulted in the same behavioral deficit. Among these was Paul Broca, who correlated clinical evidence of a severe deficit in speech production with specific cortical brain lesions. Today, researchers gather such evidence from living brains using imaging techniques that can light up the regions that are hard at work or can draw attention to the silent regions that, as a result of injury or disease, will never again contribute to a thought or deed. We know that our visual world is constructed for us courtesy of the occipital lobe in the back of the head, that understanding speech is chiefly delegated to a bit of brain just above the ear, on the left side for most people, and that if you should be unfortunate enough to damage a dime-sized piece of your right temporal cortex you might not be able to recognize faces – only faces, not other complex visual patterns. And it's not just chunks of the brain that can show specificity. In the 1950s Wilder Penfield[12] tickled tiny cortical areas in people who had their brains exposed for other reasons and found each spot gave a different, specific response: a leg might twitch or the patient would report, 'Hey, I smell my father's aftershave!' or 'I see sparkles.' These results led to some pretty strong general statements about the brain's structure.

As you can probably guess, the story isn't quite so clean. If, for instance, you take a group of people who meet the clinical

[12] Penfield and Rasmussen, 1950.

criteria associated with damage to Broca's area, the location and extent of their lesions is quite variable.[13] Those neat diagrams in textbooks with an oval drawn around a section of cortex are showing the average or typical location of damage that affects speech production. Some of that variability is simply poor quality control: individuals vary in nearly all respects, including the exact position of different anatomical areas. Moreover, we know little about people who might have damage in that area but fail to show that collection of behavioral problems; it's hard to gather data on clinically silent populations. The term 'speech production center' may also be too strong: an anatomical module may be more of a statistical consensus than a clearly defined physical area. Also, for an extreme modularist position to hold any water, the brain areas dedicated to a particular function should not only light up when that bit of cogitating is on the agenda, but should also stay quiet during anything *except* that function. That, of course, would be very hard to prove decisively – a lot like trying to prove that an animal is incapable of jumping through a certain cognitive hoop. But the objection stands: it is one thing to say that this brain morsel is involved in this or that process but quite another to say that this is what this part of the brain does – *period*.

Whatever we eventually decide about the modularity of the brain, the mind may not be obligated to follow the same organizational blueprint. That is, the structural architecture of the brain doesn't necessarily dictate the functional architecture of the mind (although the physical nature of the brain may impose some constraints and the functional nature of the mind may impose others). Neurons in the same neighborhood may or may not be part of the same functional cohort; it all depends on how they are wired together. Indeed, what neural imaging studies have highlighted so graphically is the distributed nature of certain mental activity – how, for example, the act of reading a word sets off a pattern of cortical impulses resembling a

---

[13] Kimura and Watson, 1989.

wildfire consuming much of the cortex, with localized hot spots flashing brightly, then smoldering. That is not to say that the brain/mind is not highly organized. Division of labor is one aspect of that organization: not all neurons are participants in every act or passing fancy. This division of labor is quite strict for certain functions and firmer at some levels of organization. For example, in their book *Wet Mind*, Kosslyn and Koenig argue that the brain is 'weakly modular', with more obvious independence of function at higher levels (this handful of the cortex is for seeing, that handful for believing), and more sharing of processing routines at finer levels, just as in the mouse grooming example.[14] Any model of mental activity must strike a balance between promising efficient organization and offering access to knowledge that is both deep and wide.

A team of British and German researchers recently isolated a part of the human brain that is remarkably egalitarian in coping with a hodgepodge of information types. This wine-cork-sized bit of cortex lights up like Disneyland whenever the person breaks out into a cognitive sweat, regardless of whether the problem being attacked is verbal, spatial, or perceptual. Easy problems, the same ones that make lousy measures of general intelligence, don't activate this part of the lateral prefrontal cortex. Other intellectual challenges, however, such as novel tasks, things that are difficult to perceive, and trying to do two demanding things at once also trigger activity in this region. The title of the report summarizes neatly how the researchers feel about these results: 'A Neural Basis for General Intelligence'.[15] I'll leave it to you to ponder whether a specific area of the brain devoted to general intelligence supports or undermines modularity. (It taxes my lateral prefrontal cortex just to think about it.)

We know our own minds better than those of any other species and yet have not settled the issue of how autonomously our modules run, assuming we should be labeling them 'modules' at all. Cognitive psychologists and neuroscientists are still building

[14] Kosslyn and Koenig, 1995, p. 44–45.
[15] Duncan, Seitz, Kolodny, Bor, Herzog, Ahmed, Newell, and Emslie, 2000.

plausible models for how as many as 100 billion neurons can get along so productively. The architecture of the mind that is eventually agreed upon will have implications not only for whether we believe human intelligence is best described as one entity or many, but also for how we believe intelligence evolved, in whatever creature it is found.

The Shell Game

You don't need a degree in evolutionary biology to see how natural selection worked its slow but relentless magic on the beaks of birds: pelicans have a fish scooper with a built-in holding sack, seed-eating finches have short, thick bills (some even have ridges inside to help grip the seeds), and waders have thin sand probes. Take the oystercatcher, which has a bill like a chisel. Way back when, there were birds with modest bills that could only manage to pry apart oyster shells that were already substantially opened, like the wide-open pistachio nuts my kids select from the bowl. Along came a mutant oystercatcher with a somewhat heftier bill that could exploit the better-sealed oysters without any change in its technique – just a better tool for the job. With a corner on the closed oyster market, it was bound to out-compete its weaker-billed relatives. Natural selection makes mountains out of fortuitous molehills. As Darwin said: 'The smallest grain in the balance, in the long run, will tell on which death shall fall, and which shall survive.'[16]

Adaptive, evolutionary stories about the bodies of animals are not always straightforward but they are, as a rule, easier to discern than are the evolutionary stories about animal behaviors. To understand the selective forces shaping behavior, the yea and nay of adaptive opinion, we need to know how the behavior is accomplished. Consider this example of a good behavioral trick: beachcombing crows in British Columbia open whelks (a marine snail) by flying to a height of five meters and dropping

[16] Darwin, 1859, p. 433.

the whelk on the rocks.[17] If the shell doesn't shatter, the crow picks it up and drops the shell until it does. What, exactly, is the adaptation? If the behavior currently improves the reproductive success of crows that adopt it, what aspect of shell dropping could be passed on to the next generation of crows? To discern what selective forces lurk behind this behavior we need to know how the trick is done: what mental processes is the crow using when it decides which shell to select, how high to fly, on what surface to drop the shell, and how many times to retrieve an unbroken shell? When the crow, whelk in beak, flies slowly over a large flat rock, what mechanism says: 'Drop it . . . *now'*?

There are only three possibilities. First, shell-dropping crows may have a one-of-a-kind, custom-built shell drop module, a snap-in add-on to the typical design of a northwestern crow. The shell drop module requires input from the visual system, motivation centers, and flight control units, and provides limited output to motor functions controlling the beak and wings. Like all encapsulated products, use of the shell drop module for purposes other than shell dropping is strictly prohibited. The shell drop module is an out-of-the-box module, but incorporates certain user-specific information.

The second possibility is that there is no shell-dropping mechanism per se. Rather, the behavior relies on cognitive mechanisms already installed and paid for. The preexisting mechanisms would have to be relatively plastic, with operations specified somewhat generally so that the peculiarities of shell dropping would not make it throw a wobbly. A learning mechanism, plus a few other crow-standard features, might do the trick. Here's one scenario: a crow, bored with picking at discarded sandwich crusts, grabs a whelk and flies up toward a familiar spot to take a crack at cracking it. Along the way, it slips out of the crow's beak, shattering on the rocks below. The crow obtains a salty, nutritious reinforcement for its Skinnerian

---

[17] Zach, 1979.

slip. Once one crow has gotten the shell-dropping habit, other crows have the opportunity to employ an observational learning mechanism, if they happen to have one handy. The details of this hypothetical history are not very important. The point is that the pre-shell-dropping crow isn't obligated to make a mechanism from scratch; an existing mechanism, one without blinders, could be co-opted for the job. In this example, a learning mechanism is an obvious choice, but the design of other cognitive processes could leave enough wiggle room to be readily reengineered to take on new adaptive behaviors.

The final possibility for a shell-dropping mechanism (and I apologize for this fence straddling) employs some combination of restricted and generalized components. Crows might, for instance, learn to drop whelks using a flexible learning mechanism, but then develop routines peculiar to shell dropping (e.g., a template for appraising droppable whelks, or a route finder connecting harvest points to the best nearest dropping site) that optimize the payback from the behavior.

The Greening of Psychology

How do we decide which possibility is correct? The answer boils down to finding out how concretely or how abstractly cognitive processes are designed. The way behavioral scientists have approached the problem has a curious history. Around the time that philosophy, psychology, and computer science developed the hybrid called cognitive science, studies of behavioral adaptation suddenly became very popular. Ecologists, who had until then spent most of their time tracking how populations of animals responded to ecological circumstances, saw that the behavior of individuals within a population was a powerful force driving the larger scale processes hither and thither. Although ecologists had always known that natural selection operates on the little guy, it wasn't until at least the 1970s that the decisions made by this lion or that salamander were seen as the cornerstone for understanding the fit between animals and their environments. Ecologists wandered toward psychology.

Psychologists met them halfway. Scrambling out from under the wreckage of Behaviorism, a significant minority of animal psychologists got natural. The main impetus for the shift was a handful of papers known collectively as the 'constraints on learning' literature.[18] These papers described results that made perfect sense given an animal's natural history, but made no sense given pure behaviorist-style learning theory. It seems so blindingly obvious now, but resistance to the implications of the data was extreme. Garcia and Koelling showed that rats that dined on a novel cuisine that later made them ill learned to avoid that food.[19] Behaviorists couldn't swallow it because the behaviorist Bible said that animals shalt not learn in one trial and shalt not learn anything about an aversive consequence (indigestion) that comes hours later. In fact, someone stood up at the meeting where this research was first reported and said, 'The probability of obtaining these results is the same as finding bird shit in a cuckoo clock.' Breland and Breland (students of Skinner – oh, the perfidy!) used conditioning techniques to train circus animals to do silly things and found that a species' natural tendencies often interfered with the performance.[20] Raccoons would obsessively rub tokens that they should have cashed in for food. Pigs behaved similarly, rooted their tokens, tossing them in the air, rooting them again, all to the exclusion of completing the trained sequence and getting the goodies. All these natural behaviors would begin intruding *after* the tricks had been learned, so it wasn't a simple failure of training. Even Thorndike noted that it was easy to get cats to scratch at something to get out of his puzzle box, but laborious to teach a cat to lick itself to get out, presumably because

[18] Shettleworth, 1972; Seligman, 1970.
[19] Garcia and Koelling, 1966.
[20] Breland and Breland, 1961.

grooming is in no way associated with getting food.[21] The bottom line was, when you pit conditioning principles against ecologically driven behaviors, animals do what nature has told them worked best over evolutionary time. Learning was not an agent of the environment, helpfully connecting any old stimulus to the consequences that gave it meaning. Rather, learning was an agent of evolution, just another tool of some selfish genes, constrained, like everything else, by ecological necessity.

The Right Tool for the Job

If you cross a cognitive psychologist with a psychologist hip to evolution, what do you get? Adaptive modules. Lots of them. Here's the logic. Step 1: Learning mechanisms are neither general between species nor all-purpose within an individual animal. The original 'constraints on learning' literature (and many other studies that we've already discussed) showed that each animal has an uneven report card. Birds that can remember their father's song for months can't remember the color of a triangle for twenty seconds.[22] Pigeons are great at rote learning but unclear on the concepts.[23] Zebras are aces at discriminating one stripe width over another, but no better than horses at other visual discrimination tasks.[24] Step 2: All cognitive processes, not just learning mechanisms, are designed to species-specific requirements. This is simply an extension of Step 1 in recognition that, in the post-behaviorist world, there is more to the mind than learning. Step 3: Because the peculiarities of an animal's niche are specific, the design response to pressures from that niche must also be specific; competition and natural selection work to force apart the characteristics of different species' cognitive processes as surely as they differentiated the thirteen beaks of Darwin's

[21] Thorndike, 1911.
[22] Sherry and Schacter, 1987.
[23] Mackintosh, 1988.
[24] Geibel, 1958, cited in Kalat, 1983.

finches. Voilá – adaptive modules.

Some researchers in comparative cognition have adopted the metaphor of 'mental tools' in lieu of 'adaptive modules'. It may have started with Tooby and Cosmides, known for their pioneering efforts to account for human behavior in terms of specific selective pressures operating in our dim past.[25] They likened the modular human mind to a Swiss Army knife, a survival kit consisting of an assemblage of specially adapted tools. Marc Hauser, in his book *Wild Minds*, also talks tools, arguing that most species share a core set of modules that reflect universal challenges (such as those relating to space, number, and objects), plus additional specializations that are special-ordered according to need.[26] (Swiss Army knives work this way, too. You always get a couple of blades, but you only get the toothpick if you really need it.)

The idea of a black box filled with tools is so appealing, I almost hate to criticize it, especially because the logic that ushered in the metaphor is, in large part, sound. The evidence for adaptive specializations of bodies, behaviors, minds, and brains is *everywhere*. Learning *is* constrained. Animals are not adapted to all possible environments – species change to fill the space that is their physical, ecological, and psychological niche. But something is amiss, starting with the tool metaphor. Tools are always designed for specific purposes: a hammer makes a lousy screwdriver and needle-nose pliers are hopeless wire cutters. The design of a tool begins in the mind of the person who makes it. But who is making the mind tools? Evolution doesn't walk up to the pre-oystercatcher and say, 'I see you're struggling a bit with that bivalve. Have I got the tool for you!' No, as Richard Dawkins put it, evolution is a tinkerer, not a designer.[27] If you are dependent on the arrival of a genetic hiccup to get you out of a competitive fix, you can't afford to be choosy. Maybe you get a custom-designed module to solve your particular little

[25] Tooby and Cosmides, 1995; Barkow, Cosmides and Tooby, 1992.
[26] Hauser, 2000.
[27] Dawkins, 1986.

problem, or maybe, just maybe, you get something a bit richer, something that happens to be the right tool for the job in hand but also the right tool for another job down the road. Lucky you! Remember, it doesn't even have to be the perfect tool for either job. It just has to work better than what's hiding in the boxes of your competitors. When you go to Darwin's hardware store, you never know what you'll come home with. Most of the inventory is pure rubbish, but you just might end up with a real treasure.

Too Stupid to Live

There's more to say about multipurpose tools, but first we need to consider what the concept of adaptive modules has done to the study of animal intelligence. Curiously, an extreme adaptive module view can take the wind out of the sails of comparative intelligence as quickly as did extreme behaviorism. One way this happens is by fusing the idea of intelligence with that of adaptation:

> If the notion of intelligence has any role to play in the study of animal minds, it is in terms of how each species solves the problem of making a living. In the struggle to survive, nature is the only arbiter of intelligence. The survivors are smart enough to carry on living, while those that became extinct were not. [28]

There can be no dispute about the validity of the first two sentences; whatever we conclude about animal intelligence must be compatible with evolutionary principles. The third sentence, however, warps the sense of the word 'smart'. We may disagree on the precise definition of the word 'intelligence' but it has not commonly been used to describe the trait that, say, allowed cockroaches or certain viruses to win out over their competitors.

[28] Hauser, 2000, p.256.

As Peter Sellers's character in *Being There* so vividly demon-strated, you don't have to be smart to be a success. Shettleworth agrees with Hauser in her otherwise cogent book, *Cognition, Evolution and Behavior*, stating that if 'intelligence is seen as solving problems of ecological relevance in the environment in which the species evolved, then all species still extant are equally intelligent in their own ways, and the question becomes what different species' intelligence consists of.'[29] Adaptation cannot be equated with intelligence for two very concrete reasons. First, all species in attendance in the year 2000 are not equally well-adapted to their present environments; like gold-medal athletes from an Olympics of the previous decade, they have a history of superior adaptation that may or may not give them the necessary edge in the next culling. (We don't know who outsmarted the competition, only who outscrewed them!) Time will tell who is 'stupid' in this sense. Second, any conclusion about comparative animal intelligence must, to make any sense at all, support this: chimpanzees are smarter than blowflies.

Eco-logical

Extreme cognitive modularity also throws a bucket of cold water onto a comparative study of intelligence by stressing the specificity of cognitive mechanisms. If every species' mind is a confederation of adaptive specializations, a box of tools designed for myriad disparate jobs, then how can species be sensibly compared? The landscape of each animal's mind would, in this view, resemble the Himalayas, with a lofty peak corresponding to each adaptive ability and sharp drop-offs between abilities where natural selection had no urgent purpose. Like our hypothetical idiot savant with ten or forty or a hundred miraculous but lonely talents, each species would have a nearly idiosyncratic profile to which no single measure could ever begin to do justice. We would be left only with a large number of qualitative differences

[29] Shettleworth, 1998, p. 570.

and no stable vantage point from which to survey the entire intellectual landscape.

But can this be right? No individual is assembled from raw materials by a competent engineer with an eye toward the future prosperity of his handiwork. Individuals are always cobbled together out of recycled parts and half-finished projects, bearing a legacy of eons of blind watchmaking.[30] Why couldn't some of those designs be a little more multipurpose than what was specified by the ecological problem? The familiar answer is that there can be no general intelligence because there are no general problems. This thinking, however, may be flawed:

> There is no such thing as a general wound either; each wound has a quite specific shape, but there can still be a general wound-healer, capable of healing wounds of an almost limitless variety of shapes – simply because it is cheaper for Mother Nature to make a (quite) general wound-healer than a specialist wound-healer. [31]

Compelling logic aside, the specificity of cognitive mechanisms is ultimately an empirical question, and a tough one at that. We can readily witness the outcome of whatever design solution evolution has, for the moment, settled on, but describing that design requires clever probing.

All laboratory experiments are, to a greater or lesser degree, demonstrations of the ability of cognitive mechanisms to function outside the boundaries of a narrow, ecologically defined problem. A rat pushing a bar for food, a chimpanzee punching symbols on a keyboard, and a parrot using English words are all pressing into service machinery designed for other purposes. The weirder the environment in which an animal can perform with some competence, the more accepting those underlying cognitive mechanisms must be to varying input. But if you start with the artificial environment, then it is harder to know what cognitive

[30] Dawkins, 1986.
[31] Dennett, 1995, p. 491.

capacities you are querying and to what natural situation they may, at one time or another, have been attuned. Better to turn the question around and start with behavior that appears to require cognitive specialization: if natural selection requires a tight fit between ecological demand and cognitive design, then animals should perform better at natural, ecologically relevant tasks than at more abstract or more artificial tasks that are remote from the environment of evolutionary adaptation.

Thanks for the Memory

The Clark's nutcracker, if you remember from chapter 1, has an extraordinary ability to find the thousands of seed caches it had made months before. The question is, is the Clark's nutcracker an idiot savant, a bird with a stored seed retrieval module attached to an otherwise unremarkable mind, or is its memory for cached seeds the tip of an intellectual iceberg? We can't answer this question by just testing the nutcracker on a series of problems that are further and further away from the natural caching situation because there would be no basis for comparison across problems. If we predicted that a cheetah would be a better sprinter than a high jumper, what high-jump result would confirm or refute that prediction? We need some other species to provide a yardstick against which to measure the nutcracker's performance across tasks. A series of experiments compared the nutcracker to several other seed-caching corvids that vary in their reliance on hidden seeds for survival and reproduction. Pinyon jays are caching fanatics like the nutcracker, but are a little less dependent on the food they store. Mexican jays cache less than both the nutcracker and the pinyon jay. The least dependent on food caching is the scrub jay. These four species entered a mini Cognitive Olympics, beginning with a cache-and-retrieve test.[32]

Clark's nutcrackers were a bit better at finding the seeds that they had hidden than were pinyon jays, which, in turn, were a lot

---

[32] Olson, 1991; Olson, Kamil, Balda, and Nims, 1995.

more accurate than scrub jays. (Mexican jays sat this one out.) The next question was whether these species differences were specific to seed-caching (the output of a stored seed retrieval module in the nutcracker and pinyon jay), or whether the differences were evidence of a broader superiority. All four species were given a spatial memory test involving finding food (hidden by the experimenter, not the bird) in a small number of locations. The nutcrackers and pinyon jays again outperformed the species less obsessed with caching. The third test was yet further removed from the natural circumstances that presumably fostered the specialization of memory. The birds were tested in an operant chamber. Their assignment was to remember the position of one of three circular lights – still a test of memory for something's location, but not a test involving hidden seeds. The top scores again went to the Clark's nutcrackers, with the pinyon jays performing comparably to the two other species of jays. In the final test of the series, the birds were again placed in operant chambers. This time, however, they had to remember not the *position* of one of three lights, but the *color*. In this nonspatial memory test, the Clark's nutcracker, for the first time, came in second. First place was a draw between the pinyon jay and Mexican jay.

So the Clark's nutcracker's memory is not a tool practical only for the purpose of remembering where the bird left pine seeds. It works better than other related species' memory as long as the question is 'Where?' For the nutcracker, location is everything. It is reasonable to suppose that this enhanced spatial memory was one gift (among several) that allowed the Clark's nutcracker to carve out its niche among the highest, snowiest mountains; in that sense, the spatial memory is probably an adaptive specialization. It is, however, wrong to suppose that this gift (or others) could not keep on giving in other contexts: the results obtained already imply that the nutcracker, as well as the pinyon jay, might have an aptitude for remembering other ecologically relevant spatial facts, such as nesting sites, harvesting sites, and human picnicking sites (which both species are known to exploit). Until we pose the empirical question we cannot know how precise a gift evolution gave for the simple reason that evolution never means to give anything in particular. There may nevertheless be guidelines that tell us who might get the more general design, the larger gift.

Gaining Access

The idea that the shell-dropping crow might adopt a preexisting cognitive mechanism might have struck a chord with Paul Rozin, who originated the concept of cognitive accessibility. Rozin says that intelligence is a hierarchical organization of subcomponents. These subcomponents were, at one time in the species' history, adaptive specializations – that is, each was an evolutionary gift that helped solve a particular problem of niche fulfillment. Rozin conceives of these adaptive specializations as extremely modular: 'specific, tightly-wired, limited-access machinery'[33] and gives some familiar examples, including the song-learning template in many bird species, imprinting mechanisms, and perceptual systems. While the outputs of these mechanisms certainly seem to contribute to adaptation, they are not necessarily what we would call intelligent. According to Rozin, intelligence evolves when these adaptive specializations become emancipated from slavish adherence to their original purpose and become available to other systems for other functions. Instead of running to the hardware store for a new tool, you adapt one you've already got. Rozin suggests two methods for making specialized components more accessible: the entire component could be copied to another functional or physical location (such as the mechanisms for seeing in three dimensions being replicated in auditory centers), or new connections between the component and other brain areas could be forged. However accessibility is accomplished, such co-opting of specializations would increase 'flexibility and power over the environment, surely hallmarks of intelligence'.[34]

[33] Rozin, 1976, p.256.
[34] Rozin, 1976, p.256.

All animals sporting more circuitry than a hair dryer seem to have at least a handful of adaptive specializations that could, in theory, be appropriated for other cognitive tasks. Yet it is clear that some species are more flexible in their behavior and show greater aptitude for a wider variety of natural and artificial puzzles than others. Why? Dennett suggests that the design of some cognitive mechanisms (or control structures, as he calls them) precludes the kind of accessibility upon which increased intelligence depends. While Dennett uses this argument primarily to cleave humans away from all other species, there's no reason not to apply the logic more generally. Some animal brains are designed as 'a collection of interlocking special-purpose minimalist subroutines'[35] – a package of idiot savant abilities – that constrain the possibilities of innovation toward a more powerful design. Repeatedly, a specific adaptation solved a specific problem; the species won round after round. But the nature of those specific solutions closed off the option for more general design solutions, solutions more easily tweaked the next time the ground shifted. Evolution (unwittingly, always unwittingly) had painted the animal into a corner. Other species also faced specific problems but in solving them, hit upon design solutions that could, with modification, support mental operations not necessarily limited to the current problem. Think of it as a design to grow into. The last time I went into a computer store to buy a printer, I spent less than I thought I'd have to and got a printer, color copier, fax machine, and scanner all in one. This more general design, in which common components are shared, preadapted my home office for all sorts of communicating, replicating, and transmutating even before I knew I needed to do all that. And the machine printed. You'd be right in thinking that evolution is not as goal-directed as Hewlett-Packard, but then again, the engineers at Hewlett-Packard haven't got all the time in the world. Evolution does.

Accessing specialized mechanisms for other purposes may also

[35] Dennett, 1995, p. 373.

allow the background knowledge associated with that mechanism to be become available. What the animal knew about in one domain becomes information that could be applied to another domain, like fusing libraries. Of course, all that extra information is worthless unless its organization permits ready access; this is one reason that many cognitive scientists hold the human mind apart from that of other beasts. What we've got that they don't is words and the other mind tools that go along with using them.[36] The claim is that without language, the highest levels of abstraction, foresight, and knowledge mining are impossible. Words facilitate the design of efficient knowledge search engines. Without words, the argument goes, other species are mired waist-deep in an information junk heap. While there is no doubt that language enables us to be smart and to keep getting smarter, it remains to be seen just what informational and organizational constraints wordlessness has imposed on the animal mind.

Enough with the theory. Is there any evidence for specialized cognitive adaptations that have been made more generally accessible? While there is nothing unassailable, there are some strong candidates. Language in humans has to be the top pick. It is, as Pinker and others have so persuasively argued, a specialized adaptation – unique to our species and, largely, bred in the bone.[37] But this specialized adaptation has nearly taken over our minds by storm. Human cognition is so steeped in words that some believe no thought is possible without linguistic facility. What started out, presumably, as a communication system became the newest, most powerful way of using the other existing mind components to get ahead in life. There are no retarded savants with amazing linguistic skills because if one has amazing linguistic skills, the high mountains in the cognitive landscape would be so numerous (or the average altitude so great) that retardation would be impossible. Note also that scores on five of the six verbal subtests of the Weschler

[36] Dennett, 1995; Gregory, 1981.
[37] Pinker, 1994.

Adult Intelligence Scale predict I.Q. scores better than any of the five performance subtests.

Another candidate might be sensory (especially visual) integration. Many reptiles rely heavily on vision but, unlike mammals, they process most visual information in the eye. Jerison hypothesizes that this design has limited the accessibility of this processing to other sensory systems.[38] The first mammals were largely nocturnal and therefore had to rely on their ears and noses to know what was going on around them; this processing, for mysterious reasons, occurred centrally, in the brain rather than in the ear or the nose. When some mammals, like the primates, decided to see what life in the sun was like, their visual systems became very sophisticated. Visual processing took up residence centrally, where there happened to be ready access to information from the nose and ears. With multiple sensory systems operating side by side, the evolution of design integration and resource sharing was feasible. Indeed, mammals more easily transfer information across sensory modalities; if they learn a trick via one sensory system, they can often transfer that learning to other modalities. Pinker argues that fancy vision itself can put an animal on the fast track to higher intelligence, noting that the primacy of primate color vision permits a cognitive organization in which object content (what it is) and object location (where it is) are handled distinctly.[39] Again, we don't know any of this for sure, but it seems as though specific design changes in response to one type of adaptive problem (e.g., entering a daylight niche or seeing better) can, incidentally, open opportunities for more sophisticated structures that make use of existing components that have already been road-tested.

Learning mechanisms are also candidates for specialized plug-ins that may have been co-opted for more general use. As mentioned in chapter 5, many apparently reasonable people believed that learning was general enough to account for all

[38] Jerison, 1973.
[39] Pinker, 1997.

behavior both within and between species! We know now that learning mechanisms are not *that* general, but we should be careful not to throw the baby out with the bathwater. Associative learning is a nearly universal learning mechanism; there are common properties across species as different as honeybees and honey badgers, suggesting a very old, favored cognitive routine. It would be very surprising if such a basic, useful mechanism were not an accessible multipurpose tool. In fact, psychologists have found that associative learning helps animals accomplish a huge variety of behaviors. The implication for comparative intelligence is that animals that expanded the domain of the existing mechanisms, like those governing learning, could behave more intelligently at little extra cost. When animals learn in a new, expanded context, they don't learn just one thing; a door opens to another realm of possible behavioral success. The world becomes their oyster – or their whelk, in the case of the northwestern crow. Indeed, the most likely explanation of shell dropping is that it represents a feeding innovation, a local cuisine invented by the crows and passed on through some learning mechanism. LeFebevre and his colleagues collected published reports of feeding innovations by North American, European, and Australasian birds from every professional journal they could find.[40] Some groups of birds, notably corvids, storks, hawks, falcons, woodpeckers, and parrots, show a much higher rate of feeding innovation than you would expect by chance: expanding their diet, creating new ways to eat, or both. Not surprisingly, the rate of feeding innovation correlates positively with the size of the bird species' forebrains. Having a relatively bigger brain may entail running a learning mechanism that is both flexible and accessible – characteristics that permit the animal to improvise wisely.

Unfortunately we know little about the range of natural circumstances to which a given animal would apply specific mechanisms, such as those governing learning, memory, or the

---

[40] Lefebvre, Whittle, Lascaris, and Finkelstein, 1997; Lefebvre, Gaxiola, Dawson, Timmermans, Rosza, and Kabai, 1998.

ability to abstract. One reason for this ignorance is the concentration on adaptive specializations. Cognitive ethologists, quite understandably, are focused on linking an animal's ecological circumstances to its cognitive features. When that is the goal, it makes sense to choose species with a narrow view on life (corvids specialized to cache seed or bees with flowers to find) or to concentrate on one aspect of the species' behavior (frogs with mates to attract or cowbirds with nests to find and parasitize). But this tack will not tell us to what other uses the animal might be putting its 'specialized' mechanism. In order to know how inaccessible (modular) or accessible (general) mechanisms are, we should conduct investigations of the animal mind that are at once broad (to examine generality) and deep (to get the details of the design). The nutcracker uses its seedy spatial memory to remember the location of more abstract objects, but for what else can it use this mechanism, or components of it? Recent experiments have shown that nutcrackers can learn to use a number of abstract geometric principles (such as 'in the middle') to locate cached seeds; their spatial system is remarkably flexible.[41] Can they abstract similar principles about time and number? Until we know the answers to questions such as these, claims concerning the modularity of the animal mind are extremely premature. We have hardly begun to ask the questions!

The field of primate cognition is furthest along the path to identifying the breadth and depth of mental capacities. The adaptive 'specialization' that cognitive primatologists worry about most is that for social living, and because sociality in primates is such a complex, multidimensional problem, a more generalized intelligence may be the only successful design solution. In studying how primates manage their social lives, primatologists could see that they were also building a framework for studying intelligence. (Social complexity does correlate nicely with brain size in primates, but doesn't explain why great apes can outthink

---

[41] Kamil and Jones, 1997.

146

monkeys). Also, because primatologists have evolutionary continuity to back them up, they have never been shy of addressing the question of comparative intelligence. The question of where human intelligence came from was always lurking nearby. Why shouldn't questions parallel to those asked of humans be asked of nonhuman primates? Researchers were highly motivated to look for missing cognitive links and to explore just how different (how less flexible and generally adaptable) the mind of the ape is from that of a person. We'll discuss some of those distinctions in the following chapter.

Who's in Charge?

The emancipation of restricted cognitive mechanisms does more than save an animal from having to design and build a new mechanism from scratch. The biggest payoff to having at least a modicum of general-mindedness is in the power of executive control. At the most rudimentary level, executive control means that your left hand knows what your right hand is doing – some mechanism keeps track of bimanual coordination. That problem, however, has been solved more than once by animals with no more complexity than that Hewlett-Packard printer mentioned earlier. Higher levels of control also exist, most commonly organized in a hierarchy. Think about the rat in the radial maze that kept solving the problem in different ways: what agency was telling the rat which solution to apply? We do not have to invoke a special little commandant of the Mind; executive control is just another process made out of the same stuff as the rest of the brain. That process just needs to have *access*.

The highest level of executive control involves implementing useful solutions by calling on whatever mental resources are accessible and relevant to the job. However, if all you've got is a Balkanized brain, with this module over here doing its thing and that module over there doing its (very different) thing, then you'll have a hard time rounding up the information and processes you need to get a solution on the table and out the behavioral door. Sure, specialized modules can keep an animal on the adaptive straight and narrow as long as life is *predictable* – some simpler animals get along with little more – but not everyone's niche runs like a Swiss train. Because of the complexity and unprogrammability of some niches, certain animals have greater need to integrate, to surmise, and to make informed guesses about what to do next, taking into account information that is geometric, numerical, temporal, long-term, temporary, conceptual, concrete, visual, auditory, kinesthetic, and object-related, just to name a few. Complex social environments, in which predicting the behavior of other animals is key, are one example. For that kind of intricate, seat-of-the-pants cogitating, something has to be the arbiter. It is that arbitration, the sense that a person or an animal has considered (by whatever mechanism) the scope of a problem, the logical options it poses, and decided what to do, that compels us to use the word 'intelligent'. As Dennett said about human learning:

> Learning is not a general-purpose process, but human beings have so many special-purpose gadgets, and learn to harness them with such versatility, that learning often can be treated as if it were an entirely medium-neutral and content-neutral gift of non-stupidity.[42]

Some animals (e.g., primates, dolphins, corvids, and parrots) also show learning abilities that, to a lesser degree, fit this description. This is what makes us feel that Kohler's ape was very different from Epstein's pigeons. The learning set performance of jays and rhesus monkeys also demonstrates such 'content-neutral' learning. Learning of abstract concepts entails cutting across domains and extracting a general attribute out of a set of exemplars. Alex the parrot can respond correctly to the questions 'What's same?' and 'What's different?' as applied to the color, shape, or material of objects. When his trainer asked, 'What's

[42] Dennett, 1995, p. 491.

same?' and presented a red square key and a red triangular piece of wood, Alex answered, 'Color'.[43] Some chimpanzees can use information gleaned from a scale model of a room to find treats in its real-world counterpart.[44] All of these feats require more high-level integration than can be bought with narrow, specialized modules. This is not to say that there are not gaps in these animals' abilities, tell-tale stupidities caused by a specialization being tripped up by some environmental irregularity. As Tooby and Cosmides have been so clever to point out, people are also prone occasionally to such stumbling, but that doesn't alter the conclusion that despite our dependence on routines that adhere to specific Darwinian cause, we show a tremendous ability to solve problems, think abstractly, and plan – to be intelligent.

The Beak of the Crow

Despite all the problems with measurement, adherence to the idea of human general intelligence is strong. If evolution had a hand in shaping this cognitive design for us, wouldn't similar processes be expected to apply, to some degree, in the evolutionary history of other species?

Maybe not. We learned that evolutionary continuity does not guarantee uniformity of behavior or cognition, that a primate and a bird may be more similar than two primates species. Maybe general intelligence is like being a mammal that walks on two legs – it's our innovation and no one else's. Maybe, as some cognitive scientists argue, thinking that transcends context must piggyback on language. You can't think the think if you can't talk the talk. Maybe.

The Clark's nutcracker is not an idiot savant. Neither is it an avian Einstein. There *are* species, mostly insects and invertebrates (but perhaps not *Portia*), which could be characterized as idiot savants; their mental talents show sharp specificity and

[43] Pepperberg, 1987, 1990.
[44] Kuhlmeier, Boysen and Mukobi, 1999.

remain beholden to the precise adaptive cause that assured their perpetuation. For other species, cognitive abilities appear to have become emancipated from slavish adherence to particular inputs, under particular circumstances, for particular ends. Some cognitive mechanisms may indeed have always been a few sizes bigger than needed for the problem they originally solved; these mechanisms would be prepared to transcend context, should the need arise. (Imagine the ad: Find dinner! Choose a mate! Get rid of those embarrassing parasites! Optimally care for your young! All with one, space-saving, energy-efficient neural gadget! Brainstem not included.) The opportunity to develop a more general mechanism seems to have arisen in certain species; we know that we are part of this in-group, but we are not sure who else is a member. The data are very scarce.

In Shettleworth's book there is a figure depicting the specialized adaptations of birds' bills for different kinds of foraging techniques.[45] There's a cardinal (seed-cracker), a parrot (nut-cracker), and several others. The one that caught my eye was the beak of the crow. It's a Goldilocks beak: not too long, not too short, not too thick, not too thin. The caption describes it this way: 'generalized forager.'

[45] Shettleworth, 1998, p. 43.

Chapter 8

Hotbeds of Intelligence

The intellect must have been all-important to [man], even at a very remote period, as enabling him to invent and use language, to make weapons, tools, traps, etc., whereby with the aid of his social habits, he long ago became the most dominant of all living creatures.

C. Darwin, 1874[1]

Perky Primates

Tamarins and marmosets are tiny South American primates; one species is barely six inches long, not counting the tail. If Yoda overdosed on Rogane, he'd pass for one. Unlike most primates, the callithricids are monogamous, with the Dad usually doing more than his share of carting the kids around. Most species forage in groups, scrambling through the forest canopy in search of ripe fruit. Menzel and Juno studied memory and social foraging in a group of saddle-back tamarins.[2] Each day, the tamarins were released into a large room in which two new objects had been placed. One new object, a red bow, contained some candy while the other new object (a bag, a tin can, or an aspirin bottle) did not. The objects never left the room so, as the days went by, there were more and more hiding places to choose among. Even when there were thirty objects, the tamarins zipped into the room, looked around quickly, and raced over to the new ones which might conceal a treat. Other tests showed that the tamarins were doing more than just noting novelty; they were remembering the location and identity of all thirty objects.

In the discussion section of the paper, after commenting on the meaning of their results, Menzel and Juno had this to say:

[1] Darwin, 1874/1998, p. 633.
[2] Menzel and Juno, 1985.

To most of humanity some animals quite simply look smarter and seem to act smarter than others . . . the first time we ever laid eyes on [the tamarins] they impressed us as highly intelligent, largely because they seemed so alert, visually curious, and reactive towards us as strangers or indeed toward almost any novel event in their inferred visual and auditory field. All of the tests we devised amount, in retrospect, to little more than introducing some additional minor novelty or change into their environment, to test whether these first impressions were true or false, or in what sense they were true or false. [3]

The authors deserve credit for being so honest about how the tamarins' bright-eyed appearance affected the estimate of its intellect. Most researchers wouldn't feel secure enough to present their biases right next to their data. The deeper issue is, however, why tamarins and other similarly perky species give the impression of intelligence. What is it about being a success in a tamarin's niche that makes these animals look – and act – as if they're on the ball? In the last chapter we asked whether cognitive mechanisms could be designed with sufficient generality to support the kind of intelligence that spans the peaks of adaptive specializations. We made steps toward reconciling the idea of context-flexible (if not context-transcendent) processes with the idea of evolutionary design. Now we are working at the same question from the other side: do the environments that intelligent animals inhabit have anything in common? If there's not something in the water, where is it?

Curiouser and Curiouser

The observation that the tamarins were 'visually curious' and strongly attracted to novelty led Menzel and Juno, as it would lead you, to the hypothesis that tamarins are smart. Curiosity, the quality of actively interrogating the world, would seem to be a

[3] Menzel and Juno, 1985, p. 156.

sister quality to intelligence, if not an integral part of intelligence itself. Curiosity moves the animal into new worlds where it can acquire knowledge, test developing skills, and sample niche boundaries. We see this most unmistakably in children, who toddle and then run into ever-increasing spheres of novelty, eyes wide open, questions erupting unremittingly. (When my daughter, Rachel, was a preschooler she was such an incessant questioner I dubbed her 'The Why Machine'.) Curiously, comparative curiosity has been little studied, with one prominent exception. In 1966, Glickman and Sroges observed the reactions of more than 100 species of zoo animals to a variety of novel objects.[4] The objects were scaled for species ranging in size between a gerbil and a gorilla and included wood blocks, steel chain, rubber tubing, wood dowels, and crumpled paper (although the data from the crumpled paper were excluded because 10 percent of the subjects ate it). The experimenters observed in detail how each animal oriented toward and manipulated each new object. The combination of orienting responses and object contacts was labeled 'reactivity'.

For sheer number of hits on objects, the primates (forty-nine species) and carnivores (twenty-three species) were at the head of the class, followed by the rodents (fifteen species), with the reptiles (nineteen species) bringing up the rear. Carnivores, as a group, messed with the objects the most, often using characteristic hunting and prey-handling tactics; they batted the objects around the cage, chased after them, subdued the unruly blocks and tubing with their paws and jaws, chewing them to bits. The primates had the highest orienting scores, conducting much of their information gathering with their eyes. Like the carnivores (and human infants), they stuck nearly everything into the mouth, but also twisted, banged, poked, rolled, bent, and otherwise tested the limits of each object, typically with the forepaws. These comparisons between large sections of the evolutionary tree, however, are not nearly as intriguing as those

[4] Glickman and Sroges, 1966.

between smaller branches: within each broad taxonomic group is striking variability in reactivity that doesn't correspond to which species sits on a more recent branch of the evolutionary tree. For example, nearly all the reptiles were flatliners on these tests, failing to orient to or interact with the objects in any way (although the spotted monitor and Cook's tree boa both struck at the experimenter!). The exception was the Orinoco crocodile, which seemed to appreciate this break in the usual zoo routine. It lunged at and bit every object, and pushed some around the cage – a distinctly mammalian response. Among the rodents, the squirrelly types were more curious than the mouse/rat types, even though the squirrels are modern representatives of an older group. By far the most reactive rodents were, oddly, the porcupines, which confidently approached each object placed in the cage, often bristling aggressively at the experimenter. Although the high reactivity of the baboons and chimps surprised no one, other primates were also dark horses; the prosimians, an ancestral group of primates including lemurs and galagos, were as curious as both New and Old World monkeys.

What's for Dinner?

What are we to make of this confusing pattern of results? Phylogenetic relationships alone fail to separate the inquisitive from the indifferent. Glickman and Sroges hypothesize that a consideration of natural habits can help explain why Curious George was a monkey rather than a mouse or a monitor lizard. First, to favor curiosity, the animal's metabolic rate needs to be high enough to make eating a regular necessity. Animals like the bushmaster (a snake) that eat only every few months are unlikely to develop a sustained interest in manipulating and investigating food sources; most of the time they just don't have the energy for it. Second, those animals at great risk of becoming someone else's dinner can ill afford to poke around satisfying curiosity. Looking over one's shoulder is incompatible with examining a whelk or exploring the uses of a stick. Well-defended animals, like the porcupine and most carnivores, can therefore invest in a little curiosity without paying the ultimate penalty. An organized social structure can also effectively operate as a defense system, since vigilance is typically shared across members of a group. Animals that benefit in this way from sociality, like many Old World monkeys and apes, are thereby more at leisure to explore and manipulate.

The third and most significant natural promoter of curiosity is a species' feeding habits. An animal whose diet requires complicated handling (think of eating a lobster) is equipped with the motor and sensory capacities that would easily transfer to fiddling with objects. This was apparent in the reaction of the carnivores to the objects tossed into their cages: they treated them as prey. Similarly, an animal that must get a nut out of a shell, coax a termite from its mound, peel the rind from a fruit, or dig for water has the behavioral infrastructure to do some exploring during downtime and, perhaps, the cognitive infrastructure to make use of the new information. As others have argued, it isn't usually a particular foraging trick that predicts further mental dexterity, but rather having a bagful of tricks.[5] The nectar-feeding hummingbird is a whiz at getting nectar from hard-to-reach places, but what the hummingbird has is pretty much a one-trick act. The same holds true with the kangaroo rat's ability to harvest minuscule desert seeds at a blinding rate, and the sea otter's use of rocks to break open abalone shells. The kind of animal that we can expect to be insatiably curious is one that, upon arising hungry, sets off to see what in the world looks good today. Like the best chefs, they defer deciding what's on the menu until they know what the market has to offer; these berries are not ripe today, it's already too warm for the fish to linger in the shallows and – hey! – a lizard just ran across the path! To feed in this way,

[5] Parker and Gibson, 1979; Byrne, 1995.

an animal has to be omnivorous, opportunistic, and inventive. The bear and the blue jay, the raccoon and the raven, the rat and the gorilla match the profile. So do humans. To be a successful omnivore, you have to be curious. You have to be willing to sample and test, to poke and prod, to experiment with novel ways of getting all the vitamins, minerals, and calories you need.

Picking with your Brain

Following an omnivorous diet seems to favor curiosity: is there a consistent relationship, or set of relationships, between feeding habits and intelligence? Having an omnivorous diet is only one way to lead a cognitively challenging life. Sometimes even relatively specialized diets carry a heavy mental burden. In the tropics, animals that eat mostly fruits and flowers survive only by mastering a complex scheduling problem. Spider monkeys, for example, are surrounded by hundreds of plant species varying in density, fruiting time, and nutritional payoff. Their home ranges must be huge to harbor enough edible food year-round. To make efficient use of this space, the monkeys have to keep track of what's ripe where and when. Katherine Milton compared the spider monkey's brain to that of the howler monkey, a leaf-eater of similar size.[6] Unchallenged by the puzzle of where the next meal could be found (if you can't find leaves in the rainforest, you've got issues), the howler monkey's brain is only half as big as the spider monkey's. The howler also can't keep up with its fruit-eating cousin in tests of learning ability. Compared to their leaf-eating relatives, fruit-eating rodents, bats, and primates all have bigger brains relative to body size. Sometimes, though, fruit isn't the issue: frugivorous monkeys in Sri Lanka have ripe fruit most of the time, but have large ranges anyway because of the need to balance their diet with scarce, premium foods such as fungi, shoots, and

[6] Milton, 1981, 1988.

insects.[7] For vegetarians that can easily end up a few amino acids shy of a protein, remembering scarce and transient food sources, paying attention to subtle signs of valuable foods (like the shoot of a legume hiding in the grass), and testing out new foraging techniques, routes, and schedules can result in a competitive intellectual edge. Some ambitious animals actually *create* foraging brainteasers for themselves, by way of outwitting rivals. Caching animals (like Clark's nutcrackers, pinyon jays, chickadees, and squirrels) hide abundant food to make it available only to themselves later.[8] Territorial nectar-feeding honeycreepers visit flowers on a large tree using a random route so that an intruding bird cannot know which flowers still contain nectar; the resident bird's memory is the key to eating well on a budget.[9]

Having to think about where the next meal is hiding is one way to put a premium on brainpower. Another way is to have to do something complicated to your food once you've located it. As we've already learned, developing a single procedure that can be executed without much variation will not require a general boost in cognition; whatever smarts the nutcracker has are probably not traceable to its ability to crack open pinecones. If there is more to animal intellect than a confederation of specialized abilities, then we might expect this more general intelligence to arise in species with lots of different complicated puzzles to solve. A more general intelligence could be used, not for general problems, but for whatever specific problems happen to come along. Richard Byrne has shown that mountain gorillas exploit a variety of foods that require plant-specific technical skill.[10] For instance, mature gorillas handle nettles in a practiced way that minimizes painful stings, while young gorillas cannot manage the techniques very well. Bears have broad, opportunistic feeding habits[11] that become yet broader in the presence

[7] Hladik, 1975.
[8] Vander Wall, 1990; Vander Wall and Balda, 1981; Sherry, 1989.
[9] Kamil, 1978.
[10] Byrne, 1995.
[11] Holcroft and Herrero, 1991.

of campers. Park officials warn overnight visitors to conceal popular brands of coolers stored inside their cars; the bears appear to selectively break into cars (i.e., smash a window) that hold familiar food-containers. Ravens, like most other corvids, are omnivorous. Because of their size and their love of meat, ravens have been spotted engaging in a bewildering variety of complex foraging behaviors: pulling two dozen trout out of a stream by the dorsal fin, catching birds on the wing, excavating moles, robbing bird nests, pecking apart any carcass (eyes first) and, incredibly, attacking reindeer.[12] As indicated in the previous chapter, because of the focus on specialized adaptations, we lack detailed knowledge of behavioral capacities of most species with more generalist foraging habits.

Primates are the exception.

If I Had a Hammer . . .

Circumventing food extraction and handling problems by using tools may, in some cases, indicate a special kind of improvisation by foragers. Many species use objects to aid in acquiring something (usually food): gulls drop rocks to break open shellfish, the Galápagos cactus finch uses a cactus spine to probe for insects lurking under bark, and certain ant species use a piece of leaf or wood as a sponge to soak up fruit juice or the runny bits of their prey.[13] But these cases, like the use of the stepping box by Epstein's pigeons (but not by Kohler's chimps?), may not reflect the kind of improvisational tool use that we would expect from a nimble intellect. Why not? The use of a tool for a single job, however ingenious, doesn't require an understanding of the function of the tool. The behavior may be hardwired or, alternatively, the animal could have stumbled onto the solution; in that case the smartest part would have been recognizing that the tool did in fact do the job. If we want to know what tool use says about intelligence we need to know how the behaviors

[12] Heinrich, 1999.
[13] Beck, 1980.

develop and what mental abilities underlie them. Let's say a raccoon used a garage door opener to raid the garbage bins. The raccoon might have only accidentally stepped on a remote control unit carelessly left on the driveway, then snooped around in the garage until it hit pay dirt. Now, if the raccoon repeated the trick on another night, we'd be impressed with the rapidity of the learning. If the raccoon had observed a person letting himself into the garage using the remote and then had imitated the maneuver on its own, we'd probably report it to the *National Inquirer*. Behavioral history is key to understanding which mechanisms are on board.

We don't know for certain whether *any* animal really understands the function of the tool it employs, but some cases are better candidates than others. When the animal has to modify the tool, for example, in order to make it work, and when different individuals use a similar tool differently, we begin to suspect that a more intelligent process is at work – one of design, not happenstance. Some chimpanzees use special stones to break open nuts: a flat stone for an anvil and another stone as a hammer.[14] The tools are sometimes left under the nut tree where they will be used, but at other times the chimps cart them around like prized possessions. Females appear to coach young chimps on proper technique. In contrast to the nut-cracking stones, twigs used for ant-dipping and grass stems used for termite fishing are tools made by the chimps.[15] New Caledonian crows also modify objects for use as tools, bending twigs in different shapes for different extraction problems.[16]

In the absence of developmental histories from the field, the best we can do is test animals' tool know-how in experimental situations. For example, Visalberghi and Limongelli gave capuchin monkeys and chimpanzees a clear tube with a peanut inside and a stick to use to poke the peanut out. This was simple enough for all the contestants until a devious wrinkle was added: the

[14] Boesch, 1991; Boesch-Achermann and Boesch, 1993.
[15] Sugiyama and Koman, 1979; Goodall, 1986; Beck, 1980.
[16] Hunt, 1996.

clear tube contained a trap, a bulge in the underside of the tube's center. If the animals inserted the stick into the wrong end of the tube, the peanut would be pushed into the trap. Different versions of the trap tube test have shown that capuchin monkeys, if they can solve the trap tube problem at all, use a rule something like: 'Put the stick into the end farther away from the peanut.' Two of five chimpanzees were able to solve the problem even when the trap was not centered (when the capuchin rule would have failed). Orangutans, bonobos, and chimpanzees, if given a bundle of sticks too big to fit into the tube, will not only remove a single poker more suited to the task, but will do so without first trying to cram the bundle into the tube. Capuchins, by contrast, don't seem to realize the tool's inappropriate shape until after they've tried to ram the whole bundle into the tube.[17] Studies such as these are our first glimpses into the machinery behind the use of tools as an aid to niche exploration and exploitation. It is almost certainly no coincidence that the flexible use of tools has only been recorded in species with broad diets. A curious animal who can't keep its paws to itself is much more likely to discover what objects can do. Curiosity, idle though it may be, is the mark of a mind seeking to enlarge itself.

Stalking up on Brainpower

It may be difficult to recall when you last checked the mango tree, but at least the mangoes aren't taking evasive action. Constructing a diet around meals that have brains has its own consequences for mental abilities: while the hunter works out how to catch and subdue, the hunted works out how to scram. We've already discussed how a predatory appearance is associated in people's minds with intelligence. Now we will assess whether this common deduction has a scientific basis. The relative size of the carnivore brain has increased remarkably since the first pint-sized specialized meat-eaters appeared on the scene

[17] Visalberghi and Limongelli, 1994, 1996; Limongelli, Boysen and Visalberghi, 1995.

during the early Cenozoic period. This progressive brain expansion probably answered the need to develop more sophisticated hunting methods. Instead of wandering around hoping to happen on a meal, savvy hunters could stalk, ambush, and seek prey not just directly, but by signs. Carnivores flourished.

Of course, if the prey species hadn't also wised up, they would soon have become extinct, dragging the carnivores into the fossil record behind them. As Paul Shepard put it, 'Only a progressive prey could withstand the emphasis on intelligent assault.'[18] Prey that could not develop morphological solutions to more cunning predation, such as the armadillo's armor, had to develop behavioral, hence cognitive, tricks. For that they needed, it seems, more brain, setting up an intellectual arms race with the carnivores: 'Terrestrial predators and prey honed their respective intelligences on the whetstone of each other's strategies.'[19] But the carnivores have stayed ahead at each stage of evolution, as Jerison has shown using cranial fossil casts of extinct herbivores and carnivores.[20] Interestingly, in South America, which is devoid of advanced carnivores, the herbivores have tiny brains. Unchallenged by the mind behind the hungry jaws, these grass munchers lived fruitfully and multiplied in blissful ignorance. In any contest of wits, never bet on the llama.

Brain size is at best, however, a very rough estimate of intelligence. What's more, there have been no studies of the intellectual requirements of hunting; in the social hunters, such as lions, hyenas, and wild dogs, some active cooperation between individuals may occur, but it is yet unclear how severe a cognitive load this or other hunting strategies produce. Our preanalytic intuition that keen-eyed predatory animals are sharper than their prey is a reasonable working hypothesis, but one with few data behind it.

[18] Shepard, 1978, p. 9.
[19] Shepard, 1978, p. 18.
[20] Jerison, 1973.

Menu-Driven Intelligence

The breadth of the diet, its distribution in time and space, its packaging, and the agility with which it can elude the grasp all determine how much mental effort must be expended to get a meal. Any one of these factors might be sufficient to promote a more general ability to solve problems flexibly, assuming that door has not been slammed shut by restrictive cognitive design. But given that the data relating specifics of foraging behavior to cognitive capacities are so thin, our bets will be safer if we consider species in which the factors occur together. Chimpanzees, for example, have very broad diets, with complex spatial and seasonal distribution. Many of their favorite foods require extensive handling. Chimpanzees in different areas have developed the use of foraging tools to aid in extraction and processing. Three separate populations of chimps are documented hunters, chasing down colobus monkeys, forest antelope, and giant rats.[21] In short, if we had to draw conclusions about comparative intelligence based on foraging data alone, chimps would be high on the list. Some smaller carnivores, such as foxes (at long last!), mustelids (the weasel and mink family), and raccoons, also match the profile; they sample among reptiles, birds, small mammals, eggs, and insects in response to opportunity and seasonal availability. Foxes cache extensively and remember, rather than sniff out, the location.[22] The stashes reveal the breadth of the foxes' diet: one cache contained thirty-six little auks, two guillemots (seabirds), four snow buntings, and a stash of auk eggs, while another held three voles, two mice, a chunk of garter snake, and six grasshoppers.[23] Bears are also omnivorous, occasionally predatory, multitactic feeders. No rigorous cognitive research has targeted the bear, but the field evidence for their resourcefulness and ability to improvise is strong.[24] As we've already mentioned,

[21] Teleki, 1973; Boesch and Boesch, 1989; Nishida, Uehara and Nyundo, 1979.
[22] Macdonald, 1976.
[23] Fisher, 1951.
[24] Herrero, 1985.

many corvid species are foraging generalists, as happy to nosh a few berries or crack open a nut as nab a salamander or steal some eggs. Gulls are also opportunistic, exploiting any food source within reach, including food found in garbage dumps and in the claws of other birds. Of course the quintessential omnivorous, predatory, tool-using, food-fiddling species is the human. Say what you will about the intricate feeding habits of other species: we remain the world's only garnishing animal.

Lack of data notwithstanding, a comparative analysis of cognition and calories will take us only so far. If asked to guess which animals will medal in the Cognitive Olympics, you could do worse than put your money on one of the species mentioned above. But the link between feeding habits and intelligence is far from ironclad. Dolphins, for example, do not appear to have a mentally taxing foraging habit: lots of animals eat fish without needing a human-sized brain – what does the dolphin do with such expensive hardware? And while herbivorous primates tend to have smaller brains than their fruit-loving relatives, not all the scatter in brain-size measures in fruit-eating primates and in leaf-eating primates can be readily explained by diet. For instance, Dunbar has shown that neither the amount of fruit in the diet nor the range size of primates correlate well with the size of the neocortex; there is more to being a clever monkey than being able to remember when the guavas ripen.[25] Slipping into a niche that rewarded culinary curiosity, dietary dexterity, and robust memory for a good meal may be one way to get smart, but not the only way.

Social Smarts

Thinking back to chapter 2, you may recall that experts and nonscientists agreed on the two primary abilities of the ideally intelligent person: problem-solving ability and verbal ability. Nonscientists also pegged 'social competence' as a component of intelligence, identifying characteristics such as these as being

[25] Dunbar, 1992.

typical of a smart person: 'accepts others for what they are', 'admits mistakes', 'displays interest in the world at large', and 'has social conscience'. In contrast, the experts failed to see most of these traits as relevant to intelligence, picking out instead traits that gathered under the label of 'practical intelligence', such as 'sizes up situations well' and 'determines how to achieve goals'.[26] Who's right? What, if anything, does knowledge of other people and their behavior have to do with being intelligent? Everything, if you buy in to some recent theories of the influence of sociality on the evolution of primate intelligence.

There are as many versions of this idea as fleas on a gibbon, but the essence is the same. Forget mapping fruit trees, forget learning how to peel a banana, forget outfoxing a wildebeest – that's all intellectual child's play. If you want to sharpen your wits against something really tough, try the mind of one of your pals. Nicolas Humphrey was one of the first to air the idea that intelligence was evolution's answer, not to practical dilemmas, but to social ones:

> [The desert island of Robinson Crusoe] is a lonely, hostile environment, full of technological challenge, a world in which Crusoe depends for his survival on his skill in gathering food, finding shelter, conserving energy, avoiding danger . . . But was that the kind of world in which creative intellect evolved? . . . My view – and Defoe's, as I understand him – is that it was the arrival of Man Friday on the scene which really made things difficult for Crusoe. If Monday and Tuesday, Wednesday and Thursday had turned up as well then Crusoe would have had every need to keep his wits about him.[27]

Lots of animal species like to hang out with others of their kind; sardines school, finches flock, hartebeest herd, geese gaggle. They do it for good reasons, usually to reduce predatory risk, improve foraging success, or get more dates. Researchers interested in

[26] Sternberg, Conway, Ketron and Bernstein, 1981.
[27] Humphrey, 1976, p. 305.

the social induction of intelligence focus on primates because so many primate species live in social groups comprised of relationships as convoluted as a daytime television drama. Having chosen the evolutionary path that led them to group living, social primates, the argument goes, have to play those relationships for every fitness point they are worth. Thrown together into a group, but really only pulling for themselves (and, to some degree, their kin), the social primate uses her cognitive wherewithal to figure out what the other guy is doing with his cognitive wherewithal so she can do better than he can. I would much rather be a carrion-shredding vulture or a blood-sucking leech than a baboon in a troop of fifty. They are *nasty*.

For those unlucky enough to be baboons, the only way to have any peace at all and get ahead in life is to know a few things about the troop. The advantage of knowing your enemies and friends (and being able to tell the difference) is that, in a social world, every behavior is like a chess move – the board can change instantaneously. The better that an animal can predict what others in the group will do in a particular situation, the more effectively it can position itself to take the greatest advantage. Let's say you're a male baboon with an eye on a female named Martha. If Joe's friend Bruce is sneaking off into the bushes with Martha, and Joe is dominant to you, then whether you try to intervene might depend on whether Joe is watching. The possibility of a tryst with Martha may not be worth the combined force of Bruce and Joe's wrath. To evaluate the situation and compute the recommended behavioral decision would appear to require not only considerable knowledge of social relationships but also the cognitive perspicacity to put two and two together. It is precisely this type of 'Machiavellian' intelligence[28] that has been proposed as the hotbed of most of our fancy thinking. Primates that could psych out the competition would do better (in a Darwinian sense), thereby paying off the cost of running a larger brain.

[28] Byrne and Whiten, 1988.

Wildlife Psychologists

For sociality to have special status as the main ingredient in the recipe for intelligence, it has to make cognitive demands that other factors, such as feeding habits, do not. What is exceptional about the social mind? And do those exceptional properties account for differences in intelligence among primates, including the gap between our intelligence and the rest?

We won't be reviewing all the relevant data; the literature is a mess of methodological pitfalls (and pratfalls), ingenious designs, reckless overinterpretation, muddled theory, fascinating possibilities, and philosophical and moral dark alleys. It sounds like fun, but we could drown in those data before we'd get anywhere. It all boils down to whether social knowledge is different in kind from other knowledge, and therefore whether special cognitive equipment is necessary to handle it. If any animal that needs to keep track of social information can employ the same mechanisms that it uses to keep track of herd movements or fruiting trees, then we don't need a social theory of intelligence. Why upgrade unnecessarily? The modularity folks want there to be special cognitive equipment for every kind of knowledge; any alleged peculiarities of social knowledge should, in their view, force the development of specialized cognitive mechanisms. As we saw in the previous chapter, however, it's perfectly reasonable to suppose that even a 'relationship module' or a 'social information module' might have been usurped for more general purposes. If that is true, then looking only at the behavior of living species (much preferable to the behavior of extinct species) makes it very hard to distinguish between the (now) generally intelligent species that used to be only socially competent and the (now) generally intelligent that used to be foraging aces. The possibility of cognitive accessibility derails attempts to discern the evolutionary origins of psychological faculties.

If the original wise guy were a party animal, then there should be something particularly vexing about problem solving in the social realm. At the core, the definition of a social animal is one whose behavior is dependent on the behavior of others of its kind. If eating, mating, and staying safe all depend on getting information about what others are doing (or, more importantly, what they are going to do), then the successful social animal needs to be a skilled psychologist. In some ways, this problem is the same as that faced by predators; accurately anticipating the prey's movements can mean the difference between a full and an empty belly. A lion that interprets the meaning of a flick of the gazelle's tail is doing just what a vervet monkey does when it interprets the flash of a fear grimace on the face of another monkey.

So why is within-species psychology (monkey studying monkey) supposedly a more difficult subject than between-species psychology (lion studying gazelle)? The answer to this question is not very clear. Researchers usually point to the need to know about *relationships* between group members, not just about the individuals themselves; members of stable, long-standing social groups in which friendship and kinship determine power will be more likely to play their cards right if they pay attention to group dynamics.[29] The data on this point are somewhat equivocal because in practice it is very hard to control all the confounding factors. For example, when vervet monkeys hear an infant's cry played on a tape, they are more likely to look at the infant's mother than at other mothers in the group.[30] One interpretation is that the vervets understand, in some sense, the mother-infant relationship. The problem is that other mechanisms that don't rely on special social concepts can also explain the result. Mother-infant pairs are usually together, so the looking response might just reflect generalization from the infant to the mother. The association might also be based on resemblance between infants and mothers. If either of these explanations is correct, then learning about social relationships

[29] Cheney and Seyfarth, 1990; Kummer, 1995.
[30] Cheney and Seyfarth, 1990.

may not be a qualitatively different task than learning about most other things, such as what predators learn about prey and what fruit-eaters learn about fruit. In a different study, however, Seyfarth and Cheney suggested that vervets might know enough about relationships to carry out a vendetta. Like miniature Hatfields and McCoys, the monkeys tend to threaten the relatives of monkeys who recently harassed their relatives. Acquiring and maintaining relationship data on a large number of group members may require additional cognitive resources, but we don't yet know how much or what type.

I Know What You're Thinking

The brouhaha over social theories of intelligence is not, however, so much about whether it takes a new mega-gigabyte module to remember which of those guys in the tree are your third cousins. The critical psychological gambit is knowing what those guys are *thinking*. The question that is typically posed is whether animals attribute mental states to other animals, that is, whether animals have concepts about 'knowing', 'wanting', and 'believing' and use those concepts to predict, explain, and manipulate the behavior of their friends and enemies. (This is also called having a 'theory of mind'.) People attribute mental states incessantly. We assume that other people know things, want things, and need things, and base much of our behavior on our beliefs about how those mental states drive their behavior. As we learned in chapter 4, we often attribute mental states to animals. My dog is sitting in front of the door because she *wants* to go out, she follows me around because she *believes* I might leave her alone in the house, and she barks because she *knows* that person in the backyard is a stranger. (Although if she barks because she *wants* me to *know* that there is a stranger, then I am not only attributing mental states to her but am also allowing her to attribute mental states back to me.) People are such irrepressible mental state attributors that we slap mentality onto just about anything: the sun is *trying* to burn off the fog, the vending machine *wants* another quarter, and a broken thermostat *thinks* it's hotter than it really is. Of course, we don't really mean what we say in all these instances, but they do illustrate just how natural it is for us to view animals – any animate object, really – as having inner existences that refer explicitly to behavior. Ask people to describe what happens in films showing little boxes and circles moving around, bumping into one another, going in and out of gates, and you get language referring to a wealth of intention, desire, and knowledge contained in a black outline on a white background.[31] Humans are predisposed to think: if it moves, it believes.

The million-dollar question is whether other species have the same inclination. Are they haves or have-nots? Many experimental shots have been fired at this question, but none has been a direct hit. There have been studies of imitation (does the imitator ascribe goals to the animal modeling the behavior?), self-recognition (does the animal know this is the face that others see?), deception (does the deceiving animal mean to take advantage of ignorance or plant a false belief in another's mind?), and perspective-taking (do animals understand that seeing something gives people or animals privileged knowledge?). Each of these abilities with a presumptive relationship to a theory of mind has been assessed using several different experimental paradigms. Whatever field data exists on each subject has been picked over repeatedly. It turns out to be very very difficult to tell the difference between an animal that is responding to another animal's behavior and one that is responding to inferences about mental states based on that behavior. We've already reviewed some of the literature on mirror-guided 'self-recognition' in primates; the conclusion was that the mechanisms underlying the distinctive performance of great apes in the vanity test are unknown. The similarity of the apes' performance to what two-year-old humans do in front of a mirror has to be balanced by their similarity to what Epstein's pigeons did with the blue dots. Granted, phylogenetic considerations should lead us to pay

---

[31] Heider and Simmel, 1944.

more attention to the human data, but we already know that if we lean too heavily on those evolutionary twigs, they might snap. If we are going to let 'evolutionary parsimony' decide the matter, then the primatologists at work on the problem can just pack it up today. What we need are better experiments.

Easier said than done. Here's an example: The Knower-Guesser paradigm has been used to assess whether primates can take into account someone else's knowledge. In these experiments, the primate 'chooses the advice' of one of two people in deciding which of four cups is baited with food. The primate can't see the cup being baited, but it can see which of the two people baits the cup. The other person is either out of the room or behind a screen during the baiting, or has a bag or bucket over the head. The Knower and the Guesser then each point to one cup; the primate must decide whose 'advice' to follow. Pretty straightforward, right? Not quite. First, the data. Rhesus monkeys never pick the Knower more often than the Guesser, even after 400 trials. Chimpanzees learn to pick the Knower after several trials, but choose randomly on the first two trials. Children pick the Knower right away starting at about age four and give explanations for their choices that reflect mental state attribution, e.g., 'The other guy couldn't see where it was.'[32] The chimp data in particular are open to multiple interpretations. Given that the chimps did not choose the Knower on the first trials, they could have solved the problem by rapidly learning a rule such as 'Pick the one who stayed near the cups,' or 'Never choose a guy with a bucket over his head.' Why rhesus monkeys never followed suit is a mystery. Interestingly, if some human adults are rewarded for choosing the Knower (the natural choice) and other adults are rewarded for choosing the Guesser (who pointed to the correct cup despite never seeing it), the groups learn at the same rate. These results counter the idea that mental state attribution is always the dominant determinant of social assessment; the learned association between the actor and the

[32] Povinelli, Parks, and Novak, 1991; Povinelli, Nelson, and Boysen, 1990; Povinelli and deBlois, 1992.

reward carried more weight than responding to who supposedly had the knowledge.

Can we make tests of mental state attribution by animals more conclusive? At one extreme are those researchers, primarily field primatologists, who consider the evidence in hand fifteen years ago sufficient to justify the conclusion that apes (at the very least) have a theory of mind (and probably theories of political justice, social malfeasance, and moral turpitude as well):

> Our daily observations ('anecdotes') make [a theory of mind] the most plausible interpretation of many kinds of behavior; it offers the clearest explanation for many problem-solving actions. Imputing theory of mind to other beings is a product of everyday experience with other primates, whether human or nonhuman. [33]

Griffin echoes this view in each of his books, as do popular authors such as Masson and McCarthy. Theory of mind experiments, however, have failed to show that mental state attribution provides the 'clearest explanation'; alternative explanations (such as those based on rapid, flexible learning) are still alive and kicking.[34] A more moderate position is that while we should strive to improve experimental design, there never will be an experimental silver bullet. In this view, the data from a variety of laboratories employing a variety of techniques, plus anecdotal accounts from the field already converge on the idea that apes (but not monkeys) have a theory of mind. No single datum is watertight but taken together it makes a pretty picture.[35] The skeptic's counterpoint is that stacking leaky experiments atop one another will not make the whole structure watertight. Field reports of deception and the like, while intriguing, are difficult to interpret without complete behavioral histories. According to these folks (and I count myself among them), we must remain

[33] Green, Wilson, and Evans, 1998, p. 122.
[34] Heyes, 1998; Hauser, 2000.
[35] Byrne and Whiten, 1991, 1992.

agnostic on the point. The lack of valid, confirmatory data for other species means that, at least for now, only humans can be awarded a theory of mind. This conclusion would, of course, be revised if stronger data emerged. The most extreme position on the skeptics' end of the spectrum belongs (no surprise here) to the radical behaviorists: 'The most one might hope to learn from [experiments on theory of mind] is what cues are required before someone in our culture with training in cognitive psychology will start to talk about "theory of mind" in a chimpanzee.' [36]

Join the Club

So where does the dispute on which species have a theory of mind leave the social theory of intelligence? Let's pretend that some genius designs and executes the perfect, definitive theory of mind test and all the primates fail, except people over the age of four. Does that mean social living was not the engine behind primate intelligence? Hardly. Attribution of mental states is not the only possible intellectual consequence of having an active social life; social complexity might have spurred the development of other cognitive mechanisms, or embellished the operation of existing ones. Highly social primates might, for example, have perfected the art of translating gestures of the face and body into behavioral propensities, using those visible signs to predict what behavior was likely to occur next. Primates might have developed enhanced memory for keeping track of transgressions and favors, alliances and dalliances. They might also have steepened the learning curve for any events involving other group members, improved vigilance for social interactions, and increased their sensitivity to the consequences of social gaffes and triumphs. Any of these upgraded abilities might have then become more generally accessible, allowing the more social primates, the apes in particular, to impress us with their cognitive acumen in laboratory tasks.

[36] Baum, 1998, p. 116.

If improving your social life results in increasing your I.Q., then any highly social animal should be subject to the same selective pressures. We have focused our discussion on primates because that's where most of our information lies, but data on other species are beginning to accumulate. The social carnivores, such as lions, wolves, and wild dogs, also live in long-standing, structured groups. Because of their nocturnal lifestyle, however, behavioral detail is tricky to get, and because of their intractability, rarity, and size, laboratory work is absent or limited. Spotted hyenas win the prize among carnivores for social complexity (though perhaps not the Miss Congeniality Award). Hyena clans exhibit cooperative territorial defense, group hunting, and a matrilineal inheritance of dominance rank like that of baboons, which is strictly enforced with the threat of retribution from the strongest jaws in the animal kingdom.[37] Unlike vervet monkeys, however, the hyenas did not respond to a tape of a whooping infant by looking at the infant's mother, although the hyenas could discern whether a whoop belonged to a relative or not.[38] This raises the possibility that comparable social structure, especially in phylogenetically distant species, may not always have the same cognitive outcome, either due to design constraints or due to selective pressures in other realms, such as foraging. Dolphins also live in long-term groups, forming coalitions within coalitions for the purpose of garnering females.[39] Whether this social structure has been instrumental in enlarging the mind of the dolphin is unknown. Some bird species, such as bee-eaters, acorn woodpeckers, and Florida scrub jays, live in stable groups, with group foraging areas and cooperative territorial defense. The gregarious pinyon jay, for example, learned a motor task faster when another jay was demonstrating the technique, but the more solitary Clark's nutcracker learned the task at the same rate whether a nutcracker demonstrator was present or absent. Because the jays' and the nutcrackers' overall performance did

[37] Kruuk, 1972 ; Frank, 1986.
[38] Holekamp, Boydston, Szykman, Graham, Nutt, Birch, Piskiel, and Singh, 1999.
[39] Connor, Smolker and Richards, 1992.

not differ, sociality, in this case, may not have conferred an overall cognitive boost to the pinyon jay.[40] Nevertheless, in order for the social theory of intellect to hold water, data from highly social nonprimate species must either conform to the same pattern or the failure to conform must be adequately explained.

The idea that keeping one mental step ahead of your friends and enemies is nature's greatest cognitive challenge is not without appeal or support. It is not yet, however, entirely clear what it is about social life that requires a sharp mind; we can see that brain size increases with social complexity in primates, but we can't yet pin down experimentally what those more social primates are doing with that extra neural tissue. Until we can, we won't know whether sociality did, or continues to, propel intelligence upward. An additional complication is that some of the biggest brained and most social animals are also the kind of foragers we'd predict could use some extra computing power. Chimps and gorillas, as we've mentioned, are both culinary artists and social divas. Hyenas, lions, wolves, and wild dogs live, but also hunt, cooperatively. The sociality of the omnivorous and carnivorous raven is still poorly understood, but juveniles tend to hang out in gangs, and pairs may remain together through the year.[41] As the evolutionary tree branched and grew, hotbeds for intelligence might have arisen more than once, breeding solutions to parallel problems or divergent ones. It is proving far easier to tease apart the origins and function of intelligence in our theories than in our animals.

[40] Templeton, Kamil, and Balda, 1999.
[41] Heinrich, 1999.

Chapter 9

Crocodile Tears and Alligator Shoes

Her speech is nothing,
Yet the unshaped use of it doth move
The hearers to collection. They aim at it
And botch the words up fit to their own thoughts;
Which, as her winks, and nods, and gestures yield them,
Indeed would make one think there would be thought.

W. Shakespeare, 1623[1]

Three times in the last month, a female house finch has ended up on the wrong side of our kitchen windows. Each time, it was the male's calling and fluttering on the sensible side of the window that alerted me to his beloved's plight. The female was so flooded with stress hormones that she didn't know which end was up; wide-eyed and trembling, she didn't struggle a bit as I picked her up and escorted her to the door. A very confused lizard that thought it would set up a territory in the fireplace received the same treatment; I am also in charge of returning bees and wasps to their homeland, but displaced pillbugs are strictly my daughters' department. They carry the tiny rolled-up balls in the palm of their hands, lecturing them firmly but gently on the proper habitat for their kind. All very heartwarming, I know, but our repatriation program has its dark side. Black widow spiders are dealt with severely, and I mean *severely*. The local protocol upon encountering a rattlesnake on one's property is to call the animal control folks (who, rest assured, do not drop the snake off at a shelter) or to chop off its head with a spade.

Whatever your opinion about the particulars of these decisions, we all have to make them. Do you wear leather? Do you eat meat

---

[1] Shakespeare, 1623.

or fish? Would you eat a monkey? How many spotted owls are worth a logger's livelihood? Did you consider all the nesting sites you destroyed when you cleared some property to put in a lawn or a pool? Would you buy a mahogany table? Is it ecologically correct to allow your cat to hunt birds? What if he proudly deposited rare lizards at your feet? While there are many angles from which to address the issues inherent in these questions, we are primarily interested in their relationship to animal intelligence. In the last chapter, we discovered some reasons why natural selection might value intelligence; there seem to be certain ecological and social circumstances that favor improvements in problem-solving and learning ability. In this chapter, we will ask under what circumstances *we* value intelligence in animals, how the perceived intellectual moxie of a species affects our decisions about its worth and, therefore, its welfare.

Polly on a Cracker?

One simple metric we might use to discern which species we value and why emerges from a consideration of human diets. Take the Great Chain of Being and break it off at any randomly chosen link and you'll describe the diet of some human culture; the animals below the break end up on a plate while the animals above the break end up on laps, religious icons, or advertisements. In the standard Western diet, everything on the ladder below dogs and cats is edible. For the white-meat only group, mammals are out, but everything below birds is fair game. Some people break the chain just above fish and shellfish, while vegans spare everything incapable of photosynthesis. Cultural influences and individual experiences play a huge role in determining what we think is good eats. I know people for whom 'facelessness' is the dietary defining criterion. Species that have dual status as food and family introduce special conflicts, as we learned with respect to pigs. Jeffrey Masson, one of the authors of *When Elephants Weep*, doesn't eat anything with eyes, stemming from a childhood incident involving a neighbor who offered to duck-sit. 'How's my duck?' Masson asked upon his return. 'Delicious,' said the neighbor.

The Great Chain of Being is, in one sense, a generalization gradient of rights, with species more proximal to us favored with protection and species more distant flavored with sauces. As you may recall from chapter 4, studies showed that people rank a species' intelligence according to its position on the Chain of Being; this effect seemed to be driven by a crude sense of evolutionary continuity – the smarter species are 'more like us'. Can we disentangle how much our moral concern (or lack thereof) for a particular animal is influenced by its intelligence, independent of its perceived, or actual, relationship to us? It proves difficult to tease these dimensions apart. In a study by Herzog and Galvin, college students rated eighteen animals on the degree to which they possessed human-like levels of eight mental states, including intelligence (though intelligence isn't really a mental state).[2] Overall, the ordering of the species was predictable enough, although the subjects' willingness to ascribe moderate to high levels of mentality to animals was striking. Forty percent said that chimps are just as smart as people and felt emotions the same way. Dolphins received similar scores.

When it comes down to who deserves moral consideration, however, being brainy and emotional was found to be irrelevant; if you want college students to care what happens to you, you'd better be capable of suffering. The researchers also measured attitudes toward animal welfare in the same subjects. People who cared more about animal welfare issues tended to rate every animal higher on both their capacity to suffer and feel pain and on their likability. Interestingly, animal welfare attitudes had nothing to do with how people rated the animals' intelligence; people with a high dose of moral concern for animals tended to see all the animals as being more sentient and more lovable, but not necessarily smarter.

[2] Herzog and Galvin, 1997.

Beetle Bashing

One way to separate whether we value an animal because it is smart or because it is simply more like us is to manipulate our perceptions of the animal. Susan Opotow chose the bombardier beetle as the unlikely star in this role because most people, being beetle-ignorant, would believe almost anything about them. The central question was under what conditions would people include beetles in their 'scope of justice', 'the psychological boundary within which considerations of fairness and moral rules and values govern our conduct.'[3] Animals that fall outside of the scope of justice would be treated as expendable nonentities, undeserving of protection or concern. Opotow manipulated the beetle's reputation along three dimensions: similarity and utility to people and degree of conflict with them. In one scenario, beetles were portrayed as sharing many characteristics of people. Beetles were said to be similar biologically, share common learning processes, and have social mores more commendable than the average person: the beetle is 'communicative, an industrious worker, a protective parent and homeowner, a brave fighter, and a responsible provider for its young.'[4] In the other scenario presented to different subjects, beetles were described as biologically primitive (and therefore very unhuman) and hardwired. In fact, the beetle could survive if you cut off one of its brain centers, e.g., its head. Beetles lay eggs on dead flesh and then abandon them. Not the sort of neighbors anyone would welcome.

For the second manipulation the beetle's utility was the subject. The beetles were portrayed as either beneficial or harmful to humans, including an assessment of their economic impact. Finally, the severity of the conflict between the beetle and people was manipulated. In both cases the issue was a land grab, which, if the beetle were to lose, would result in its endangerment. In

[3] Opotow, 1993, p. 71; Opotow, 1994.
[4] Opotow, 1993, p. 75.

the low conflict scenario, the beetle habitat would be used for an industrial project of questionable need while in the high-conflict scenario a badly needed reservoir was proposed. After the scenarios were presented, the subjects were asked what protective actions they would recommend (such as create a refuge, allocate the habitat to the beetle, and punish people who harm the beetle) and whether considerations of fairness should apply.

The manipulations worked. People who read the human-like scenarios thought beetles were more intelligent, conscious, inventive, and complex than those that read the lowly beetle scenarios. People who read the beneficent beetle descriptions saw beetles as friendlier and more helpful than those who read the bad beetle descriptions. As expected, greater perceived complexity translated into an increased willingness to include the beetle in the scope of justice. But – and this is the kicker – being more intelligent hurt the beetle! People who saw the beetle as smarter were more reticent to extend fairness to the beetle and move to protect its habitat. This was particularly true when the stakes were high, as in the high conflict scenario.

> Emphasizing an environmental entity's intelligence in the context of a conflict of interest may label that stakeholder as a wily or cunning competitor, abet its exclusion from the scope of justice and reduce support for its protection.[5]

The feature that could have spared the beetle from this hypothetical demise was its usefulness to people. People who thought the beetle carried an economic bonus also found the beetle more attractive, lovable, and intrinsically valuable. Similarity to humans did not have the same effect.

Why should intelligence give the beetle a bad reputation? Perhaps, as Opotow suggests, when we are competing with

[5] Opotow, 1994, p. 60.

animals we prefer that they are stupid. Intelligence is fine for pets, which have their roles and know their place, but animals on the loose are another matter. This idea may help explain why, in the studies of animal rankings, the perceived gap between the intellect of pets and nonpets was so vast. The only nonpet species that are consistently viewed as smarter than dogs and cats are primates and dolphins – species that we Westerners very rarely, if ever, see in the wild, much less compete with directly. In West Africa, where the Mende rub shoulders with the chimpanzees, similarity to humans is sometimes used to justify killing chimps.[6] The Mende recognize a common heritage with the chimpanzee, but think chimps are degraded and are bringing down the neighborhood. (Chimps are also threatening: there is evidence that chimpanzees make off with Mende infants. When in Gombe, Jane Goodall kept her young son in a large cage for just this reason.[7]) The evolutionary process is called competitive exclusion: when two species are similar enough to sit in the same niche, someone's got to go. If that direct competitor is intelligent like you, all the more reason to get rid of them before they get the best of the situation, as intelligent creatures are wont to do. Of course, the bombardier beetle doesn't occupy the same niche as humans. Nevertheless, conservation issues are almost always about direct competition between humans and another species over a specific resource and nobody likes a 'wily or cunning competitor'. The age-old struggle between ranchers and farmers on the one hand and foxes and wolves on the other must, at least in part, be responsible for those animals being not only feared and reviled, but also earning the labels 'wily', 'sly', and 'clever', instead of the more neutral term 'intelligent'.

So maybe a beetle that could qualify for *Who Wants to Be a Millionaire?* is a bit daunting, just as *Portia*'s hunting tactics make it a little spooky. But inasmuch as humans are highly intelligent, we should still expect that we would exercise our

[6] Richards, 1995.
[7] Goodall, 1971.

narcissism and value intelligence wherever it is found. There is, however, an aspect of intelligence that runs counter to this expectation, something we might call the Nerd Factor. It's part of our cultural wisdom (stored somewhere in that compendium of background knowledge) that thinking is the antithesis to feeling, that there is something *inhumane* about relying too much on your brain and failing to follow your heart. Many philosophers and scholars have argued that it is human morality, rather than problem-solving skill, that sets us apart from other species. In this light, it makes perfect sense that the compassion of subjects in the Herzog and Galvin study was connected to their perceptions of the animals' ability to feel pain and suffer, not intellectual capacity. The extent to which we find a correspondence between our sentience and that of other animals will determine where we place our compassion. If they think, we may either be impressed or afraid. If they feel, we care.

Razing Animal Consciousness

Sentience is one aspect of consciousness, the I-know-I-just-bashed-my-toe-because-it-hurts-like-hell aspect. How do we decide in whose head the chandelier is lit? We approached the consciousness question from another angle in the last chapter in the discussion of mental state attribution. At issue then was whether, say, a chimp named Donald moves his behavioral chess piece in response to some inferred subjective state that controls the moves of his ally, Marian. But as some people see it, the stakes are higher and deeper than that: they want to know (or claim that they already know) whether Marian is consciously aware of the mental state that propels her in one direction and not the other, and whether Donald is consciously aware of his own psychological states including – why not? – his theories of Marian's mind. Consciousness is the bubble inside whose membrane we tirelessly mold evanescent physical sensation into the solidity of simply being. It is not only undeniably real to us;

it's the only reality we have. And while we are magnanimous in granting each human being a gossamer cloud within which to hope, know, and dream, passing out consciousness to animals is more contentious. Do some animals have consciousness or is it, like rave clubs, prosthetic devices, and lawsuits, distinctly human? And if animals do have consciousness, what do they do with it?

The simplest way to settle the issue is to argue by analogy with humans: if we've got it and we behave like other animals in so many ways, then they've got it, too! This desire to 'penetrate the animal's consciousness by way of analogy' to human introspective accounts[8] was characteristic of psychology at the turn of the twentieth century. Drowned for several decades by the relentless rigor of behaviorism, the idea that consciousness is widespread in the animal kingdom, if not ubiquitous, has recently come sputtering to the surface: 'Special pleading is going to be needed to maintain that similarities in behaviour coexist [in people and animals] with a lack of similarity in conscious awareness.'[9] According to the Herzog and Galvin study, a lot of people agree with Dawkins; more than 90 percent think dogs are at least moderately conscious and about 15 percent believe that ants and spiders are, too.

As we learned in chapter 6, concepts of consciousness and thinking have been intermingled, resulting in an impenetrable thicket of gnarled logic and unsubstantiated criticism of how cognitive science has tackled, or failed to tackle, this issue. Griffin is the ringleader of those who would make the study of subjective experience in animals a research priority, claiming, 'the taboo against considering subjective mental experiences of nonhuman animals has become a serious impediment to scientific investigation'.[10] He chides cognitive scientists for 'clinging to the security blanket of conventional reductionism'[11] and accuses animal researchers of betraying their finer intuitions about the

[8] Boring, 1929, p. 551.
[9] Dawkins, 1993, p. 176.
[10] Griffin, 1992, p. 21.
[11] Griffin, 1992, p. 6.

patent reality of animal consciousness and succumbing to 'self-inflicted paralysis'. [12]

A tacit assumption behind the call for studies of animal consciousness is that consciousness is where all the intelligent action takes place. It may surprise you to realize, then, that you know things that you don't know you know and can acquire conditioned responses (like an eye blink) without knowing you learned them – even as you are doing it.[13] Intelligent mental activity doesn't necessarily take place on center stage where you can view it. The cognitive scientist James McClelland and others have noted that experts often handle a situation 'without any deliberate conscious cogitation,' but instead immediately perceive a solution, bringing to bear 'an indefinite amount of background, relevant experience, and knowledge.'[14] The conscious thoughts of a less expert person, though perhaps eventually arriving at the same solution, are plodding and deliberate. And for those of you who are very attached to your consciousness, there is the disturbing possibility that it is epiphenomenal, or even only an afterthought. Libet, a neuroscientist, has shown that the conscious thoughts that seemed to the thinker to activate a simple action ('I think I'll move my little finger') actually occurred *after* the neural pattern that sparked the movement.[15] That stream of consciousness in which we live might only be a cover story our brain releases to account for decisions made outside of conscious awareness.

Contrary to Griffin's assessment, the animal behavior researchers that I know are hip to the subject of consciousness and most, I would venture, retain an open mind as to whether animals devise their actions from within a membrane of awareness. There remain, however, nagging questions. First, if an animal were conscious, how would you know? We've seen how difficult it has been to obtain solid data on whether animals

[12] Griffin, 1992, p. 117.
[13] Nisbett and Wilson, 1977.
[14] McClelland, 1995, p. 141.
[15] Libet, 1985.

attribute mental states; all the same problems, plus a few more, attend experiments on animal consciousness. Inevitably, some researchers will be drawn to pursue questions of mental state attribution and awareness. However, as I have stated elsewhere, it isn't a project I'd recommend for anyone without tenure.[16] If Griffin writes the definitive grant proposal and gets the funding, he'll have no problem finding someone to run the experiments. As they say in Missouri: 'Show me.'

The second, more immediately germane question is, if an animal were conscious, would it make any difference to our theories of animal intelligence? In more than 800 pages of accumulated evidence in Griffin's three books (and add to that any scientific paper on animal behavior that I have ever heard of), there is not a single piece of evidence that requires the prop of consciousness. It seems we could add a little consciousness (or a lot – why not be generous?) to all of our theories without altering the predictions at all! Perhaps, though, we've been turning over the wrong stones. To direct our attention to the likely hiding places of consciousness, we need to ask what, if anything, does being aware buy an animal, in the evolutionary sense? Humphrey conjectured that consciousness serves a modeling function,[17] improving an animal's ability to keep a behavioral step ahead: Donald runs the parameters of Marian's situation through his own mind, deduces how she should behave given what he knows about her (and the chimp consciousness they have in common), and makes his moves accordingly. On this view, consciousness may be a component of the theory of mind gift package. Considering the thin empirical ice on which the theory of mind theory in animals currently rests, Griffin might have time to write a couple more books before we know the answer.

[16] Yoerg, 1992.
[17] Humphrey, 1978.

Parsing Sentience

In *How the Mind Works*, Steven Pinker comes to the guarded conclusion that conscious awareness, real as it is, is just one of those things that our minds aren't built to understand. Like free will, knowledge, and meaning (but not intelligence!), consciousness has the annoying habit of being 'peculiarly holistic and everywhere-at-once and nowhere-at-all and all-at-the-same-time'[18]; our minds are designed, Pinker says, to grasp relations and combinations, not irreducible, free-floating mental ooze. Certainly the lack of progress in nailing down these phenomena suggests something is fishy.

It's fine for us to close the door on the study of consciousness if we please, considering that the reality of our consciousness is not at stake. We are all snug and dry under the moral umbrella that protects those who feel and suffer. Even babies and people with damaged brains are welcomed because, although their current grip on awareness is uncertain, their trajectory will bring them in, or might have. But if the barometer that tells us which species merit our moral concern is marked off in units of sentience, then we may be up a critical creek without a logical or methodological paddle. How can we know so little about something that seems to matter so much?

Pain is that aspect of sentience which, when welded to morality, yields suffering. For starters, think of pain as a functional biological signal, one that prevents further damage in the here and now (like putting weight on a broken leg or leaving your hand on the broiler pan) and, via the glue of conditioned association, makes sure a lesson was learned for future reference, such as 'give thorn bushes a wide margin,' 'refrain from taunting a dominant male in a bad mood,' and 'always eat fish head first.' The only true requirement of a pain mechanism is to ensure that behavior, current or future, takes into consideration tissue

---

[18] Pinker, 1997, p. 564.

damage or other harm. Although it's difficult for us to imagine it, the trick could work without involving sentience. Why does pain have to hurt, anyway? As Yossarian in *Catch*-22 suggested, couldn't a doorbell chime instead?[19] Like eye blinks that can be conditioned beyond our awareness, couldn't our bodies learn the lesson without underscoring it with conscious pain? We can speculate that this masochistic feature of humanity probably has some function, but I cannot tell you what it is. People do experience pain, but couldn't other species, at least some of them, have developed mechanisms that deliver the behavior-modifying goods without the painful side effects? If a worm retreats from a sharp tweak, did it feel pain? Does the bird that crashed into my closed window have a painful headache, or does it simply thereafter avoid that part of my house?

Again we struggle to differentiate between the information evident in the behavioral emissaries of internal processes and the (redundant? additional?) information in the internal processes themselves. We are at a loss to identify what may have been lost in translation. When I accidentally step on my dog's paw, her startled yelp sure sounds like authentic pain – that is, it sounded as I would have sounded if I had the voice of a dog and had my foot pinched by a bigger animal wearing hard-soled shoes. But is my take on the authenticity of my dog's painful experience accurate or is just my tear-jerk reflex on behalf of a member of my in-group? Just as people attribute more intelligence to familiar animals, they may also attribute more sentience. Any dog has a big intrinsic advantage over a worm in winning my empathy; the characteristics of dogs that resonate to human emotions have been carefully selected over generations upon generations. We have chosen and molded the dog for its social, responsive qualities; we like that the dog behaves much as we would in so many circumstances, cowering in fear, furrowing its brow in confusion, gamboling about in joy. (Cats are typically more aloof and self-contained, accepting human social ministrations

[19] Heller, 1955.

according to their needs, not ours.) We nimbly make the intuitive leap across the divide to other minds and assume that analogous behavior means analogous mental states. It is inevitably human. Daniel Dennett argues that there may, however, be a downside to breeding and enculturating sentience in man's best friend.[20] Think of a two-year-old who trips and falls with a thunk onto his knees. What is his first reaction? He looks around at his mother, father, or whoever is handy, eager to know whether this is one of those times when he should burst into tears. If the adult jumps up and laughs and the toddler laughs, too, where is his pain? If the adult had rushed to him in concern, would his tears then be those of a crocodile? In selecting for canine expressiveness and sociality, we may have unwittingly given the dog a fuller experience of pain. Or it may be that social animals (like dogs, but not cats) are designed to communicate distress, so as to enlist the aid of group members, especially kin.

The truth is, we just don't know. We are not going to be able to peer into a secret window and see, or fail to see, the suffering that behavior suggests is concealed within. On this point, however, because the stakes are higher than in the intellectual pillow fights of animal intelligence, we cannot deny that animals experience any pain whatsoever pending the accumulation of better data. What we can do is use the best objective measures we have to guide animal welfare decisions. For example, we understand in considerable detail the action of analgesics on the physiology and psychology of pain in people. If those same analgesics help an animal recover from an injury, it's sensible to hypothesize that pain mitigation was involved. After all, we *test* these analgesics on animals first! Behavioral measures of pain are fraught because some species' typical responses may not be easily interpreted by us. If a horse with a broken leg eats normally, what are we to think? Measuring suffering that is not caused by tissue damage, such as distress and loneliness, is a taller order, one more susceptible to well-meaning, but possibly misguided, attribution

[20] Dennett, 1996.

of human-like experience. For captive animals, one alternative involves giving animals choices of different rearing and housing conditions; animals vote with their feet whether they like straw better than sawdust, whether to live with others of their kind or alone. Such studies are not tests of subjective states; they rely on the principle that animals know, by and large, what is best for them, having been designed by evolution to do just that.[21]

The fixation on sentience during debates about animal welfare draws attention away from other factors that should matter to people who care about animals. If the subjective experiences of animals were all that counted, it would follow that we could do whatever we wished to any anesthetized animal without staining our ethical reputation. We focus on pain and suffering because of their importance and salience to us and because it allows us to worry more about the species connected to us phylogenetically and emotionally. We can assuage our guilt for trashing the planet and still reach for the insecticide whenever we feel like it.

Undaunted by lack of evidence, animal rights advocates have bravely drawn firm lines between the feeling and the unfeeling, so that we humans, with bulldozers and forks at our disposal, might know where to unload our compassion. Tom Regan, author of *The Case for Animal Rights*, hands out coupons for moral favors only to mammals over one year of age.[22] Peter Singer originally argued for bringing shrimp into the charmed circle, but kept oysters out. Based on studies of cephalopods, such as octopi, Singer is now rewriting his guest list.[23] (Implicit in all these have and have-not disputes is our old friend, the *scala naturae*: everyone talks about drawing *one* line, not many.) Herzog and Galvin note that many animal rights writers maintain that 'common sense' offers a steady hand with which to draw the line that defines the sentient, and therefore morally worthy,

[21] Bateson, 1991; Dawkins, 1993; Dolins, 1999.
[22] Regan, 1983.
[23] Singer, 1975, 1990.

species.[24] Naturally, there are vast potential problems with using common sense as a guide: common sense may not be 'common' in the sense of 'consensual', and what is consensual may not be true. Do we really want our decisions about animal welfare to be based on unsubstantiated hunches about what some of us supposedly believe?

People cling to common sense when they have nothing better to go by, and in the realm of animal consciousness and sentience, animal psychology hasn't delivered any reasonable alternatives. This is hardly sharp criticism; the problem of how we tell the difference, on the basis of overt behavior, between an animal with subjective states and an animal without them is, as we have seen, hardly simple. Some people are hopeful that studies of the neurophysiology of awareness will render the problem soluble; others are as certain that the neural blips that correlate with consciousness are no closer to the experience of consciousness than are the behavioral markers we have before us. Meanwhile, the moral issue of what we should and should not do to animals persists.

Pet Peeves

In my view, the concept of rights for individual animals has limited value. Animal rights activism is sometimes an embarrassingly flimsy cover for an infantile longing for the world of Beatrix Potter, in which all the animals are sweet, well-dressed, immortal vegetarians. The fantasy of a Peaceable Kingdom, in which death and killing never sullies the park-like beauty of nature, may go unchallenged when people lose regular contact with biological reality. As a basis for policy on slaughtering practices, animal experimentation, and the treatment of pets, it may represent an extreme position, but, at least in principle, it is neither untenable nor crazy. Be nice to all the mammals, some of the birds, and maybe the fish, and everyone can sleep

[24] Herzog and Galvin, 1997.

with a clear conscience. Who cares about sparing cockroaches, mosquitoes, and slugs anyway?

But try applying this Disneyland ideal to real ecosystems and the result is downright ludicrous. In the natural world, the fortunes of species rise and fall with and because of myriad complicated relationships, not the least of which are those with species we'd just as soon heedlessly crush under the heel of our Vibram soles as save. The squishies and crunchies (not to mention fungi, bacteria, and plants) whose foreignness guarantees that they lie far beyond our empathic concern, are nevertheless vital. At the risk of evoking nauseating associations with crystal-swinging diatribes about the holistic interconnectedness of the Web of Life, a sharp focus on the 'rights' of species at the top of ladder is simply bad ecology. Every schoolboy knows this and yet conservation agencies are forced to rely on the winning caricatures of 'flagship species' to whip up even a modicum of popular interest in the plight of natural habitats. It may ease our guilt to protect only the appealing, the noble, and the most nearly human, but as sustainable conservation policy it won't work. For years I was a member of the Endangered Species Recovery Team for the Morro Bay Kangaroo Rat. The team took it for granted that there would never be a popular wellspsring of support – a 'Friends of the Rat' campaign; I suggested we have the species renamed the 'Morro Bay cuddle bunny' to improve its cachet and, thereby, its chances. Without this sort of PR, few people could work up any sympathy for a rat. The irony is that kangaroo rats *are* adorable; they have huge dark eyes, large heads, long tufted tails, and hind feet so big they look like wind-up toys – not that it should have mattered. By the way, the rats are now extinct.

For animals that currently exist for our benefit, such as pets, livestock, and research animals, a discussion of the ethics of their use is inevitable; because we wield the power, we have the responsibility to make informed decisions. As it stands, the decisions typically involve the application of some complex formula that weighs the species' similarity to humans against its instrumental value. Chimps are too like us to ever be eaten, given that beefsteak is readily available, but, according to some people's formulae, they may be used in medical research if absolutely necessary. They are also welcome to sit in zoos for their entire lives for our education and amusement. Dogs are not food (except in some cultures, creating a huge social rift) but may be kept, worked, traded, dressed, neutered, hospitalized, and tethered. Dogs are 'companion animals', more akin to humans, in feelings, needs, and rights, than to any wild dog or wolf. The practice of using dogs for research is, no surprise here, extremely controversial. Dogs and cats are obligate carnivores, meaning that they can't help it that something else has to die to help them live. Pet cats eat cans of veal and lamb, and also tuna in whose nets dolphins may be snared. (Your moral instincts should make your head spin on that one!) In the United States alone, that's over ten million pounds of vertebrates down house cats' throats every day, not counting the songbirds. Cats puncture the tidy boundary that separates the bourgeois pets from the wild animals by snatching birds whose rights under these schemes are ill-defined, whose consciousness is more than a little suspect, and whose utility is vague. Herzog estimates that 'if each pet cat in the United States ate only two mice, chipmunks, or baby birds each year, the number of animals slaughtered by pets would greatly exceed the number of animals used for research.'[25]

Don't get me wrong: I like cats, I really do. But the emotional tie we have to domestic animals tends to trump all the others factors that could weigh on welfare decisions: how fair is that? How does one justify, except on selfish, emotional grounds, the common belief that house cats (or feral goats, or minks) should always be spared, even when doing so directly threatens the existence of native species? If we are going to talk about animal rights and sentience, however, we are obligated by virtue of having the fanciest brain on the planet to talk *sensibly*.

[25] Herzog, 1991, p. 247.

Chapter 10

Meaningful Arrangements

Oh! Blessed rage for order, pale Ramon,
The maker's rage to order words of the sea,
Words of the fragrant portals, dimly-starred,
And of ourselves and of our origins,
In ghostlier demarcations, keener sounds.

W. Stevens, 1923[1]

When I was a little girl in Vermont, I spent a lot of time lying on the rooty ground under shady trees, looking up through the overlapping layers of impossible green, to catch glimpses of sky and cloud. Sometimes I'd watch the dappling patterns in the canopy. Sometimes I'd follow the route of a beetle from the base of the trunk until I lost it somewhere in the branching maze. And sometimes I searched for the perfect leaf – the leaf that had not been trimmed by a caterpillar, given a lacy patch by a leaf miner, bent by a squirrel hanging from a branch, discolored by a nutrient shortage, edge-rolled to make a cottony egg sack, spotted with fungus, or developed asymmetrically from some glitch during budding. I did occasionally find leaves that seemed, at least in the moment they appeared before me, to have escaped the nearly inescapable assaults of imperfection, but even those, beautiful as they were, nevertheless bore a fragile and transitory essence. Perfect or not, in a few short weeks, all would flame out in red, orange, and yellow, take the dive of Newton's apple, and contribute to the leaf pile goal line for touch football.

Variability is the theme song of life. The fate of a leaf, the fate of a tree, the fate of a forest is spun by the hands of so many blind forces that we are still, even with our sciences and tools,

[1] Stevens, 1923.

192

mostly clueless as to how it all works; we can name the forces (climate, geology, life cycles, season, gene flow, ecosystem) but not yet piece it all together. The deep, inexorable variability of the natural world attracts us. We don't tire of watching a fire or a sunset because it's always different. Wave upon wave coil and roll shoreward, each making a signature splash; winds make the dunes crawl; river bottoms tumble and slide away; seas rise to the tide; cloud shadows pass over a mountainside. This variability exists at every level: in the color of the ocean from an airplane, in the contours of a rocky cliff, in the shape of trees blowing in the wind, in the timing of the blossoms on a flower. For living things the variability doesn't stop there: go inside and you'll see that it varies from others of its kind and even from itself moments ago. DNA is being repaired constantly, like the painting of a huge bridge that begins again as soon as it is complete. Every so often, the DNA patch job is sloppy and the animal or plant is, in a very fundamental way, different from what it was before, adding grist to the mill of natural selection. If nature were merely complex we might still find it beautiful. But it is because nature is always *different* that we find it fascinating.

Categorical Imperatives

The problem with all that fractal variability is getting your mind to make some sense of it for you. While on a walk through the woods with a full belly, we can idly admire the intricate, ever-changing display before us. But several thousand years ago, we'd more likely have been in those woods running an errand with fitness consequences. The natural world was not a destination, it *was* the world. Our job, and that of every other creature, was to cut through some of the variability – trim off the noise – and get hold of the signal, whether it be a significant smell, melody, or pattern. Bombarded by more information than any animal could ever use, brains evolved largely as filters, sifting through the haystack of sensory data to find the needle through whose eye the camel of survival might be threaded.

The lion's share of filtering, sorting, and categorizing occurs before we even know what's before us; in that sense all animals have a dim and clouded eye through which they perceive the world. Your auditory system subtracts background noise and sharpens up other sounds, especially those in the range of human speech. Your visual system enhances contrast, adjusts for overall brightness, closes circles. As that tuned and sifted information goes a little higher up, perceptual systems compute how far away something is given its expected size (either that hill has gotten higher or that's a *big* bear up there), keep the world from spinning every time you turn to look behind you, and fantasize the spaces between spoken words, which do not usually exist – you just hear them that way. Animals, of course, have their own versions of these cut-to-the-chase devices, at both sensory and perceptual levels. Cheetahs' vision, for example, is more acute in the central horizontal strip of their visual field that typically corresponds to the horizon: they have a filter that favors detecting things to chase on the savannah. The ears of some female frogs are tuned to a component of the males' mating call. And we already know what red bellies, on almost anything, do to male sticklebacks. Some species delight in foiling the filters of other species, as when palatable butterflies mimic the paint job of poisonous ones.

For simpler animals, the nervous system has done its job at this point. Having sluiced away 99.997 per cent of the variability the world has to offer, they are now free to react to this dumbed-down version of reality. If it's about the right size and moving at about the right speed, it's probably a fly – out goes the tongue! We know that for some animals, life is played out at about that level. For other animals, and certainly for us, there's obviously still plenty of variability on the upstream side of these filters: we live in an information-rich world. As we have been discussing, the study of cognition is about what minds do with this information to generate the behavioral options.

Your mind is like a closet designed by a professional organizer: a place for everything and everything in its place – with coordinating hangers. Arguably the most important component of your tidy mind closet are the labels, the words you use to say 'Here is a rose,' 'Yesterday was Tuesday,' and 'Susan can't be trusted.' Some words – and the concepts they attach to – act like boxes: what belongs in them is defined by a set of rules: Tuesday is the day of the week between Monday and Wednesday. Either a day is Tuesday or it isn't. And Tuesday has a relationship to the other six days of the week that other words do not. They belong to a category with its own label (days of the week); membership in the category is unequivocal. You can't be a little bit pregnant or partly Friday. Other words (most of them, as it turns out) have fuzzy boundaries rather than sharp edges. 'Tree' seems like a clear enough word, until you try to define it. When does a shrub graduate to being a tree? Is an oak seedling a tree?

Eleanor Rosch and others[2] have studied how people use categories and concepts to make Venn diagrams that sort the masses of stuff in the world. A robin is an 'ideal' bird; a penguin, while still a bird, is not a very good one because it does not fly and it puts eggs on its feet. Penguins live on the margins of the bird circle, while robins and sparrows are smack dab in the middle of the category 'bird'. In the center of each of the thousands of fuzzy categories we hold is the quintessential member, the one that has the most properties of whatever it is that defines the category. People tend to see all members of the same category as sharing the properties of the quintessential member; we apply the stereotype from the center of the category right out to the edges, where membership may be tenuous. We do this to tidy up the world, to make infinite variation comprehensible. Partial similarity is readily reconfigured as pervasive similarity. For the box labeled 'animal intelligence', we spin a theory of similarity between ourselves and other species based on the history of domestication, emotional hunches, and a *Reader's Digest* version of evolution. If we see human emotions on an animal's face, we

---

[2] Rosch, 1978; Smith and Medin, 1981.

divine that they harbor human feelings and thoughts. If we see behavior that resembles our own, we assume that the similarity is more than fur-deep. With ourselves in the center, we draw a circle that includes other primates and another wider circle that includes all mammals. Categorizing and circle drawing is useful – indeed, absolutely necessary; we'd be snowed under the details otherwise. Our commitment to the circles we draw is strong; we are biased toward confirming whatever hypothesis we have selected and ignore data that is inconsistent with it. For example, people are stubbornly resistant to reshuffling information about other people, what Fiske calls being a 'cognitive miser'.[3] As we learned in chapter 4, we attribute others' behavior to stable personality traits. Then, to support our pet theories, we discount any data that suggest our take on them is off the mark: 'I've made a box for you, now lie still in it!'

Theoretical Fashion Statements

We have repeatedly witnessed our cognitive tidying in action during the history of the study of animal intelligence. The Great Chain of Being is an intriguing simplifying structure; each species has its reserved spot on the chain, resulting in an orderly, though category-less, sequence of worthiness. It is a little weak on the details (just how *would* you rank, say, the varieties of coral reef fish?), but strong on the overall message: there is but one dimension. Then Darwin stepped up to the plate and hit one out of the park. From the standpoint of evolutionary theory as a whole, Darwin was even-handed in attending to similarities and differences. The gradualism that he espoused, that his version of evolution required, was based on the idea that tiny little differences (things we would normally just lump together) may become big important differences – differences that might eventually expand to become as vast as that between an ant and an anteater. As the Grants have demonstrated, a millimeter's

[3] Fiske, 1995.

difference in the depth of the beak in one of Darwin's finches did, during a drought, make all the difference in the world.[4] Scientists can now also see, at a molecular level, those minute differences that shake up the categories. However, when the subject was animal mentality, Darwin blurred the differences and concocted a melting pot of thinking and feeling from which each species had a generous dollop. That dream of continuity, of intellectual kinship, continues to have emotional and intellectual appeal to many people. It is not, as far as we can tell, in complete harmony either with evolutionary theory or the empirical facts.

Behaviorism wins the prize for most egregious oversimplification: all of animal behavior comprised a single category (learning) governed by a single mechanism (conditioning). In its one-size-fits-all view of behavior, behaviorism glossed over so much of the variability in animal behavior that it put itself out of business as a theory, if it ever was more theory than religion. Similarity, indeed unity, of process guaranteed the continuity we craved. Then came cognitive psychology, with its promise of rediscovering animal intelligence as an engineering triumph. But engineered exactly how, and to what purpose? With survival and fitness as end points, there are, as nature has shown us, a million ways to get there. This is the core attraction of cognitive science: the design of the mind is a puzzle with a large number of plausible solutions but only one correct one. For a species that thrives on puzzles, the study of our own mind (and those of other animals) may be one brainteaser that defines the limits of our intellect. Adaptation, though a pertinent and handy guide, doesn't come close to drawing the blueprint for the mental mechanisms that serve its cause in each of the varied installations before us. As cognitive science as a whole grapples with this problem, many animal researchers are already closing certain doors: cognitive mechanisms must be modular at all levels, specializations are more significant than general mechanisms, the principle of adaptation renders comparative intelligence

[4] Weiner, 1994.

meaningless. Having attached their intellectual strings to the high-flying kite of evolutionary psychology, every aspect of animal (and human) psychology must now fit into the box of adaptation, often narrowly conceived. Intelligence has been dropped like a hot potato; it's a gigantic square peg that won't fit into any of the round little holes. Of course, adaptation to specific ecological circumstance *has* been a primary shaper of cognitive process, but that historical fact may tell us less than we wish about what animals know.

Being only human, we want very badly to have a compact box or two – a comprehensive theory – into which to place the phenomena of animal mind and behavior. After 100 years of scientific study on the topic, we feel we should at least know the essential outlines of the theoretical framework and recognize what our assumptions ought to be. We are eager to close some doors, narrow the possibilities. But if you have taken away nothing else from this book, you now know that doors closed in haste tend to swing open again (sometimes giving us a good smack on the head); we have barely begun to understand what shape our theories of animal mind should take. If we pretend otherwise, then our assumptions will lead us by the nose to certain facts and straight over others; we might be led astray, as we have been in the past.

Adherence to intellectual fashion is not necessarily wrong; think of the confusion if scientists jumped ship every time a datum did not support a theory. Scientists can't be fickle about their theories for the same reason that people can't bring a clean slate to their social interactions. Being a cognitive miser in the social realm stops us from changing our opinions about other people based on a meager sample; if we allow our cognitive boxes and circles to be perturbed by every fleeting mood and misspoken word, we couldn't make sense of the social landscape and we wouldn't know what to do. We need our simplifying schemes. In science as in life, the goal is to find that elusive middle ground somewhere between chaos and dogma, a theory that is a meaningful arrangement of everything we know about how animal minds work. At their best, theories are headquarters for facts. At their worst, they are prisons.

Three Cheers for Intelligence

Here's one likely retort to my contention that much of current theory in animal cognition is barking up a spindly tree: 'OK, so our theories need a little work. But what makes you think pursuing the idea of intelligence will get us further?' Plenty. For starters, the study of human intelligence, while not exactly a smooth ride, is nevertheless a lively field. There are competing, testable theories about what intelligence is and how best to measure it. The information derived thus far has, despite the surrounding controversy, proved useful in applied settings. Only a very small minority of psychologists would like to toss out the entire concept of intelligence; it is recognized as a difficult but essential aspect of human mind and behavior. The artificial intelligence folks have built an entire discipline around the idea. If regular people were asked to put in their two cents, I'd wager most would agree that intelligence is a legitimate topic for human psychology. To put it bluntly, if intelligence is good enough for people psychology, isn't it good enough for animal psychology? Intelligence evolved, by whatever means, as a cognitive strategy in humans; we might reasonably hypothesize that it evolved similarly in other species. As we discussed earlier, primatology has always accepted intelligence as part of what must be explained. They have, at times, come under fire for their methods and interpretations, but that does not mean that their *questions* were wrong.

Another reason to pursue the study of animal intelligence is that it's a 'big picture' topic. While it is undoubtedly important to understand how this little function relates to that little piece of behavior, we will never discern the organizational principles of animal minds with our faces pressed up to the window. We can't wait for all the little pieces to fall into place before we start to look at how, say, an animal decides which bit of its intellectual arsenal to deploy because there will be constraints imposed by the larger organization. Remember, it isn't only the nutcracker's spatial memory or the monkey's tool use that is vulnerable to the scythe of natural selection: it's the whole nutcracker that makes more nutcrackers (or doesn't) and the whole monkey that makes more monkeys (or doesn't). Yes, a particular trait can make or break an animal's chances, but who says the critical trait is the one we happen to be staring at during an empirical moment? If we only illuminate animal minds with a narrow beam, then we may fail to observe how a more general trait may have figured in the behavioral decisions that contribute to selective outcomes.

Within the dizzying complexity of the mind we have taken pains to distinguish between functions, between abilities, and between mechanisms. We are disassembling cognition. Modularity theorists claim that the mind is not a single domain, that our theories of separable functions will never coalesce. It is too soon to know for sure, but the evidence from neuroscience and from human cognition already suggests this idea has been oversold. If we obstinately ignore the fact that the parts of the mind interlock within a single behaving animal, our explanations for how the parts work may be feeble, limited, or, quite possibly, dead wrong. Contrary to Gardner's prediction, psychology isn't and never will be a holding company, as long as, having taken apart the mind, we eventually remember to put it back together. Studying general abilities (such as intelligence) and overarching structural properties (such as neural network integration) will aid in the reassembly.

The final reason for advocating the study of intelligence is that it meshes nicely with an evolutionary perspective; there can be designs for intelligence that interpolate and subsume the peaks of specialized abilities. We understand little of how general abilities lace together with specific ones, either as a species develops over evolutionary time or as the environment poses an immediate question to the individual animal. We can see in our own lives, however, the advantage of a more general intelligence: it can get us out of all sorts of tight fixes, ones that evolution hasn't had the time or opportunity to throw us a genetic rope. For us it has meant curing and curbing disease, producing food, modifying microclimates, and overcoming distances, to name just a few. Wouldn't it be interesting to know what broad intellectual capacities might be doing for other species?

A tantalizing case involves yet more of Darwin's finches.[5] These inhabit a tiny rainy island far off the coast of Costa Rica. Tracey Werner and Tom Sherry discovered that, like their Galápagos cousins, Cocos finches share the island by exploiting different food resources: some glean bugs from green leaves, some from dry leaves, some probe for bugs under bark, and some prefer nectar. Like housemates with completely different diets, there are no arguments over food. Unlike the thirteen species of Galápagos finches, however, the Cocos finches are a single species! The island is just too small and too isolated to allow the birds to get away from each other genetically. There is no opportunity for selection for morphological specialization for the different feeding regimes, so all the finches have the same all-purpose beak – a miniature version of the crow's beak. Because geography blocked the exits that would have allowed the birds to radiate into different species, the birds get away from each other *behaviorally*. Each bird adopts one, and only one, behavioral strategy. Finches specializing on bugs on dead leaves one day will be eating the same things next week, next season, and next year. Finches majoring in bark probing or leaf gleaning or ground pecking stay with the program forever. And – incredibly – the finches appear to learn what their specialty will be from following their parents around.

The mind of a Cocos finchling must be malleable enough to be molded by early experience into a shape suitable for its particular trade. Human infants emit universal babble because there is no way for their brains to know whether they will end up communicating in French, Swahili, or Tagalog. Similarly, in order to become specialized the birds must first be cognitively

[5] Werner and Sherry, 1987.

labile. Whether they retain any of that lability is unknown; an adult Cocos finch might or might not have the psychological elasticity of classically opportunistic foragers such as raccoons, bears, and ravens. The implications, however, for the significance of intelligence are clear: there are situations in which leaving your cognitive and behavioral options open is a winning adaptive strategy. It worked for us.

Tell Me a Story

In *In the Shadow of Man*, Jane Goodall describes what happened when Fifi, a young chimpanzee, became separated from her mother.

> As soon as Fifi realized her mother was no longer in the group she became agitated. Whimpering softly to herself, she rushed up a tall tree and ran from one side to the other, staring across the valley in different directions. Her soft calls of distress became loud grating screams. All at once she swung down and, still crying, hurried along a track. She chose the direction exactly opposite to the one her mother had taken. I followed Fifi. Every so often she climbed a tree and stared all about, and then, with her hair on end, started along the track again, crying and whimpering.
>
> Just before dusk she came upon Olly and Gilka, but though Gilka kept approaching Fifi, grooming her, trying to play, Fifi ignored her friendly advances, and instead of remaining to sleep near Olly hurried off by herself again. She made a lonely nest at the top of a tall tree. I spent the night nearby; three times during the darkness I heard her calling out, screaming and whimpering.[6]

Goodall tells a good story. You can see little Fifi, her brow crinkled in distress, lower lip jutting in a sad and worried pout, and you'd have to have a cold heart indeed not to sympathize

[6] Goodall, 1971, p. 169.

202

with her, even just a little. Fifi's story might remind you of yourself at the age of four or five, getting lost in a large store, or wandering off while visiting a zoo, more intent on the animals than the adults. You might remember feeling utterly bereft, then immensely relieved when you were returned to your family. But even if you never temporarily misplaced yourself, the power of Fifi's story remains.

Stories are central to humanity. We start out our lives listening to bedtime stories (about real and imagined events) and family stories (more real and imagined events). Soon we graduate to creating our own stories during play and reworking our short histories into stories about ourselves. We are told parables to teach us morality, gossip to exercise our social skills, and legends to glimpse the scope of history – a very long story itself. As part of living we narrate the details to those closest to us, the Daily Events Dump, offering the day as a story that functions as verbal glue for time spent apart: 'Tell me about your day.' We organize our past into stories that match our perceptions of ourselves, usually retaining the script in lengths suitable to different occasions. Would you like to hear the story of my [college days, most recent job, first boyfriend, backpacking trip, childhood, relationship with my mother, knee injury] in the twenty-five-word, five minute, or full-hour version?

Stories are powerful because the characters have agency: we attach purpose and will to them whether they are people or peep frogs. Agency gives the narrative arrangements of information that we call stories power beyond that imposed by categories and other simplifying structures. In telling stories, we create and grant meaning. The stories we tell, even of our own lives, take on a life of their own. Wallace Stevens captured this idea in a poem, the last stanza of which began this chapter. It's about a woman singing along the sea's edge:

> She was the single artificer of the world
> In which she sang. And when she sang, the sea,
> Whatever self it had, became the self

That was her song, for she was the maker. Then we,
As we beheld her striding there alone,
Knew that there never was a world for her
Except the one she sang and, singing, made.

The problem that most scientists have with anecdotes about animal behavior is that anecdotes, like the song that makes the sea, are stories that help define what we believe animals know. We say that a good anecdote is 'telling' – it reveals the true story. I've told you quite a few myself. But is the story they reveal the biological and psychological truth, or merely what runs smoothly on the narrative track that has been laid in our minds?

Spin Doctors of Science

Science tells us that unless a story relates an event that can be repeated (unless the data are replicable), it tells no tale whatsoever. Stories, after all, don't begin 'Nineteen times out of twenty upon a time . . .' It's not that the observation described in an anecdote is typically in doubt, but the interpretation of that observation as a sign of greater intelligence may be. To scientists, isolated stories about Those Amazing Animals may be suggestive, but never definitive. Anecdotes are teases, dangling the possibility of animal mental magic just beyond our grasp. People who study animal behavior learn to tell their anecdotes (who can resist?) without necessarily believing the implicit message. It can be a narrow fence to straddle.

You have undoubtedly heard that the loose language animal behaviorists use to describe animals in casual conversation is stifled once the data is packaged in a paper bound for peer review. Language that, in the mind of the scientist, may have been full of mentalese (the animal wants, tries, fools, decides, figures out) is translated into neutral-speak; the obvious story elements are excised so as not to lead the reader down the garden path. But even if scientific papers do not portray animals as willful agents, the papers nevertheless tell a kind of story:

the research is framed in light of some theories and not others, certain analyses are ditched to emphasize a result, alternative hypotheses are weakly acknowledged and then buried under the favored one. None of this is devious. It is the necessary work of the mind of the scientist trying to make sense of a finding.

Each scientific finding that I have described in this book took a near Herculean effort to produce. Most represent years of work, not even counting the training of the scientists. When the experiment is over or the field observations have reached a critical mass, the results go public. The scientist who offers up a hard-won result is like someone fitting an irregular shard into a mosaic. What is so difficult about this process is how small each piece is and how little of the entire mosaic can be seen from the perspective of one scientist, or even a group of scientists with a more or less common perspective. To decide where to place a shard of data, we study the colors and patterns that we can see are already in the mortar and find the place where our piece contributes most to a meaningful arrangement. In the mosaic of animal mind and behavior, we almost never witness a definitive finding – one that instantly changes our perception of the larger picture; the data pieces are universally small and the scope of the mosaic vast. We call out to each other from our vantage points on the mosaic, describing what we see in a story we believe is true, but the image is far from clear. Our eye is clouded or the image itself is fuzzy – we don't know which. Probably both.

If someone points out that the mosaic appears to be taking a particular shape, many people will recognize the image and never see the individual pieces the same way again. The process is perceptual, readily demonstrated using those hidden figure problems in every introductory psychology text, usually a Dalmatian against a patchy background. The dog may be initially difficult to pick out, but once you see it, it's hard not to keep seeing it. A little of the inevitable spin on every piece of data and before you know it the image is locked in. It's *always* been a dog! And it stays a dog, at least in the minds of the majority, until someone rearranges the mosaic and gives it a new meaning that others can also see. Over generations of thinkers and stacks of journal papers on the subject of animal intelligence, one image pops out and another pops in: psychological continuity, psychological uniformity, psychological specialization; qualitative differences, quantitative differences; content-neutral mechanisms, content-specific mechanisms. The one thing that really gets under our skin is when some smart aleck comes along, disagrees with where the pieces have been laid and says, 'It's not a Dalmatian. I have no idea what it really is, but I know it's not any sort of a dog.' People, especially the scientific kind, hate that. It's like a tree full of beautiful, imperfect leaves without an organizing principle that we can yet discern.

One facet of our intelligence is a knack for meaningfully arranging the world. We build categories and fill them up with experiences, visions, and ideas, ceaselessly tending their definitions and relationships. We are obsessive collectors of fragile notions. We glean them from the world and hold them safe against the chaotic onslaught of raw sensation. Using this side of our intelligence, we choose the right word, see things for what they plainly are, and know the answer. No species can afford to approach every waking moment with an unclouded eye: we are happy to finally see the dog.

In arranging and rearranging the dizzying variety of our experience, however, we inevitably do injustice to it. Fortunately, the other facet of our intelligence is reflection, a property that can take us beyond our cognitive shortcuts and, if we're lucky, closer to the truth. Though this aspect of our intellect is less obvious and more rarely exercised, we do have the capacity to think out of the boxes we have created, disabling the categories to test whether the world can be ordered a different way, whether the mosaic harbors another, truer image. The source and structure of our very thoughts are something else to consider as our view of the world gels. Artists, by intuition or training, understand the power of disassembling and then restructuring habitual organizational routines. When learning to draw, for example, the artist must refuse the apparent three-dimensionality of the world and transfer from retina to paper only two dimensions. The artist's brain says that the tree at the top of the hill is a normal-sized tree far away. To capture that tree on paper, however, the artist must draw it as it appears in the visual field: small and high in the picture plane. Receding railroad tracks don't really converge, but the artist must feign ignorance of that fact to get the drawing right. The artist attempting verisimilitude knows that our brains lie to us in helpful ways and that sometimes the lies must be exposed.

Using this side of our intelligence, we sacrifice the perfect answer for the perfect question, we try on an irrational thought and treat those we know best as if their next move was a complete and utter mystery. Kohler plainly felt that insight counted as this type of intelligence: the chimpanzee would perceive a stick but see a tool. We don't know if this is what happened in the chimpanzees' mind, but that is what Kohler was searching for. Organization is an overarching feature of intelligent mental process, but an inflexible, albeit elaborate organization may interfere with an animal or a person recognizing an original – and winning – behavioral ploy. It is obviously very difficult to search for these properties of an intelligent mind within the rules of science, but there will be a gaping hole in the mosaic if we refuse the challenge.

BIBLIOGRAPHY

Anderson, B. 1993. Evidence from the rat for a general factor that underlies cognitive performance and that relates to brain size: intelligence? *Neuroscience Letters,* 153, 98–102.

Anderson, J.R. 1980. *Cognitive Psychology and its Implications.* San Francisco: W.H. Freeman.

Andreasen, N.C., Flaum, M., Swayze, V., O'Leary, D.S., Alliger, R., Cohen, G., Ehrhardt, J. and Yuh, W.T.C. 1993. Intelligence and brain structure in normal individuals. *American Journal of Psychiatry,* 150, 130–134.

Barkow, J.H., Cosmides, L. and Tooby, J. (eds.) 1992. *The Adapted Mind: Evolutionary Psychology and the Generation of Culture.* New York: Oxford University Press.

Bateson, P. 1991. Assessment of pain in animals. *Animal Behaviour,* 42, 827–839.

Baum, W. M. 1998. Why not ask 'Does the chimpanzee have a soul?'. *Behavioral and Brain Sciences,* 21, 116.

Beatty, W.W. and Shavalia, D.A. 1980. Rat spatial memory: resistance to retroactive interference at long retention intervals. *Animal Learning and Behavior,* 8, 550–552.

Beck, B.B. 1980. *Animal Tool Behavior: The Use and Manufacture of Tools by Animals.* New York: Garland STPM Press.

Berridge, K.C., Fentress, J.C. and Parr, H. 1987. Natural syntax rules control action sequences of rats. *Behavioural Brain Research,* 23, 59–68.

Berryman, J.C., Howells, K. and Lloyd-Evans, M. 1985. Pet-owner attitudes to pets and people: A psychological study. *Veterinary Record,* 117, 659–661.

Bitterman, M.E. 1960. Toward a comparative psychology of learning. *American Psychologist,* 15, 704–712.

Bitterman, M.E. 1965. Phyletic differences in learning. *American Psychologist,* 20, 396–410.

Blough, D.S. 1985. Discrimination of letters and random dot patterns by pigeons and humans. *Journal of Experimental Psychology: Animal Behavior Processes,* 11, 261–280.

Blumberg, M.S. and Wasserman, E.A. 1995. Animal mind and the argument from design. *American Psychologist,* 50, 133–144.

Boesch, C. 1991. Teaching among wild chimpanzees. *Animal Behaviour,* 41, 530–532.

Boesch, C. and Boesch, H. 1989. Hunting behavior of wild chimpanzees in the Taï National Park. *American Journal of Physical Anthropology*, 78, 547–573.

Boesch-Achermann, H. and Boesch, C. 1993. Tool use in wild chimpanzees: New light from dark forests. *Current Directions in Psychological Science*, 3, 93–94.

Boring, E.G. 1929. *History of Experimental Psychology*. New York: Appleton.

Breland, K. and Breland, M. 1961. The misbehavior of organisms. *American Psychologist*, 16, 681–684.

Brown, P.L. and Jenkins, H.M. 1968. Auto-shaping of the pigeon's key-peck. *Journal of the Experimental Analysis of Behavior*, 11, 1–8.

Byrne, R. 1995. *The Thinking Ape: Evolutionary Origins of Intelligence*. Cambridge: Oxford University Press.

Byrne, R. and Whiten, A. (eds.) 1988. *Machiavellian Intelligence: Social Expertise and the Evolution of Intellect in Monkeys, Apes, and Humans*. Oxford: Clarendon.

Byrne, R. W. and Whiten, A. 1991. Computation and mindreading in primate tactical deception. In A. Whiten ed. *Natural Theories of Mind*. Oxford: Basil Blackwell.

Byrne, R. W. and Whiten, A. 1992. Cognitive evolution in primates: evidence from tactical deception. *Man*, 27, 609–627.

Campbell, C.B.G. and Hodos, W. 1991. The scala naturae revisited: Evolutionary scales and amagensis in comparative psychology. *Journal of Comparative and Physiological Psychology*, 105, 211–221.

Cheney, D.L. and Seyfarth, R.M. 1990. *How Monkeys See the World*. Chicago: Chicago University Press.

Churchland, P. 1995. Neural networks and commonsense. In P. Baumgartner and S. Payr (eds.) *Speaking Minds: Interviews with Twenty Eminent Cognitive Scientists*. Princeton: Princeton University Press.

Clayton, N.S. and Dickinson, A. 1999. Scrub jays (*Aphelocoma coerulescens*) remember the relative time of caching as well as the location and content of their caches. *Journal of Comparative Psychology*, 11, 403–416.

Connor, R.C., Smolker, R.A., and Richards, A.F. 1992. Dolphin alliances and coalitions. In A.H. Harcourt and F.B. M. de Waal (eds.) *Coalitions and Alliances in Humans and Other Animals*. Oxford: Oxford University Press.

Cook, R.G., Brown, M.F. and Riley, D.A. 1985. Flexible memory processing by rats: Use of prospective and retrospective information in the radial maze. *Journal of Experimental Psychology: Animal Behavior Processes*, 11, 453–469.

Coren, S. 1994. *The Intelligence of Dogs*. New York: Bantam.

Crinella, F.M. and Yu, J. 1995. Brain mechanisms in problem-solving and intelligence: A replication and extension. *Intelligence*, 21, 225–246.

Darwin, C. 1859/1958. *The Origin of Species*. New York: New American Library.

Darwin, C. 1874/1998. *The Descent of Man*. New York: Prometheus.

Davis, S.L. and Cheeke, P.R. 1998. Do domestic animals have minds and the ability to think? A provisional sample of opinions on the question. *Journal of Animal Science*, 76, 2072–2079.

Dawkins, M. S. 1993. *Through Our Eyes Only? The Search for Animal Consciousness*. New York: W.H. Freeman.

Dawkins, R. 1986. *The Blind Watchmaker*. Harlow, Essex: Longman Scientific and Technical.

Demarest, J. 1983. The ideas of change, progress and continuity in the comparative psychology of learning. In D.W. Rajecki (ed.) *Comparing Behavior: Studying Man Studying Animals*. Hillsdale, N.J.: Erlbaum.

Dennett, D.C. 1995. *Darwin's Dangerous Idea: Evolution and the Meanings of Life*. New York: Touchstone.

Dennett, D.C. 1996. *Kinds of Minds*. New York: Basic Books.

Devlin, B., Fienberg, S.E., Resnick, D.P. and Roeder, K. (1997) *Intelligence, Genes and Success: Scientists Respond to The Bell Curve*. New York: Springer.

Dolins, F.L. (ed.) 1999. *Attitudes to Animals: Views in Animal Welfare*. Cambridge: Cambridge University Press.

Dunbar, R.I.M. 1992. Neocortex size as a constraint on group size in primates. *Journal of Human Evolution*, 20, 469–493.

Duncan, J., Seitz, R.J., Kolodny, J., Bor, D., Herzog, H., Ahmed, A., Newell, F.N., and Emslie, H. 2000. A neural basis for general intelligence. *Science*, 289, 457–460.

Durlach, P.J. and Mackintosh, N.J. 1986. Transfer of serial reversal learning in the pigeon. *Quarterly Journal of Experimental Psychology*, 38B, 81–95.

Ebbesson, S.O.E. and Northcutt, R.G. 1976. Neurology of anamniotic vertebrates. In R.B. Masterton, M.E. Bitterman, C.B.G. Campbell and N. Hotton (eds.) *Evolution of Brain and Behavior in Vertebrates*. Hillsdale, N.J.: Erlbaum.

Eddy, T.J., Gallup, G.G., Jr., and Povinelli, D.J. 1993. Attribution of cognitive states to animals: Anthropomorphism in comparative perspective. *Journal of Social Issues*, 49, 87–101.

Epstein, R. 1981. On pigeons and people: A preliminary look at the Columban Simulation Project. *Behavior Analyst*, 4, 43–55.

Epstein, R. 1986. Bringing cognition and creativity into the behavioral laboratory. In T.J. Knapp and L.C. Robertson (eds.) *Approaches to Cognition: Contrasts and Controversies*. Hillsdale, N.J.: Lawrence Erlbaum.

Epstein, R., Lanza, R.P and Skinner, B.F. 1981. 'Self-awareness' in the pigeon. *Science*, 212, 695–696.

Epstein, R., Kirshnit, C., Lanza, R.P. and Rubin, L. 1984. 'Insight' in the pigeon: Antecedents and determinants of an intelligent performance. *Nature*, 308, 61–62.

Fentress, J.C. 1972. Development and patterning of movement sequences in inbred mice. In J. Kiger (ed.) *The Biology of Behavior*. Corvallis: Oregon State University.

Fisher, E.M. 1951. Notes on the red fox (*Vulpes vulpes*) in Missouri. *Journal of Mammalogy*, 32, 296–299.

Fiske, S. 1995. Social cognition. In A. Tesser (ed.) *Advanced Social Psychology*. New York: McGraw Hill.

Fodor, J.A. 1983. *The Modularity of Mind*. Cambridge: MIT Press.

Fodor, J.A. 1995. The folly of simulation. In P. Baumgartner and S. Payr (eds.) *Speaking Minds: Interviews with Twenty Eminent Cognitive Scientists*. Princeton: Princeton University Press.

Frank, L.G. 1986. Social organisation of the spotted hyaena (*Crocuta crocuta*): II. Dominance and reproduction. *Animal Behaviour*, 35, 1510–1527.

Gallup, G.G. Jr. 1970. Chimpanzees: Self-recognition. *Science*, 167, 86–87.

Gallup, G.G. Jr. 1987. Self-awareness. In J.R. Erwin and G. Mitchell (eds.) *Comparative Primate Biology, Volume 2B: Behavior, Cognition and Motivation*. New York: Alan Liss.

Garcia, J. and Koelling, R.A. 1966. Relation of cue to consequence in avoidance learning. *Psychonomic Science*, 4, 123–124.

Gardner, H. 1983. *Frames of Mind: The Theory of Multiple Intelligences*. New York: Basic Books.

Gardner, H. 1985. *The Mind's New Science*. New York: Basic Books.

Gardner, R.A. and Gardner, B.T. 1969. Teaching sign language to a chimpanzee. *Science*, 165, 664–672.

Gardner, R.A., Gardner, B.T. and Van Cantfort, E. (eds.). 1989. *Teaching Sign Language to Chimpanzees*. Albany: State University of New York Press.

Gilbert, D.T. and Malone, P.S. 1995. The correspondence bias. *Psychological Bulletin*, 117, 21–38.

Glickman, S.E. and Sroges, R.W. 1966. Curiosity in zoo animals. *Behaviour*, 26, 151–188.

Goodall, J. 1971. *In the Shadow of Man*. Boston: Houghton Mifflin.

Goodall, J. 1986. *The Chimpanzees of Gombe: Patterns of Behavior*. Cambridge: Harvard University Press.

Gottlieb, G. 1984. Evolutionary trends and evolutionary origins: Relevance to theory in comparative psychology. *Psychological Review*, 91, 448–456.

Gould, S.J. 1980. *The Panda's Thumb*. New York: W.W. Norton.

Gould, S.J. 1983. *The Mismeasure of Man*. New York: W.W. Norton.

Green, S.M., Wilson, D.L and Evans, S. 1998. Anecdotes, omniscience and associative learning in examining the theory of mind. *Behavioral and Brain Sciences*, 21, 122.

Gregory, R.L. 1981. *Mind in Science: A History of Explanations in Psychology*. Cambridge, UK: Cambridge University Press.

Griffin, D.R. 1984. *Animal Thinking*. Cambridge: Harvard University Press.

Griffin, D.R. 1992. *Animal Minds*. Chicago: University of Chicago Press.

Grindley, G.C. 1950. *The Intelligence of Animals*, Second edition. London: Methuen.

Harlow, H.F. 1949. The formation of learning sets. *Psychological Review*, 56, 51–65.

Harlow, H.F. 1958. The evolution of learning. In A. Roe and G.G. Simpson (eds.) *Behavior and Evolution*. New Haven: Yale University Press.

Harlow, H.F. 1959. Learning set and error factor theory. In S. Koch (ed) *Psychology: A Study of a Science*, Volume 2. New York: McGraw-Hill.

Hart, B. and Hart, L. 1988. *The Perfect Puppy*. New York: Freeman.

Haugeland, J. 1995. Farewell to GOFAI. In P. Baumgartner and S. Payr (eds.). *Speaking Minds: Interviews with Twenty Eminent Cognitive Scientists*. Princeton: Princeton University Press.

Hauser, M. D. 2000. *Wild Minds: What Animals Really Think*. New York: Henry Holt.

Heider, F. and Simmel, M. 1944. An experimental study of apparent behavior. *American Journal of Psychology*, 57, 243–259.

Heinrich, H. 1995. An experimental investigation of insight in common ravens (*Corvus corax*). *Auk*, 112, 994–1003.

Heinrich, H. 1999. *Mind of the Raven*. New York: Harper Collins.

Heller, J. 1955. *Catch–22*. New York: Simon and Schuster.

Herman, L.M., Abichandani, S.L., Elhajj, A.N., Herman, E.Y.K., Sanchez, J.L., and Pack, A.A. 1999. Dolphins (*Tursiops truncatus*) comprehend the referential character of the human pointing gesture. *Journal of Comparative Psychology*, 113, 347–364.

Herrero, S. 1985. *Bear Attacks: Their Causes and Avoidance*. New York: Lyons and Burford.

Herrnstein, R.J. 1984. Objects, categories and discriminative stimuli. In H.L. Roitblat, T.G. Bever, and H.S. Terrace (eds.) *Animal Cognition*. Hillsdale, N.J.: Erlbaum.

Herrnstein, R.J. and Murray, C. 1994. *The Bell Curve: Intelligence and Class Structure in American Life*. New York: Free Press.

Herzog, A.H. 1991. Conflicts of interest: Kittens and boa constrictors, pets and research. *American Psychologist*, 247–248.

Herzog, A.H. and Galvin, S. 1997. Common sense and the mental lives of animals: An empirical approach. In R.W. Mitchell, N.S. Thompson and H.L. Miles (eds.) *Anthropomorphism, Anecdotes and Animals*. Albany: State University of New York Press.

Heyes, C.M. 1998. Theory of mind in nonhuman primates. *Behavioral and Brain Sciences*, 21, 101–148.

Hingston, R.W.G. 1929. *Instinct and Intelligence*. New York: MacMillan.

Hladik, C.M. 1975. Ecology, diet and social patterning in Old and New World monkeys. In R.H. Tuttle (ed.) *Socioecology and Psychology of Primates*. Paris: Mouton.

Hodos, W. and Campbell, C.B.G. 1969. Scala naturae: Why there is no theory in comparative psychology. *Psychological Review*, 76, 337–350.

Holcroft, A.C. and Herrero, S. 1991. Black bear, *Ursus americanus*, food habits in southwestern Alberta. *Canadian Field Naturalist*, 105, 335–345.

Holekamp, K.E., Boydston, E.E., Szykman, M., Graham, I., Nutt, K.J., Birch, S., Piskiel, A. and Singh, M. 1999. Vocal recognition in the spotted hyaena and its possible implications regarding the evolution of intelligence. *Animal Behaviour*, 58, 383–395.

Hull, C.L. 1932. The goal gradient hypothesis and maze learning. *Psychological Review*, 39, 25–43.

Humphrey, N.K. 1976. The social function of intellect. In P.P.G. Bateson and R.A. Hinde (eds.) *Growing Points in Ethology*. Cambridge: Cambridge University Press.

Humphrey, N.K. 1978. Nature's psychologists. *New Scientist*, 29 (June 1978), 900–904.

Hunt, G.R. 1996. Manufacture of hook-tools by New Caledonian crows. *Nature*, 379, 249–251.

Hunter, M.W. and Kamil, A.C. 1971. Object-discrimination learning set and hypothesis behavior in the Northern blue jay. *Psychonomic Science*, 22, 271–273.

Hunter, W.S. 1913 The delayed reaction in animals. *Behavior Monographs*, 2, 21–30.

Jennings, H. S. 1904/1962. *Behavior of the Lower Organisms*. Bloomington: Indiana University Press.

Jerison, H.J. 1973. *Evolution of Brain and Intelligence*. New York: Academic.

Jerison, H. J. 1985. Animal intelligence as encephalization. *Philosophical Transactions of the Royal Society of London B*, 308, 21–35.

Kalat, J.W. 1983. Evolutionary thinking in the history of the comparative psychology of learning. *Neuroscience and Biobehavioral Reviews*, 7, 309–314.

Kamil, A.C. 1978. Systematic foraging by a nectar-feeding bird, the amakihi (*Loxops virens*). *Journal of Comparative Psychology*, 92, 388–396.

Kamil, A.C. and Balda, R.P. 1985. Cache recovery and spatial memory in Clark's nutcrackers. *Journal of Experimental Psychology: Animal Behavior Processes*, 11, 95–111.

Kamil, A.C. and Jones, J.E. 1997. The seed-storing corvid Clark's nutcracker learns geometric relationships among landmarks. *Nature*, 390, 276–279.

Kamil, A.C. and Yoerg, S.I. 1982. Learning and foraging behavior. In P.H. Klopfer and P.P.G. Bateson (eds.) *Perspectives on Ethology*, Volume 5. New York: Plenum.

Katcher, A.H. 1989. How companion animals make us feel. In R.J. Hoage (ed.) *Perceptions of Animals in American Culture,*. Washington, D.C.: Smithsonian Institution Press.

Kellert, S.E. 1989. Perceptions of animals in America. In R.J. Hoage (ed.) *Perceptions of Animals in American Culture*. Washington, D.C.: Smithsonian Institution Press.

Kimura, D. and Watson, N. 1989. The relation between oral movement control and speech. *Brain and Language*, 37, 565–590.

Knoll, E. 1997. Dogs, Darwinism and English sensibilities. In R.W. Mitchell, N.S. Thompson and H.L. Miles (eds.) *Anthropomorphism, Anecdotes and Animals*. Albany: State University of New York Press.

Kohler, W. 1930/1971. The nature of intelligence. In M. Henle (ed.) *The Selected Papers of Wolfgang Kohler*. New York: Liveright.

Kohler, W. 1953/1971. The scientists from Europe and their new environment. In M. Henle (ed.) *The Selected Papers of Wolfgang Kohler*. New York: Liveright.

Kosslyn, S.M. and Koenig, O. 1995. *Wet Mind: The New Cognitive Neuroscience*. New York: Free Press.

Kruuk, H. 1972. *The Spotted Hyena: A Study of Predation and Social Behavior*. Chicago: Chicago University Press.

Kuhlmeier, V.A., Boysen, S.T. and Mukobi, K.L. 1999. Scale-model comprehension by chimpanzees (*Pan troglodytes*). *Journal of Comparative Psychology*, 113, 396–402.

Kummer, H. 1995. *In Quest of the Sacred Baboon*. Princeton, NJ: Princeton University Press.

Lawrence, E.A. 1993. The sacred bee, the filthy pig and the bat out of Hell: Animal symbolism as cognitive biophilia. In S.R. Kellert and E.O. Wilson (eds.) *The Biophilia Hypothesis*. Washington D.C.: Island Press.

Lawrence, E.A. 1989. Neoteny in American perception of animals. In R.J. Hoage (ed.) *Perceptions of Animals in American Culture*. Washington, D.C.: Smithsonian Institution Press.

Leach, E. 1975. Anthropological aspects of language: Animal categories and verbal abuse. In E.H. Lenneberg (ed.) *New Directions in the Study of Language*. Cambridge: MIT press.

Lefebvre, L., Whittle, P., Lascaris, E., and Finkelstein, A. 1997. Feeding innovations and forebrain size in birds. *Animal Behavior*, 53, 549–560.

Lefebvre, L., Gaxiola, A., Dawson, S., Timmermans, S., Rosza, L. and Kabai, P. 1998. Feeding innovations and forebrain size in Australasian birds. *Behaviour*, 135, 1077–1097.

Lenat, D.B. and Guha, R.V. 1990. *Building Large Knowledge-based Systems: Representations and Inference in the CYC Project*. Reading, MA: Addison-Wesley.

Libet, B. 1985. Unconscious cerebral initiative and the role of conscious will in voluntary action. *Behavioral and Brain Sciences*, 8, 529–566.

Limongelli, L., Boysen S. T. and Visalberghi, E. 1995. Comprehension of cause-effect relations in a tool-using task by chimpanzees (*Pan troglodytes*). *Journal of Comparative Psychology*, 109, 18–26.

Lloyd, J.E. 1986. Firefly communication and deception: 'Oh, what a tangled web.' In R.W. Mitchell and N.S. Thompson (eds.) *Deception:*

Perspectives on Human and Nonhuman Deceit. Albany: State University of New York Press.

Lorenz, K. 1981. *The Foundations of Ethology*. New York: Simon and Schuster.

Lovejoy, A.O. 1936. *The Great Chain of Being*. Cambridge: Harvard University Press.

Lubinski, D. and Thompson, T. 1993. Species and individual differences in communication based on private states. *Behavioral and Brain Sciences*, 16, 627–680.

Macdonald, D.W. 1976. Food caching by red foxes and some other carnivores. *Zeitschrift für Tierspsychologie*, 42, 170–185.

Mackintosh, N.J. 1988. Approaches to the study of animal intelligence. *British Journal of Psychology*, 79, 509–525.

Mason, P. 1988. The excommunication of caterpillars: Ethno-anthropological remarks on the trial and punishment of animals. *Social Science Information*, 27, 265–273.

Masson, J.M. and McCarthy, S. 1995. *When Elephants Weep: The Emotional Lives of Animals*. New York: Dell.

McClelland, J. L. 1995. Toward a pragmatic connectionism. In P. Baumgartner and S. Payr (eds.) *Speaking Minds: Interviews with Twenty Eminent Cognitive Scientists*. Princeton: Princeton University Press.

Menzel, E.W. and Juno, C. 1985. Social foraging in marmoset monkeys and the question of intelligence. *Philosophical Transactions of the Royal Society of London, B*, 308, 145–158.

Miles, R.C. and Meyer, D.R. 1956. Learning sets in marmosets. *Journal of Comparative and Physiological Psychology*, 49, 219–222.

Miles, R.C. 1957. Learning-set formation in the squirrel monkey. *Journal of Comparative and Physiological Psychology*, 50, 356–357.

Milne, A.A. 1996. *Complete Tales of Winnie-the-Pooh*. New York: Penguin

Milton, K. 1981. Distribution patterns of tropical plant foods as a stimulus to primate mental development. *American Anthropologist*, 83, 534–548.

Milton, K. 1988. Foraging behaviour and the evolution of intellect in monkeys, apes and humans. In R.W. Byrne and A. Whiten (eds.) *Machiavellian Intelligence: Social Expertise and the Evolution of Intellect in Monkeys, Apes, and Humans*. Oxford: Clarendon Press.

Minksy, M. 1980. Decentralized minds. *Behavioral and Brain Sciences*, 3, 439–440.

Mitchell, R.W. 1997. Anthropomorphic anecdotalism as method. In R.W. Mitchell, N.S. Thompson and H.L. Miles (eds.) *Anthropomorphism, Anecdotes and Animals*. Albany: State University of New York Press.

Morgan, C.L. 1900. *Animal Behaviour*. London: Edward Arnold.

Neisser, U., Boodoo, G., Bouchard, T.J.Jr., Boykin, A.W, Brody, N., Ceci, S.J., Halpern, D.F., Loehlin, J.C., Perloff, R., Sternberg, R.J., Urbina, S. 1996. Intelligence: Knowns and unknowns. *American Psychologist*, 51, 77–101.

Neiworth, J.J. and Rilling, M.E. 1987. A method for studying imagery in animals. *Journal of Experimental Psychology: Animal Behavior Processes*, 13, 203–214.

Nisbett, R.E. and Wilson, T. D. 1977. Telling more than we can know: verbal reports on mental processes. *Psychological Review*, 84, 231–259.

Nishida, T., Uehara, S. and Nyundo, R. 1979. Predatory behavior among wild chimpanzees of the Mahale Mountains. *Primates*, 20 , 1–20.

Norman, M.D., Finn, J. and Tregenza, T. 1999. Female impersonation as an alternative reproductive strategy in giant cuttlefish. *Proceedings of the Royal Society of London, Series B*, 266, 1347.

Olson, D.J. 1991. Species differences in spatial memory among Clark's nutcrackers, scrub jays and pigeons. *Journal of Experimental Psychology: Animal Behavior Processes*, 17, 363–376.

Olson, D.J., Kamil, A.C., Balda, R.P. and Nims, P.J. 1995. Performance of four seed-caching corvids in operant tests of nonspatial and spatial memory. *Journal of Comparative Psychology*, 109, 173–181.

Olton, D.S. and Collison, C. 1979. Intramaze cues and 'odor trials' fail to direct choice behavior on an elevated maze. *Animal Learning and Behavior*, 7, 221–223.

Olton, D.S. and Samuelson, R.J. 1976. Remembrance of places passed: spatial memory in rats. *Journal of Experimental Psychology: Animal Behavior Processes*, 2, 97–116.

Opotow, S. 1993. Animals and the scope of justice. *Journal of Social Issues*, 49, 71–85.

Opotow, S. 1994. Predicting protection: Scope of justice and the natural world. *Journal of Social Issues*, 50, 49–63.

Orwell, G. 1946. *Animal Farm*. New York: Harcourt, Brace and Co.

Parker, S.T. and Gibson, K.R. 1979. A developmental model for the evolution of language and intelligence in early hominids. *Behavioral and Brain Sciences*, 2, 367–408.

Paterson, D. 1990. Beastly images of childhood., *New Scientist*, 24 March.

Patterson, F.G. 1978. The gestures of a gorilla: Language acquisition in another pongid. *Brain and Language*, 5, 56–71.

Penfield, W. and Rasmussen, T. 1950. *The Cerebral Cortex of Man: A Clinical Study of Localization of Function*. New York: Macmillan.

Pepperberg, I.M. 1987. Acquisition of the same/different concept by an African grey parrot (*Psittacus erithacus*): Learning with respect to color, shape, and material. *Animal Learning and Behavior*, 15, 423–432.

Pepperberg, I.M. 1990. Cognition in an African grey parrot (*Psittacus erithacus*): Further evidence for comprehension of categories and labels. *Journal of Comparative Psychology*, 104, 41–52.

Pepperberg, I.M. 1994. Numerical competence in an African grey parrot (*Psittacus erithacus*). *Journal of Comparative Psychology*, 108 , 36–44.

Pinker, S. 1994. *The Language Instinct*. New York: Morrow.

Pinker, S. 1997. *How the Mind Works*. New York: W.W. Norton.

Plotnick, R.J. and Tallarico, R.B. 1966. Object-quality learning set formation in the young chicken. *Psychonomic Science*, 5, 195–196.

Plutarch, *Moralia, v. XII*. Translated by H. Cherniss and W.C. Helmbold, 1968. London: Routledge and Kegan Paul Limited.

Pope, A. 1733/1975. Essay on Man. In A. Allison, H. Barrows, C.R. Blake, A.J. Carr, A.E. Eastman and H.M. English, Jr. (eds.) *Norton Anthology of Poetry*, revised. New York: W.W. Norton.

Portman, A. 1947. Etudes sur la cérébralisation des oiseaux. II. Les indices intra-cérébraux. *Aluada*, 15, 1–15.

Povinelli, D.J. 1987. Monkeys, apes, mirrors and minds: The evolution of self-awareness in primates. *Human Evolution*, 2, 493–507.

Povinelli, D.J. and deBlois, S. 1992. Young children's (*Homo sapiens*) understanding of knowledge formation in themselves and others. *Journal of Comparative Psychology*, 106, 228–238.

Povinelli, D.J., Nelson, K.E. and Boysen, S.T. 1990. Inferences about guessing and knowing by chimpanzees (*Pan troglodytes*). *Journal of Comparative Psychology*, 104, 203–210.

Povinelli, D.J., Parks, K.A and Novak, M.A. 1991. Do rhesus monkeys (*Macaca mulatta*) attribute knowledge and ignorance to others? *Journal of Comparative Psychology*, 105, 318–325.

Preuschoft, S. 1999. Are primates behaviorists? Formal dominance, cognition and free-floating rationales. *Journal of Comparative Psychology*, 113, 91–95.

Rasmussen, J.L., Rajecki, D.W. and Craft, H.D. 1993. Humans' perceptions of animal mentality: Ascriptions of thinking. *Journal of Comparative Psychology*, 107, 283–290.

Reed, T.E. and Jensen, A.R. 1992. Conduction velocity in a brain nerve pathway of normal adults correlates with intelligence level. *Intelligence*, 16, 259–272.

Reed, T.E. and Jensen, A.R. 1993. Choice reaction time and visual pathway conduction velocity both correlate with intelligence but appear not to correlate with each other: Implications for information processing. *Intelligence*, 17, 191–203.

Regan, T. 1983. *The Case for Animal Rights*. Berkeley: University of California Press.

Rensch, B. 1959. *Evolution Above the Species Level*. New York: Columbia University Press.

Ricciardi, A.M. and Treichler, F.R. 1970. Prior training influences on transfer to learning set by squirrel monkeys. *Journal of Comparative and Physiological Psychology*, 73, 314–319.

Richards, P. 1995. Local understandings of primates and evolution: Some Mende beliefs concerning chimpanzees. In R. Corbey and B. Theunissen (eds.) *Ape, Man, Apeman: Changing Views since 1600*. Leiden: the Netherlands: Department of Prehistory of Leiden University.

Riopelle, A.J. 1960. Complex behavior. In R.H. Waters, D.A Rethlingshafer,. and W.E. Caldwell (eds.) *Principles of Comparative Psychology*. New York: McGraw-Hill.

Ristau, C. 1991. Aspects of the cognitive ethology of an injury-feigning bird, the piping plover. In C.A. Ristau (ed.) *Cognitive Ethology: The Minds of Other Animals*. Hillsdale, N.J.: Erlbaum.

Rizley, R.C. and Rescorla, R.A. 1972. Associations in second-order conditioning and sensory preconditioning. *Journal of Comparative and Physiological Psychology*, 81, 1–11.

Romanes, G.J. 1883/1977. *Animal Intelligence*. Washington, D.C.: United Publications of America.

Romanes, G.J. 1888. *Mental Evolution in Man: Origin of Human Faculty*. London: Paul Kegan.

Rosch, E. 1978. Principles of categorization. In E. Rosch and B.B. Lloyd (eds.) *Cognition and Categorization*. Hillsdale, NJ: Erlbaum.

Rowell, T.E. and Rowell, C.A. 1993. The social organization of the feral *Ovis aries* ram groups in the pre-rut period. *Ethology*, 95, 213–232.

Rozin, P. 1976. The evolution of intelligence and access to the cognitive unconscious. *Progress in Psychobiology and Physiological Psychology*, 6, 245–280.

Russell, B. 1927/1989. *An Outline of Philosophy*. London: Rutledge.

Russow, L-M. 1989. Changing perceptions of animals: A philosophical view. In R.J. Hoage (ed.) *Perceptions of Animals in American Culture*. Washington, D.C.: Smithsonian Institution Press.

Schusterman, R.J. 1962. Transfer effects of successive discrimination-reversal training in chimpanzees. *Science*, 137, 422–423.

Schusterman, R.J. 1964. Successive discrimination-reversal training and multiple discrimination training in one-trial learning chimpanzees. *Journal of Comparative and Physiological Psychology*, 58, 153–156.

Searle, J. R. 1992. *The Rediscovery of the Mind*. Cambridge: MIT Press.

Selfe, L. 1977. *Nadia: A Case of Extraordinary Drawing Ability in an Autistic Child*. New Yori: Academic.

Seligman, M.E.P. 1970. On the generality of the laws of learning. *Psychological Review*, 77, 406–418.

Shell, W.F. and Riopelle, A.J. 1957. Multiple discrimination learning in raccoons. *Journal of Comparative and Physiological Psychology*, 50: 585–587.

Shell, W.F. and Riopelle, A.J. 1958. Learning sets in platyrrhine monkeys. *Journal of Comparative and Physiological Psychology*, 51, 467–470.

Shepard, P. 1996. *The Others: How Animals Made Us Human*. Washington, D.C.: Island Press.

Shepard, P. 1978. *Thinking Animals*. New York: Viking.

Sherry, D.F. 1989. Food storage in the Paridae. *Wilson Bulletin*, 101, 289–304.

Sherry, D.F. and Schacter, D.L. 1987. The evolution of multiple memory systems. *Psychological Review*, 94, 439–454.

Shettleworth, S.J. 1972. Constraints on learning. *Advances in the Study of Behavior*, 4, 1–68.

Shettleworth, S.J. 1998. *Cognition, Evolution and Behavior*. New York: Oxford University Press.

Singer, P. 1975. *Animal Liberation*. New York: Avon.

Singer, P. 1990. *Animal Liberation*. Second edition. New York: New York Times Review of Books.

Skinner, B.F. 1938. *The Behavior of Organisms*. New York: D. Appleton Century.

Skinner, B.F. 1948. *Walden Two*. New York: Macmillan.

Skinner, B.F. 1956. A case history in scientific method. *American Psychologist*, 11, 221–233.

Skinner, B.F. 1974. *About Behaviorism*. New York: Random House.

Smith, E.E. and Medin, D.L. 1981. *Categories and Concepts*. Cambridge: Harvard University Press.

Snyderman, M. and Rothman, S. 1987. Survey of expert opinion on intelligence and aptitude testing. *American Psychologist*, 42, 137–144.

Spearman, C.E. 1927. *The Abilities of Man*. New York: Macmillan.

Stander, P.E. 1992. Foraging dynamics of lions in a semi-arid environment. *Canadian Journal of Zoology*, 70, 8–21.

Stephan, H., Frahm, H. and Baron, G. 1981. New and revised data on volumes of brain structures in insectivores and primates. *Folia Primatologica*, 35, 1–29.

Sternberg, R.J., Conway, B.E., Ketron, J.L. and Bernstein, M. 1981. People's conceptions of intelligence. *Journal of Personality and Social Psychology*, 41, 37–55.

Stevens, W. 1923/1975. The Idea of Order at Key West. In A. Allison, H. Barrows, C.R. Blake, A.J. Carr, A.E. Eastman and H.M. English, Jr. (eds.) *Norton Anthology of Poetry*, revised. New York: W.W. Norton.

Sugiyama, Y. and Koman, J. 1979. Tool-using and -making behavior in wild chimpanzees in Bossou, Guinea. *Primates*, 20, 513–524.

Sulloway, F. J. 1982. Darwin and his finches: The evolution of a legend. *Journal of the History of Biology*, 15, 1–53.

Teleki, G. 1973. *The Predatory Behavior of Chimpanzees*. Lewisburg, PA: Bucknell University Press.

Templeton, J.J., Kamil, A.C. and Balda, R.P 1999. Sociality and social learning in two species of corvids; the pinyon jay (*Gymnorhinus cyanocephalus*) and the Clark's nutcraker (*Nucifraga columbiana*). *Journal of Comparative Psychology*, 113, 450–455.

Thorndike, E.L. 1898/1998. Animal intelligence: An experimental study of the associate process in animals. Reprinted in *American Psychologist*, 53, 1125–1127.

Thorndike, E.L. 1911. *Animal Intelligence: Experimental Studies*. New York: Macmillan.

Tinbergen, N. 1951. *The Study of Instinct*. Oxford: Clarendon.

Tooby, J. and Cosmides, L. 1995. Mapping the evolved functional organization of mind and brain. In M. Gazzaniga (ed.) *The Cognitive Neurosciences*. Cambridge: MIT Press.

Treffert, D.A. The idiot savant: a review of the syndrome. *American Journal of Psychiatry*, 145, 563–572.

Turing, A. 1950. Computing machinery and intelligence. *Mind*, 59, 433–460.

Vander Wall, S. B. 1982. An experimental analysis of cache recovery by Clark's nutcracker. *Animal Behaviour*, 30, 84–94.

Vander Wall, S. B. 1990. *Food Hoarding in Animals*. Chicago: University of Chicago Press.

Vander Wall, S.B. and Balda, R.P. 1981. Ecology and evolution of food-storage behavior in conifer-seed-caching corvids. *Zeitschrift für Tierpsychologie*, 56, 217–242.

Vaughan, W.L. and Greene, S.L. 1983. Acquisition of absolute discrimination in pigeons. In M.L. Commons, R.J. Herrnstein and A.R. Wagner (eds.) *Quantitative Analyses of Behavior. Discrimination Processes*. Cambridge, MA: Ballinger.

Vernon, P.A. 1987. *Speed of Information Processing and Intelligence*. Norwood, NJ: Ablex.

Visalberghi, E. and Limongelli, L. 1994. Lack of comprehension of cause-effect relations in tool-using capuchin monkeys (*Cebus apella*). *Journal of Comparative Psychology*, 108, 15–22.

Visalberghi, E. and Limongelli, L. 1996. Acting and understanding: Tool-use revisited through the minds of capuchin monkeys. In A. Russon, K. Bard and S. Parker (eds.) *Reaching into Thought: The Minds of the Great Apes*. Cambridge: Cambridge University Press.

de Waal, F.B.M. 1991. Complementary methods and convergent evidence in the study of primate social cognition. *Behaviour*, 118, 297–320.

de Waal, F.B.M. 1997. Foreword to *Anthropomorphism, Anecdotes and Animals*, R.W. Mitchell, N.S. Thompson and H.L. Miles (eds.). Albany: State University of New York Press.

Warren, J.M. 1966. Reversal learning and the formation of learning sets by cats and rhesus monkeys. *Journal of Comparative and Physiological Psychology*, 61, 421–428.

Warren, J.M. 1973. Learning in vertebrates. In D.A. Dewsbury and D.A. Rethlingshafer (eds.) *Comparative Psychology*. New York: McGraw-Hill.

Warren, J.M. and Baron 1956. The formation of learning sets by cats. *Journal of Comparative and Physiological Psychology*, 49, 227–231.

Washburn, M.F. 1917. *The Animal Mind*, Second edition. New York: Macmillan.

Washburn, M.F. 1936. *The Animal Mind*, Fourth edition. New York: Macmillan.

Watson, J.B. 1914. *Behavior: An Introduction to Comparative Psychology*. New York: Henry Holt.

Watson, R. I. 1978. *The Great Psychologists*. Fourth edition. Philadelphia: Lipincott.

Weiner, J. 1994. *The Beak of the Finch*. New York: Random House.

Werner, T.K. and Sherry, T.W. 1987. Behavioral feeding specialization in *Pinaroloxias inornata*, the 'Darwin's finch' of Cocos Island, Costa Rica. *Proceedings of the National Academy of Sciences*, 84, 5506–5510.

White, E.B. 1952. *Charlotte's Web*. New York: Harper and Row.

Wilcox, R.S. and Jackson, R.R. 1998. Cognitive abilities of araneophagic jumping spiders. In R.P. Balda, I.M. Pepperberg and A.C. Kamil (eds.) *Animal Cognition in Nature: The Convergence of Psychology and Biology in Laboratory and Field*. New York: Academic.

Wilsson, L. 1971. Observations and experiments on the ethology of the European beaver (*Castor fiber L.*): A study in the development of a phylogenetically adapted behaviour in a highly specialized mammal. *Viltrevy, Swedish Wildlife*, 8, 115–266.

Woodhouse, B. 1994. *Barbara Woodhouse on How Your Dog Thinks*. Lydney, UK: Ringpress Books.

Woodworth, R.S. 1929. *Psychology*, Second edition. New York: Henry Holt.

Yarczower, M. and Hazlett, L. 1977. Evolutionary scales and anagenesis. *Psychological Bulletin*, 84, 1088–1097.

Yarczower, M. and Yarczower, B.S. 1979. In defense of anagenesis, grades and evolutionary scales. *Psychological Bulletin*, 86, 880–883.

Yerkes, R.M. 1912. The intelligence of earthworms. *Journal of Animal Behavior*, 2, 332–352.

Yoerg, S.I. 1992. Mentalist imputations. *Science*, 258, 830–831.

Yoerg, S.I. 1994. Development of foraging behaviour in the Eurasian dipper, *Cinclus cinclus*, from fledging until dispersal. *Animal Behaviour*, 47, 577–588.

Yoerg, S.I. 1998. Foraging behaviour predicts age at independence in juvenile Eurasian dippers (*Cinclus cinclus*). *Behavioral Ecology*, 9, 471–477.

Yoerg, S.I. and O'Halloran, J. 1991. Feeding of dipper nestlings by a grey wagtail. *Auk*, 108, 427–429.

Young, R.K. and Theissen, D.D. 1991. Washing, drying and anointing in adult humans (*Homo sapiens*): Commonalities with grooming sequences in rodents. *Journal of Comparative Psychology*, 105, 340–344.

Zach, R. 1979. Shell-dropping: decision making and optimal foraging in northwestern crows. *Behaviour*, 68, 106–117.

Zajonc, R.B. 1968. Attitudinal effects of mere exposure. *Journal of Personality and Social Psychology Monographs*, 9, 1–27.

Zeigler, H.P. 1961. Learning set formation in pigeons. *Journal of Comparative and Physiological Psychology*, 54, 252–254.

Zoladek, L. and Roberts, W.A. 1978. The sensory basis of spatial memory in the rat. *Animal Learning and Behavior*, 6, 77–81.

Index

Index

Evans, S., 171n
evolution. *See also* adaptation
  anagenesis, 49–52
  branching tree model, 41–44, 44–45
  continuity, 4–6, 43–47, 81–83
  convergence, 49
evolutionary parsimony, 46–47, 53
executive control, 147–149

familiarity
  and attributing sentience, 186–187
  and experimental bias, 63–65
  and fundamental attribution error, 65–66
  pets and, 13–14, 57–61
  role of the media, 14, 61–63
Fentress, J. C., 126n
Fienberg, 24n
finches. *See* Cocos finches; Galápagos finches
Finkelstein, A., 145n
Finn, J., 54n
firefly *(Photurus)*, 54
fish, 30–31, 50–51
Fisher, E. M., 162n
Fiske, S., 196
Flaum, M., 111n
Flipper (TV show), 56, 61
Fodor, Jerry, 95, 122
food
  caching, 1–3, 139–141, 157, 162
  feeding habits and curiosity, 154–156
  feeding habits and intelligence, 162–163
  locating, 156–157
  manipulating or extracting, 157–158
  use of tools, 158–160
foxes, 162
Frahm, H., 111n
Frank, L. G., 173n
fundamental attribution error, 65–66

Galápagos finches, 81–82
Gallup, Gordon G., Jr., 45, 56n, 59n, 90
Galton, Francis, 18–19
Galvin, S., 56n, 177, 182, 188–189
Garcia, J., 133
Gardner, B. T., 107n
Gardner, Howard, 18n, 122–123
Gardner, R. A., 107n
Gaxiola, A., 145n
general intelligence. *See* intelligence, general
Gestalt psychology, 84–87, 97
'g' factor, 18–20
Gibson, K. R., 155n
Gilbert, D. T., 65n
Glickman, S. E., 153
Goodall, Jane, 159n, 180, 202
gorilla, mountain, 157
Gottlieb, G., 50n
Gould, Stephen Jay, 24n, 67
Graham, I., 173n
Great Chain of Being, 3–6, 37–39, 52, 176–177, 196
Green, S. M. (1998), 171n
Green Acres (TV show), 74
Greene, S. L., 118
Gregory, 143n
Griffin, Donald R., 114–115, 171, 182–183
Grindley, G. C., 43n
grooming patterns of mice, 126
Guha, R. V., 124n
gulls, 163

Halpern, D. F., 18n
Harlow, H. F., 35n, 43n

Hart, B., 16n
Hart, L., 16n
Haugeland, John, 125
Hauser, Marc, 135, 136n, 171n
Hazlett, L., 50n
Heider, F., 169n
Heinrich, H., 107n, 158n
Heller, J., 186n
Herman, E. Y. K., 104n
Herman, L. M., 104n
Herrero, S., 157n, 162n
Herrnstein, R. J., 18n, 24n, 107n
Herzog, A. H., 56n, 177, 182, 188–189, 191
Herzog, H., 129n
Heyes, C. M., 171n
Hingston, R. W. G., 32
Hladik, C. M., 157n
Hodos, W., 29n, 41n, 51n, 52
Hoffman, Dustin, 120
Holcroft, A. C., 157n
Holekamp, K. E., 173n
honeycreepers, 157
Howells, K., 58n
How the Mind Works (Pinker), 185
Hull, C. L., 78
hummingbirds, 23, 155
Humphrey, Nicolas K., 13–14, 164, 184
Hunt, G. R., 159n
Hunter, M. W., 47–49
Hunter, W. S., 25–26
hyena, spotted, 173

idiot savants, 120–122, 123
immigrants, intelligence testing of, 24
insight, 85, 87–90
instinctive behavior, 30–32
intelligence, defining, 16–17, 33, 100–101
intelligence, general
  accessibility of specialized mechanisms, 141–147
  logic and evidence of, 104–105, 129, 138, 200–201
  only in some species, 149–150, 157–158
  power of executive control, 147–149
  unitary factor 'g,' 18–20
intelligence, measuring, 20–33
  difficulties of, 20–23
  distinguishing instinctive behavior, 30–32
  environmental effects, 27–29
  fairness issues, 23–26
  human, 20–21, 24
  systematic variation, 24
  using related or disparate species, 29–30
intelligence, reasons to study, 199–202
In the Shadow of Man (Goodall), 202

Jackson, R. R., 108–110
jays, 139–141
Jenkins, H. M., 28n
Jennings, H. S., 83n
Jensen, A. R., 19n
Jenyns, Soame, 40n
Jerison, H. J., 111n, 112, 144, 161
Jones, J. E., 146n
Juno, C., 151–152
justice, scope of, 178
juvenile features, 67–69

Kabai, P., 145n
Kalat, J. W., 24n, 134n
Kamil, A. C., 2n, 27n, 47–49, 139n, 146n, 157n
kangaroo rat, 190
kangaroos, 62–63

225

Index

Parr, H., 126n
parrots, 104–105, 111
Paterson, D., 69n
Patterson, F. G., 107n
Penfield, Wilder, 127n
Pepperberg, Irene M., 104–105, 149n
perception, 84–87
Perloff, R., 18n
pets
    as food, 176–177
    fundamental attribution error, 13–14, 65–66
    moral concern for, 191–192
    in other cultures, 62
    pigs as, 73
    preference for neotenized characteristics, 67–68
    prejudicial effects of familiarity, 13–14, 57–60
Photurus (firefly), 54
phylogeny, 44–46, 50–51
Piaget, Jean, 97
pigeons
    brain size, 111
    cognitive abilities, 103, 118–119
    insight experiments, 87–90
    mirror self-recognition experiments, 90–94
    thinking, 117–118, 119
pigs, 70–74, 75
Pikachu, 67
Pinker, Steven, 32, 124, 143, 144, 185
Pinyon jays, 139–141
Piskiel, A., 173n
Plato, 37–38
Plotnick, R. J., 37n
Plutarch, *Moralia*, v. XII, 4–5
Pokémon, 67
Pope, A., 34
porcupines, 154, 155
porpoises, 61
Portia (Australian jumping spider), 108–110, 112–113
Portman, A., 111n
Povinelli, D. J., 45, 56n, 59n, 90n, 170n
predators
    brain size, 160–161
    curiosity of, 153
    intelligence of, 69–70
    as psychologists, 167
prejudice. *See* bias
Preuschoft, S., 107n
prey species
    brain size, 161
    curiosity of, 154–155
    intelligence of, 69–70
primates
    bias toward, 3–4, 52–55, 63–65, 151–152
    brain size, 111, 112
    curiosity of, 153, 154
    evolutionary history, 41–42
    food caching, 3
    food locating, 156–157, 163
    learning set experiments, 34–37, 47–49
    mirror self-recognition experiments, 64–65, 90–94
    sensory integration, 144
    sociality, 146–147, 165, 167–168, 172
    spontaneous ambush, 53–54
    theory of mind experiments, 170–172
    thinking, 114, 115–116
    tool use, 159–160
primatology, 52–53, 63–64
psychological skills of social animals, 166–168
psychology
    Behaviorism, 77–83, 87–90
    cognitive, 80–81, 87, 97–100, 197

comparative, 44, 52–53
    Gestalt, 84–87, 97

quasi-evolutionary series, 39–40

raccoons, 159, 162
Rainman (movie), 120
Rajecki, D. W., 56n
ranking species
    animal popularity, 61–62, 75
    based on similarity, 45–46
    college students rankings of eight mental states, 177
    Great Chain of Being, 3–6, 37–39, 52, 176–177, 196
    intelligence surveys, 56–57
    Ladder of Being, 39–42
    zoo animal preferences, 69
Rasmussen, J. L., 56
Rasmussen, T., 127n
rats
    behaviorally silent learning, 98
    and behaviorists, 79, 80
    cognitive abilities, 103–104
    conditioning experiments, 28–29
    general intelligence testing, 22
    radial maze experiments, 105–106
ravens, 158, 174
rays and sharks, 111–112
Reed, T. E., 19n
Regan, Tom, 188
reinforcement theory, 94
relatedness, 6–8, 29–30
Rensch, B., 51n
reptiles, 153, 154
Rescorla, R. A., 98n
research. *See* scientific research
Resnick, D. P., 24n
rhesus monkey, 47–49
Ricciardi, A. M., 48n
Richards, A. F., 173n
Richards, P., 180
Riley, D. A., 104n
Rilling, M. E., 107n, 117
Riopelle, A. J., 37n
Ristau, C., 107n
Rizley, R. C., 98n
Roberts, W. A., 106n
rodents. *See also specific rodents*
    curiosity of, 153, 154
Roeder, K., 24n
Romanes, G. J., 44–45, 99n
Rosch, Eleanor, 195
Rosza, L., 145n
Rothman, S., 21n
Rowell, C. A., 61n
Rowell, T. E., 61n
Rozin, Paul, 141
Rubin, L., 87n
Russell, Bertrand, 85
Russow, L-M, 62n

Samuelson, R. J., 106n
Sanchez, J. L., 104n
savants, 120–122, 123
scala naturae (Ladder of Being), 39–42, 44–45, 49
Schacter, D. L., 134n
Schusterman, R. J., 48n
scientific research. *See also* bias
    anecdotes and, 202–204
    difficulties of, 7–8, 15, 20–30, 204–206
scope of justice, 178
Searle, John R., 124n, 125

A NOTE ON THE AUTHOR

Sonja Yoerg was a researcher and lecturer at the University of California at Berkeley in the Department of Psychology and the Museum of Vertebrate Zoology. She received her Ph.D. in biological psychology from U.C. Berkeley and has published research articles on the ecology and evolution of learning, development, and social behavior of a variety of species. Her theoretical papers on the integration of psychological and biological approaches to behavioral research have made her a recognized expert in this field. She is often called upon by popular media, such as *The New York Times* and ABC's *Dateline*, to comment on intelligence, emotion, and consciousness in animals. Dr. Yoerg lives in San Diego with her husband and two daughters.